Big Dead Place

Inside the Strange and Menacing World of Antarctica

BY
Nicholas Johnson

FERAL HOUSE

Big Dead Place © 2005 by Nicholas Johnson

ISBN: 0922915997

10 9 8 7 6 5 4 3 2 1

Feral House
PO Box 39910
Los Angeles, CA 90039

Send SASE for complete catalogue of publications

www.feralhouse.com — a site for sore eyes

Design: Sean Tejaratchi

FOR MOM

AUTHOR'S NOTE

Though this book is non-fiction, most of the dialogue herein is reconstructed from notes I made at the end of the workday, with the exception of recorded dialogue, which is inset.

Because the United States Antarctic Program is a very small world, I have changed the names of most of those who work in The Program, unless they have given permission, or unless their positions have already brought them media attention in other instances.

In my menial position as an Antarctic garbageman, I was exposed to a wide array of unusual official documents that had been discarded in the White Paper category. My deep research in this area (sometimes to the bottom of the bin) would not have been possible without the conscientious recycling program of the National Science Foundation, for which I am grateful.

Contents

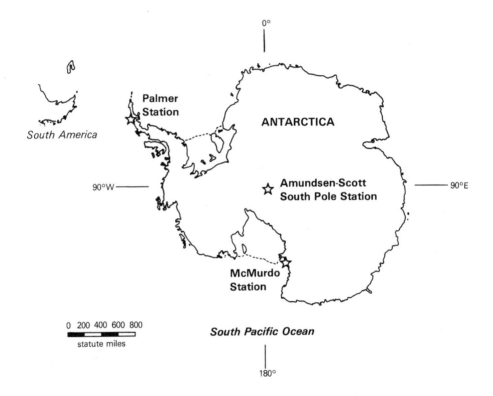

0°

Palmer
Station

ANTARCTICA

South America

90°W —— Amundsen-Scott — 90°E
South Pole Station

McMurdo
Station

0 200 400 600 800

statute miles

South Pacific Ocean

180°

Map Courtesy of National Science Foundation

FOREWORD

by Eirik Sønneland

M<small>Y FIRST MEETING</small> with McMurdo was the smell of diesel. The same that disturbed our noses when over a month earlier Rolf Bae and I had skied into the U.S. South Pole base. The clean and cold air of Antarctica's wilderness had reset our senses. Approaching McMurdo Station, we could smell humans as far as 20 kilometres outside the heart of the largest infrastructure on this frozen continent.

I looked at the GPS Monday 5th February 01.00 a.m. Behind us lies a ski trek of close to 3800 kilometres, from Gjelsvikfjella in Queen Maud Land, via South Pole to McMurdo Station. 105 days on skies, 11 months as the first winter crew at the Norwegian Research station, "Troll." Research, station upgrades, a year's worth of maintenance, and the world longest ski trek had been a success. It almost seemed like our minds and bodies didn't know how to react—all this would soon be over. A strong feeling of humility is the best description I can give today. Feeling fragile but at the same time strong.

Near McMurdo, the first building we arrived at turned out to be part of the fire department at the airfield. Five guys stepped from the small barracks and walked toward us. They looked confused. "Where are you coming from?" was the first question. We explained. It was silence for something that felt like a long time, and then one guy said, "You must be tired!" I didn't feel tired, nor happy. To be quite honest I didn't feel a thing. It was unreal. The firefighters invited us in for food and hot chocolate. They treated us very well and were calm and polite. It seemed easy to make friends. After sleeping on their couch we were escorted to Scott Base the next day. The New Zealand Base commander asked us what had happened and why we had missed our boat, the *Khlebnikov*. We told him the truth: we hadn't made it in time. It seemed like he understood and offered us use of the phone to arrange alternative transport. He told us that only the U.S. Antarctic Program had transport at this point in the season, except for some cruise ships arriving in a couple of days.

The next day we were ordered to have a meeting with the U.S. base leader. I knew this meeting would be special. It's well known that, for various reasons, the U.S. and NSF will not support any private expeditions, which was fine with us, because we believed we could find our own way out. He arrived with his big red parka and a National Geographic cap, probably to show us that he knew all about expeditions and exploration. Obviously he didn't. He had a strange arrogant attitude and wouldn't listen to our story about our transport from McMurdo. He talked to us as though we were criminals. He told us that we were not allowed to enter the McMurdo Station area, nor to enter any buildings or vehicles, and not to speak to the employees on the base. I was in shock. Then he left. The New Zealand station manager told us not to worry and tried to excuse the American leader. It didn't help. We knew from that moment it would be an unpleasant stay at McMurdo. For a few days we spent time with the Kiwis at Scott Base, helping them with their work and getting visitors from McMurdo. The American workers were horrified by the way we were treated, and when I asked them why they dared to visit us (it was forbidden) they told me they had broken every stupid rule on base, and they might as well break this one as well. I really felt good among the workers; they are normal people with the ability to work in extreme environments. Also I believe that a majority of these people want an adventure. That's a similarity between me, as a polar expeditioner, and them.

Around this time, we learned that one of our best friends had died on a platform in the Northern seas, and Rolf and I went into almost total breakdown. A Dutch cargo ship offered us a lift but NSF, wanting to make an example of us to other expeditioners, pressured the Dutch not to accommodate us, after which NSF offered us a flight to New Zealand for a fee of $50,000. I learned a lot about bureaucracy at the American station. It appeared that orders were coming from somewhere in the U.S. where they, as the author would probably express it, "sure as shit" don't know what happens in far away Antarctica, making it impossible for "leaders" with National Geographic hats to make sensible decisions. I believe this system is crazy. That's why I agreed to write the foreword for this book.

After fighting blizzards, crevasses, extreme subzero temperatures, distance, and my own psyche, I remember when I told the expedition leader on the cruise ship that finally took us from Antarctica that "if Antarctica has an asshole, McMurdo is it!" Yes, I was angry. Not toward the workers, who are truly the reason why the stations continue to run, but toward the system of bureaucracy that serves no purpose but to treat everyone poorly. The author writes that "I have never heard one person say that the most difficult thing about Antarctica is working outside, or being cold… I have never heard of one returnee who finally quit because it's the world's highest, driest, coldest or whatever. People leave because of the bullshit." After experiencing McMurdo for myself, and reading this book, I believe him.

For people that wish to work or have worked in Antarctica, this book may be a bible. For other people it will be spectacular reading about how it can be working in the world's last wilderness in good days and bad days. The author's historical knowledge of Antarctica is very good; the book will introduce new readers to some of the well-known Antarctic expeditions, and will for those already familiar with Antarctic history consolidate some of the most obscure and interesting anecdotes. The author's straightforward language and insights into human characteristics make this book unfit for the light-hearted. It will persuade the reader to think about the difference between sane and insane behavior from normal people doing normal jobs. It may make you angry, but it will certainly make you laugh. It will provoke NSF and other U.S. officials for sure. I believe they need it, and may even learn something from it.

Eirik Sønneland
July 2004

Life at a remote station is life in a test tube; it is an environment in which men and their behavior can be subjected to searching scrutiny. I feel that observations which are made and lessons which are learnt have important implications for the more complicated urban environments in which most of us lead our daily lives.

– Philip Law

I'm more American than I am human.

– David Nelson

CHAPTER ONE

FROZEN REALM OF MYSTERY

... the general object of the expedition was a peaceful voyage, to explore and survey coasts, seas, and islands, and to make such investigations as might be found practicable in aid of science...

— Charles Wilkes, 1845

This is one of the "heights" of a polar voyage, when all one's comrades are one's bosom friends, and when every single experience is viewed through rose-coloured spectacles.

— Raymond Priestly

I STEPPED FROM MY ROOM in the upper hallway of Dorm 202 to go for a piss down the hall. It was the middle of the afternoon. A man lay on his back in the middle of the hallway. He was barefoot and wearing no shirt. I assumed he was drunk. He too must have worked nightshift. His eyes were open. As I neared the bathroom I asked groggily, "Dude, are you all right?"

Only his eyes moved. "Eventually you will make a mistake," he said.

I nodded, walked into the bathroom, and peed on a cake of pink deodorant in the urinal. I washed my hands and then dried them with a paper towel from a dispenser that someone had recently ripped from the wall and left in a sink.

"You sure you're okay?" I asked as I passed the guy in the hall again.

"Eventually you will make a mistake," he said calmly.

I shrugged and went to my room, where I curled up under the covers and started to fall asleep. Before I did, I groaned and climbed out of bed to lock the door, in case he had been talking to me.

Soon after I arrived at McMurdo Station by plane that first summer, the station manager gathered the employees in the Galley for an orientation. As he spoke, we fidgeted at the cafeteria tables. Our red parkas hung in the hall, but we still sweated in our long underwear, black wind-bibs, and heavy white boots with air-valves. Paintings of glaciers hung on the walls. I had only one question in mind: How long can I stand outside before I die? The station manager instead told us that if our neighbors were noisy, we should report them to the Firehouse. The Housing lady said a few words, and we formed two lines for keys to our dorm rooms.

From the pile of standard-issue orange bags in the hallway, I dislodged mine and sought my room. Someone else had already been assigned to my bed, so I took my key back to the Housing Office, where several people were in the hallway outside the door, not in line, but just hanging around. I couldn't tell whether they were new like me, or if they had been here before. I consoled a woman who was crying because she was not assigned her choice of roommate. I could hear people talking inside the Housing Office, so I asked a guy leaning against the wall, "What's the deal here?" He shrugged and said he also needed to talk to them, gesturing at the Housing Office door, which was locked. I knocked and got no response. After a few minutes, a woman with a crowded keychain arrived from around the corner. The crying woman shifted to a hopeful sniffle. The woman with the keys looked beyond the waiting crowd as if inspecting some grave blemish in the distant hallway. Her ready key slithered into the lock, she slipped inside, and the door slammed behind her. The sniffles reverted to sobs, and one more voice joined the merry clamor from within the Housing Office. People who for a moment had stood at attention resumed their positions against the wall. After a few more minutes, the door opened, a man emerged from within, and a woman tried to close the door.

I would have worked for free my first summer, just to go to Antarctica. Because I had little knowledge about the place, I imagined that I also had few preconceptions about it. I suspected, though, that wherever the unknown lurked, science would be there to stop it, so I expected to find radar dishes and weird machines, as at a moon base. I would not have been surprised to find myself shivering in a tent full of scientists or staggering through a blizzard pulling a sled. Mostly, though, I was free of assumptions about the frozen realm of mystery. I knew only that in Antarctica, things would be different, and I was ready to do whatever it took to adjust to the rugged frontier.

Now I was blocking the door of the Housing Office with my foot.

"Excuse me," I said with a smile. "Someone is in my bed. Where do you want me?"

The Housing woman nervously eyed the crowd closing in around the door.

"What dorm are you in now?" she asked.

"155."

We smiled at each other. She hesitated, then let me in, closed the door behind me, and established herself behind a counter.

Thereafter, my daily commute to work from Dorm 202 took seconds. I worked just across the yard in Building 155, the town hub, where the main hallway, called Highway One, is congested in the summer by people using the cash machines at one end and by people talking outside the store at the other. Along Highway One are alcoves with coat hooks, and bathrooms with orange-scented hand lotion and free condoms. There are sometimes bags of shredded documents outside the Human Resources Office and people leaning against the wall by the Housing Office or by the computer kiosk. Bulletin boards along Highway One are layered with flyers for Disco Night at the bar, stereo equipment for sale, and accident and injury statistics. There is a sign-up sheet on the door of the barbershop. Haircuts are free here.

I worked Midrats (midnight rations) as a DA (Dining Attendant) in the Galley. We washed dishes, scrubbed pots, vacuumed the dining area, scouted for spray bottles of disinfectant to wipe the tables, and mixed Bug Juice (industrial-strength Kool-Aid). Most of us on the Midrats crew were fingees (Fucking New Guys). Though our reasons for coming varied, as did our methods of getting jobs, we were all excited to be here. Flo, who referred to herself as a hip grandma, had come down to see penguins. Her husband was an important figure in McMurdo construction. Lindy, who had also married into McMurdo, was here for the penguins as well. Lindy popped her gum, kept freshly painted nails, and liked contemporary country music. June was an ornery, lip-glossed San Diegan whose sister had worked on the ice for years. She had heard McMurdo was fun. Gail was a Midrats salad-maker who had no McMurdo connections. Her résumé had escaped the slush pile because she had drawn cartoon penguins on her cover letter. Mary, our supervisor, had been applying for years to get a job of any kind in Antarctica. She also had no local connections; back in the "real world," she was a financial consultant. She planned to use her wages to buy a new metal detector, as finding metal things was one of her hobbies. Steve had been down before and had come back mostly for the money. He was from Nebraska, and told me of a recent concert there featuring Jefferson Starship and Eddie Money that drew an enthusiastic crowd. Steve said that Jefferson Starship put on a good show, but that Eddie Money got drunk and bellowed contempt for all the people who had come from afar to see him.

At work, classic rock blared from different radios around the kitchen, and our exposure to the tinny canon of riffs occupied nine hours a day, six days a week. The Galley might as well have been in Nebraska. Stainless steel, hot water, the smells of baking chicken and boiling potatoes and butterscotch, all to a repetitive soundtrack of Foreigner and The Eagles. I often forgot where I was, until I went outside in the cold and wind to dump cardboard or food waste in the dumpsters off the dock.

One night early in the summer, Gail called me to the salad room where there was a suspicious hush, with four people crowding around some spectacle.

"Look at this," she whispered.

A snail was crawling across a piece of lettuce in a one-gallon plastic sauce container. There are not supposed to be snails in Antarctica; it had hitched a lift in a box of leafy vegetables. The lucky snail had found itself amongst a sympathetic group of salad-makers rather than stern representatives of the National Science Foundation, which was decidedly anti-snail by orthodoxy of the Antarctic Treaty.

"Don't tell anyone," said Gail. "If NSF finds out, they'll make us kill it."

I suggested the snail be named Anne Frank, but the salad-makers called it Snidely. A week or so later Snidely was hand-carried back to New Zealand by someone fired for throwing rocks at his co-worker.

The summer crawled along, with only small local dramas staving off the monotony of working in the Galley. Due to our collective surplus of curiosity about any event more gripping than the burning of sauce, the Galley was a hub of station gossip, a central plaza for the town's gurgling fountain of undetected infractions and titillating punishments, an engine idling on old accounts of scandalous romances and employee misbehavior. Until the day, after a seemingly endless stretch in the kitchen, the Midrats crew was offered a boondoggle, a trip out of town. Now we would have our own stories to tell: real outdoor Antarctica stories, not common indoor stories that could have happened anywhere. After our shift, we changed into our ECW gear (Extreme Cold Weather) and jabbered with anticipation on the Galley dock, our bright red parkas still clean from disuse. A noisy orange snow vehicle arrived, and Hank from F-Stop (Field Safety Training Program) jumped out and explained that the Hagglund here cost a quarter mil because it floats. "There's exit hatches in the roof," he said, which roused a happy murmur: those hatches weren't there for nothing.

We boarded and the Hagglund rumbled out of town toward Cape Evans. I awoke when it stopped, and we climbed out in front of Barne Glacier. The face of the glacier was a massive, fissured blue wall, and its bigness stunned like that of an anchor store at a regional shopping center. The area festered with seals. Lindy began shrieking and posed beside one of the creatures. She was wearing lipstick and perfume. The indifferent brown slug was bleeding and shitting where it lay. A midget on our crew squirmed on the ice in front of a seal while we snapped photos.

Hank pointed to nearby landmarks.

"That's Big Razorback Island," he said. "And that's Inaccessible Island."

We were driving across a flat plain of ice, and I could have walked to the landforms he indicated.

"You just called that an 'island'?" I said.

"That's right," he said.

"Why is it an 'island'?"

"Because it's surrounded by water."

We were driving across the frozen sea.

We filed into the Hagglund and continued driving until the vehicle suddenly stopped and Hank hurried us out. There were two Adelies, our first penguins. A wave of giddy hysteria swept through the group, and cameras began clicking. We had received several grave warnings that we were not to molest the wildlife, and that penetrating a penguin's comfort zone entailed stiff penalties. We did not want to do anything wrong, but we wanted to be as close as possible, preferably close enough to trick one of the birds into an Antarctic buddy shot. We followed Hank's lead. To us, he came to personify the Antarctic Treaty. We knew there were limits on how close we could rightfully get to a penguin, but the Treaty did not prohibit penguins from approaching us.

Hank hunkered down on the ice. We hunkered down on the ice. The penguins stood there. They watched us. It was cold and sunny. Someone was hissing in ecstasy. Hank lifted his gloved hand in the air for just a moment. The whispers of excitement froze; breaths briefly stopped clouding the air. The penguins hesitated and then waddled toward us. There was an outburst of gurgling from the spectators. The penguins stopped and looked around. They were cute. But the distance marred them. From this far they might as well have been covered in scabs. Hank began scooting forward across the ice. As if pulled by magnets, we scooted forward too. Scooting shifted to slinking, and then to a fast crawl. A horde of perfumed dishwashers converged on two saucer-eyed penguins oblivious to our designs. I was sure one of the birds would die today, drained of life by hugs and then slung over someone's arm like a dishtowel. But then Hank halted the advance. The penguins marched forward to an eruption of unregulated giggling then, only momentarily interested in us, wandered off in another direction, probably to find and eat fish.

The excited camaraderie of the penguin adventure was soon gone. Back in the kitchen, Flo befriended the Galley Supervisor, who knew about Flo's connected husband. Flo, who had never worked in food service before, disliked Mary and reported to the Galley Supervisor that Mary always stuck her with all the hardest jobs and the most work. To make sure that workloads were evenly and fairly distributed, we were swapping duties halfway through each shift, which meant that the ice cream machine seldom got cleaned. By this time, Gail was getting headaches from the perfume Lindy wore to work each night, and with a piece of hastily cut cardboard blocked the window that separated their work areas. Getting in on the action, June informed the Galley Supervisor that Mary sometimes let us stretch our breaks, so Mary was disciplined and thereafter documented when each of us returned from break, causing even more bitterness toward her.

One day, suddenly reminding us where we were, Gail was invited by some marine mammal biologists to visit their field camp, Weddell World. A trip to a field camp could only be authorized for work purposes, but since Gail was a cook, the scientists pulled the strings for her to fix them dinner. I, loyal dishwasher, went along as her assistant.

At their camp out on the sea ice, Lee took us into the Jamesway hut that served as their lab, which boasted 11 laptop computers. In the back behind a hanging sheet was a butterball of a seal with gooey brown eyes and limber nostrils, bobbing in the water through a hole in the thick ice. This hole was so far from open water that the seal had to return here to breathe. Fastened to its head with a liberal application of industrial-strength adhesive was a video camera that recorded the seal's activities. The recordings usually featured a lot of swimming about and the attacking of prey. The scientists brought the seal (Arnold) to their camp from the ice edge after knocking it out with a cocktail of Valium, ketamine, and a breathing stimulator (because seals involuntarily hold their breath if they become unconscious). Then they spent half a day outfitting the seal with the video camera and a backpack of equipment and plopped it through the hole into the sea like a plump brown berry into cream.

Terry ushered us outside and down the Ob Tube, a hollow steel shaft poked through the ice like a toothpick through plastic wrap, with a ladder inside and a window near the bottom to observe the seal in the water. In the chill of the Ob Tube I peered up at the bottom of the blushing blue sea ice through the ice-coated window and dark water. The gadget-encumbered seal floated in the hole in the ice. Just then, some marine mammal biologists returned to camp, landing noisily on the ice in a helicopter, whereupon the seal glided over to monitor me. The blubbery graceless seal above[1] was a sleek atom bundled for warmth below.

After a dinner of omelettes, and once I had washed the dishes, we relaxed with coffee in the ironless hut, a wooden black box the size of a prison cell, which was built without ferrous metals that would have interfered with the compass readings taken there. "We even had to make sure the couch didn't have any ferrous metals in it," Lee said.

"I thought you said iron was the problem," I said.

"I was trying to be understood."

The hut was mostly windows, for calculating the sun's position without standing in the elements. We drank coffee, warmed by a sun that wouldn't set until the end of summer. Lee pointed south to White Island. He told us about an isolated seal colony there, which is odd, he said, because White Island is farther south than Ross Island and is surrounded by the permanent ice shelf, rather than the seasonal ice and open water that attract seals around McMurdo. I asked how the seals got to White Island if there was no open water there, but our hosts had not studied the seal colony, so they would not even speculate on the origins of the isolated gene pool. Terry asked Lee whether so-and-so had studied the isolated seal colony. Lee didn't know, and Terry asked if so-and-so had married such-and-such. "Marine mammal biologists," Lee said, "there's another isolated gene pool."

Someone mentioned the Botswana water owl, which flies straight into the water to catch prey. Randolph had learned owl calls counting owls in the Grand Canyon.

He began doing owl calls in the ironless hut on the sea ice.

Returning to McMurdo, the glow of our fantastic seal odyssey brightened a few weeks of drudgery, but eventually dimmed. In the kitchen, June and Flo and Lindy teamed up against Mary, whose credibility in the eyes of the Galley Supervisor was not helped by her lack of an influential spouse in town, and at her end-of-the-season work evaluation they blamed her for the accumulated problems on our DA crew. June's connection in town was, at best, lateral to that of the kitchen supervisor, so her eval suffered too, but Flo and Lindy earned praise, as did Steve and I, for steering clear of it all.

When I returned home after my first summer on the ice, I wore my Antarctica regalia proudly. I wore the casual McMurdo Station ballcap and a few t-shirts from the McMurdo station store, where such items sold well.

"I just got back from Antarctica," I would say to people.

They were curious, and would ask me what I did there, and how did I get a job there, and how cold was it. I told them that I scraped ridges of turkeyloaf from baking pans while listening to Bob Seger. I told them that I knew someone who knew someone who knew someone. I said I didn't know how cold it was by temperature, but the shutter in my camera had frozen and a ballpoint pen wouldn't work outside. More questions would follow, and I would be the star of the show.

Though the details vary, this exchange, familiar to Antarctic workers, is sometimes called "playing the Antarctica card." It can be used to impress sexual prospects, potential employers, and those who get a little too uppity about their travel experience. The main drawback of playing the Antarctica card, as people with more than a few seasons of experience know, is that playing it too often can lead to weariness, as might happen to a game-show champion repeating his name, occupation, and hometown night after night.

Some seasoned workers are careful about playing the Antarctica card, broaching the subject only when they are sure that their audience has time for details, because the place is genuinely fascinating, but not always in the ways one might expect. Some, disdainful of Antarctica's use as cheap parlor entertainment, refuse to speak of the place except to other Antarcticans, to those who can differentiate between the regimes of ITT and ASA, trace the reputation of a particular department to an interdepartmental squabble six seasons ago, or at the very least understand the impact of Offload. These workers wear highly revered regalia from past seasons with the gravitas of druids bearing ancient amulets. They have risen in the ranks on the highest, driest, coldest, and windiest continent in the world. Behind their eyes lies a calm understanding of systematic hostility. They are never surprised by the weather. They expect storms, ride them out, and find them not worth mentioning, unless to someone who knows what a real storm is like.

At nearby Cape Evans, on May 6, 1915, a fearsome storm ripped the wooden ship *Aurora* from anchor and carried it away in the night, marooning[2] ten men in Antarctica for two years. They had only offloaded a few supplies. The sea swallowed their cases of fuel, left too near the shore during the storm. The only other supplies were those scattered around the Cape Evans hut by Sir Robert Scott on his doomed expedition to the Pole a few years earlier. The treeless continent provides no firewood.

Sir Ernest Shackleton, intending to cross Antarctica from the opposite coast on foot, had sent the *Aurora* expedition to lay depots of food and fuel in a route across the far side of the continent. Distracted from his task when his ship, *Endurance*, was crushed in the ice, Shackleton and his small crew spent the next few years hopping ice floes and gobbling wildlife until he crossed the ocean in a puny boat, scaled cliffs on a remote southern island, and then strolled into a whaling station to ask for assistance. Shackleton had long since canceled his trans-Antarctic expedition, but the men at Cape Evans didn't know that. They dug through crates of musty supplies, scavenging materials for a futile sled journey to establish a supply line for an expedition that would never arrive.

Six of the men sledged continuously for seven months. They wore pants made from an old tent, shoes made from fur sleeping bags; their lives depended on worn tents and defective primus stoves left behind by Scott. They traveled in blizzards. Frostbite covered their faces. One of the party, Mackintosh, reported that his ear had turned a pale green and that his feet were "raw like steak." Fellow adventurer Ernest Joyce wrote that his nose was "one black blister."

On the return journey, the supply depots laid, they began to starve. Joyce wrote that, despite the help of their four dogs, they were still only "crawling three miles in ten hours—our food, biscuit crumbs and cocoa." They gulped down filthy wads of seal meat scraped from the bags that had held the dogs' food. Then, with no food and no fuel, they had to take supplies from the depots they had risked their lives to establish. Their salvaged tent split in the wind. While two of the men made repairs, fumbling a needle with frostbitten fingers, Hayward began ranting: "We can have meat. We can kill one of the dogs and eat its flesh. That would keep us alive." Horrified, they shushed him, imagining their black lot without the dogs there to pull their pitiful effects through the bleak nightmare.

Besides freezing and starving, they suffered from scurvy. They tied lengths of bamboo behind their knees to keep their legs from curling irreversibly while they slept, a symptom of the illness. Mackintosh, the leader of the expedition, was delirious with the disease. His gums were swollen, his knees were black and bent, and he conversed with imaginary visitors to his tent. A priest brought along on the expedition was strapped in his sleeping bag to a sled pulled by the limping men and the dogs, popping opium tablets from the medicine kit, reciting Bible verses, and bleeding steadily from the ass. He died as they approached the safety of Discovery Hut, south of Cape Evans, another shelter left by Scott.

At Discovery Hut their worst problems would be alleviated. There would be shelter, a stove, and plenty of seals. Crewman Richards wrote that as the expedition neared the hut, he "had the strongest desire to rush to one of those animals and cut its throat and drink the blood that... would hose from its neck... the blood for which my body was crying out." They arrived to find the emergency hut half full of snow and had to enter through a window. Richards wrote, "There was absolutely nothing in the way of general provisions—no flour, no sugar, no bread. The sole food we had from the middle of March until the middle of July—four whole months—was seal meat. That is all we had—morning, noon, and night." For those long stormy months, recovering from their crippling afflictions, the men gorged on seal and huddled from draughts behind a heavy canvas curtain, blackened by smoke from the seal blubber they burned in a corner of the frozen hut, which still stands just across the bay from McMurdo Station.

McMurdo lies in the shadow of Mount Erebus, a smoldering volcano encrusted with thick slabs of ice. To make room for McMurdo, a ripple of frozen hills on the edge of Ross Island have been hacked away to form an alcove sloped like the back of a shovel, and then affixed with green and brown cartridges with doors and windows. Silver fuel tanks sparkle on the hillside like giant watch batteries. As if unloosed from a specimen jar, a colony of machines scours the dirt roads among the simple buildings, digesting snow and cargo dumped by the wind and the planes, rattling like cracked armor and beeping loudly in reverse.

McMurdo is the largest of three[3] year-round American stations in Antarctica. With a summer population of around 1,200, one need not greet a passing stranger outside or in the halls. Some people drive to lunch. People like McMurdo for the natural beauty that surrounds it, and dislike it because it is loud, crowded, and industrial. In the distance, framed by ratty utility poles and twisted electrical lines, the gleaming mountains of the Royal Society Range spill glaciers that glow like molten gold onto the far rim of the frozen white sea, on which planes land, out near all the buildings with skis. Near Castle Rock, skiing toward Mount Erebus, in the middle of nowhere, you can stop at the bright red emergency shelter that looks like a giant red larva and call your bank[4] to dispute your credit card fees.

The town bustles in the summer with ships, helicopters, planes, cranes, and semis. It is the coastal hub for infiltrating the rest of the continent. By plane or helicopter, equipment and supplies radiate outward from McMurdo to field camps and to Pole, the second largest year-round base, which is officially called "Amundsen-Scott Station." The name is mildly embarrassing, and seldom used except in government documents and such. Roald Amundsen was the first person to reach the South Pole. His men and his dogs made it to Pole a month before Robert Scott. Amundsen also made it out of Antarctica alive, whereas Scott is still encased in the ice like an insect in amber. Amundsen's account of his journey is matter-of-fact, while Scott's is a heroic tale of nationalist sacrifice. Uncertain whether to honor the winner or the team player, the U.S. has given its allegiance to the hyphen. Workers usually call it "Pole." It is a smeared fleck on a hulking lobe of ice called the Polar Plateau, 800 miles inland from McMurdo, where there are no seals, whales, penguins, or ships. Pole is surrounded by a desert of ice, around which the eye glides without traction inevitably back to the crawling machines, the drums of solvent, and the clusters of cargo that, more than penguins or icebergs, characterize daily life in the United States Antarctic Program, known locally as "The Program."

The first science foundation—which fostered the work of Euclid, the first star map, the calculation of the earth's diameter, and an inkling of the steam-engine—was established in the third century B.C. by Ptolemy I. The National Science Foundation—the federal agency that manages the United

States Antarctic Program—was established during the Cold War by Congress. Ptolemy's ancient think tank, history's first endowment of science, was headquartered in Alexandria, Egypt. NSF is headquartered near Alexandria, Virginia, in the suburbs of Washington, D.C.

Congress passed the National Science Foundation Act of 1950 to "promote the progress of science; to advance the national health, prosperity, and welfare; and to secure the national defense." In Antarctic brochures, NSF describes itself merely as "the U.S. Government agency that promotes the progress of science." Someone exposed only to such brochures or to newspapers might get the inaccurate impression that most Americans in Antarctica are scientists or researchers.

Most of the population work for NSF's prime support contractor, which employs everyone from dishwashers and mechanics, to hairdressers and explosives-handlers. All prime support contractors in U.S. Antarctica have been subsidiaries of defense contractors since Holmes & Narver assumed operational control of South Pole Station in 1968. ITT Antarctic Services held the contract in the 1980s. And Antarctic Support Associates (ASA), a joint venture of defense giants EG&G and Holmes & Narver, held the contract until 2000, when ASA was displaced by Raytheon Polar Services Company (RPSC), a subsidiary of Raytheon Company. While the National Science Foundation is known as a proud sponsor of public television programming, Raytheon is known for making the Exoatmospheric Kill Vehicle and other top-shelf weapons systems.

In U.S. parlance, all 5.4 million square miles and 7 million cubic miles of ice that make up Antarctica are "The South Pole." This is understandable, because from that royal dot have arisen many of the greatest tales of misery and suffering by those whose bodies are scattered across the wasteland. The South Pole, an abstract natural nonlandmark, has no visible identifying characteristics, which only adds to its elusiveness and mystique.

In Antarctic parlance, all of the United States divides into "Washington," referring to NSF's sphere of influence, and "Denver," referring to a vague suburban belt of Sheratons and brewpubs on the outskirts of Denver, where the support contractor has long been headquartered. Toward Denver is the most immediate over-the-shoulder check for the Antarctic lackey. "I'm going to have to 'okay' that with Denver first," they say, or "I'm not the one who made the decision—if you have a problem with it, talk to Denver." Denver is where most of the managers and full-time employees work, and where strategies for improving morale are formulated. Some of the clocks in McMurdo and at South Pole are set to Denver time.

I had just arrived back in McMurdo for my third summer, but this time I would stay for the winter also: a year contract. I was in Sid's room with him and Milo, upstairs in 155. I had expected them to be wild-eyed and deranged, with big beards and lips glistening with spittle, but Sid and Milo, both on the tail end of a winter contract, didn't look so bad. Sid's face looked a bit pasty, and Milo was a little haggard, but overall they seemed fit and tranquil. A few minutes after I greeted them I realized that the winter-overs were emitting a low harmonic drone that I was overwhelming with my turbulent piercing chatter. While they were calm and steady, thoughtful and deliberate, I had arrived with the agitated enthusiasm of one who has had a break from the ice.

The curtains were open to admit the perpetual summer sun.

"I got in trouble for making toast this winter," said Milo.

All winter Milo often chose to eat toasted bagels rather than attend the meals, because in the winter simple tiresome food can become preferable to elaborate tiresome food. Because there are no restaurants, a small supply of basic foods in the Galley is available for 24-hour community access. Milo said the trouble had begun at Winfly, when the Galley reopened after remodeling, during which the winter-overs had eaten in the library. Once the Galley had been renovated, meals were served there, and the library once again became the library. One of the features in the new Galley was a heavy black curtain that could be drawn to separate the dining area from the service area. The curtain was useful at the end of meal periods for keeping mobs of people from retrieving second helpings while the Galley staff cleared away the hot trays of teriyaki chicken and Hungarian goulash.

Milo was one day toasting a bagel from the bread tray when the DA screamed at him from across the room and rushed over.

"You can't come behind the curtain during non-meal times!"

"I'm making toast," he said.

"You can only use the Galley during mealtimes."

"I always eat toast."

"You can only use the Galley during mealtimes."

He ignored her and left with his bagel.

Later Milo discovered that since the heavy black curtain had come into play, the DA had been yelling at others also, so he wrote her an email saying that she had no good reason to yell at anyone.

When she read the email she burst into tears and ran to HR. The email was abusive and threatening, she said, so Milo was brought into HR for questioning. The HR Person read the email, and asked Milo if he would be willing to apologize to the DA. He agreed to apologize, but then asked plainly:

"Is she allowed to yell at me and the others?"

"No," said the HR Person.

"Can I get toast in the Galley anytime I want?"

"Yes," said the HR Person.

Sid, whom I would be replacing as a Waste EO (Equipment Operator), ate his dinner from a blue Galley tray while explaining to me how the Housing Coordinator had received a death threat and then disappeared without warning six weeks ago. No one seemed to know just what the email threatened, but management had secretly flown the Coordinator out on one of the Winfly planes, which bring new employees and cargo near the end of winter, without listing her name on the flight manifest. This unheard-of departure from protocol added to the excitement and intrigue and promised to keep the incident on the grapevine for more than a week or two. Also, rumor had it the FBI was consulted.

The task of identifying the perpetrator of the threat was complicated by widespread dislike of the Housing Coordinator. During the winter months, winter-overs each have their own private room. Just before Winfly (the season from late August until summer begins in October) the Housing Coordinator had posted signs saying that the winter-overs would each get a roommate, without exception. Her math was poor. It was simply never the case that each of over 200 winter-overs was assigned a roommate, and old-timers who knew better wrote her emails demanding to know how the lucky few were going to be chosen to keep their private rooms. She replied that people were not paying for their rooms, that their "happiness" should fall "within the policies and procedures," and that if they didn't like it they should ask their managers if they could leave on the first plane out.

This type of counsel may have blunted contention had it come from someone more experienced, but she was a fingee. This was her first year on the ice, so even though she had been appointed head of Housing, her authority was a mirage. She wrote, "I am in the position to implement and enforce the McMurdo Housing polices and I appreciate the full support that my superiors in Denver have given me." Afterward, she received the threat, and the company scoured the network records to determine when and whence the email was sent. Since the perpetrator had not logged on, Human Resources interrogated a woman who was sitting at another computer when the email was sent, asking who was beside her. She said she didn't know.

With secrecy that caught everyone's eye, the Housing lady was sent to Denver to finish out her contract, after which she was to be flown back to New Zealand to enjoy the fringe benefit of the typical post-ice holiday. As Sid scraped at something with potatoes in it, he pointed out that under the current plan, both the victim and the perpetrator[5] would arrive in New Zealand upon completion of their winter contracts.

"Besides the death threat," Sid concluded, "it was a pretty mellow winter."

CHAPTER I
NOTES

[1] "At nine in the morning of the next day we had our first opportunity of seal-hunting; a big Weddell seal was observed on a floe right ahead. It took our approach with the utmost calmness, not thinking it worth while to budge an inch until a couple of rifle-bullets had convinced it of the seriousness of the situation." – Roald Amundsen

[2] "Perhaps the most interesting of all the reactions between the Antarctic environment and the temperament of the explorer occurs during the catastrophic period of expeditions. For the sake of clearness, this heading also needs subdivision as there are several possible types of catastrophe worthy of separate consideration. Thus we have:
1. The detention or loss of the ship in pack ice.
2. Catastrophes affecting individual sledge parties.
    a. The starvation of an inland party.
    b. The marooning of a portion of an expedition with inadequate resources on an unknown coast.
3. Polar madness generally." – Raymond Priestly

[3] Palmer Station, the newest and the smallest of the three stations, is seldom discussed at the other stations. Palmer lies across the continent, on the life-infested Antarctic Peninsula, which has been called "the banana belt of the Antarctic." While McMurdo has dirty skua gulls that

pester, Palmer has exciting seals that attack; while Pole has a rowing machine in the weight room, Palmer has sleek black rubber speedboats; while McMurdo and Pole share the bureaucracy of a thousand warring subcommittees, Palmer seems merely a nice family. When Palmer arises in conversations at McMurdo or Pole, our eyes roll back in our heads and our quivering tongues sparkle, like hogs envisioning a great feed. But mostly, we don't talk about Palmer, because it seems a different world.

[4] When trying to explain to a bank customer service representative why you don't have a phone number, or why your address has a U.S. postal code but that you can't step into the nearest bank branch to re-key your PIN because the bank cancelled your old cash card, the friendly customer service representative will hang up on you about 50 percent of the time as soon as you utter "Antarctica." After trial and error, the best workaround solution when trying to conduct business from Antarctica is to say that you are at a "foreign military installation."

[5] Throughout the summer I made known to many my interest in the details of this story, and over a year later I received an email from a dummy account by an anonymous person who claimed to have sent the death threat. "Annoniemaus" wrote: "Basically [the Housing lady] was a jerk. Everyone I knew was upset about housing, and wherever I went people were talking about it, discussing it, and upset. I was actually quite fine about it, since the way things were going was how I expected them to go. [Her] being a jerk really didn't feel like that big of an inconvenience, but the more I was around it all, the more it bothered me that someone like [her] could run around affecting people's lives so uncaringly, and then act so poorly when she was questioned in any way. I thought about it. I thought about how there was no way to show her how it feels when someone screws with your life and you are helpless to effect any change. What I came up with may have seemed rather drastic, but even in retrospect I'm glad that I did it. I made up a dummy account, just like this one, by logging on to a computer without using my login name, and then sent [her] an email that said if I saw her off the ice I would punch her in the face, or something. I never had any intention of doing so. Not even a little. In fact, like I said, I wasn't involved in any of the housing drama. I merely wanted to let her know what it felt like when you have no control over a situation that is upsetting and affects your life. Simple."

CHAPTER TWO

The Offshore Account
and the
Alien Abduction

Antarctica, perhaps more than space, conjures up in the mind images of hardship, personal valor, danger, adventure, and of course, the hero.

– Report of the U.S. Antarctic Program Safety Review Panel

It has been noted that some individuals are using the ice machines in the dorms for chilling their beer and other drinks or food. This practice can lead to illness, is unacceptable and must stop immediately.

– RPSC Safety Representative

In the middle of his first night in Antarctica, Grif woke up freezing. He huddled under the blankets trying to sleep, but his uncontrollable shivering required action. First he got out of bed, donned his standard-issue expedition-weight long underwear, added the fleece jacket, some socks, and crept back into bed. No big deal. This was exactly the kind of demanding living he had expected here. That's why the company had given him all these cold-weather clothes in the first place. After a few more minutes of shivering, he got up to find a knit cap and some mittens. Then a few minutes later he went for his parka. Lying in bed, trembling in full outdoor gear, his frozen breath dancing in the dim LED glow of the nightstand alarm clock, he thought of the next four months and the obvious mistake he had made in deciding to spend them here, where everyone wears outdoor gear to bed every night, and the government handbooks don't even mention it. When the cold became too much, he finally jumped out of bed determined to get his blood moving. He rushed from the room to find all his neighbors pacing the halls in their parkas while the UTs (Utility Technicians) fixed the furnace that had broken down a few hours earlier, leaving the dorm toilets full of ice.

This story always gets a laugh after you've just returned from the ice machine with a full bucket to freshen the drinks of people wearing shorts and slugging margaritas in a stuffy dorm room after work. It is a classic story of fingee awakening, and it makes old-timers laugh because everyone remembers that brief period where going to Antarctica somehow meant going back in time to a world without technology. Before I came down I imagined I would be sleeping in a hollowed-out pit of snow and braining seals for food. I had never imagined institutional modular dorms with laundry rooms and foosball tables. Few come to the ice prepared for relatively comfortable quarters. So it is no surprise that neither are they prepared for the entrenched class structure by which comfortable quarters are allocated.

In McMurdo, the central currency for buying a larger room with a sink (so you don't have to walk in the bone-dry air down the hall to the bathroom to fill your humidifier) or a shared shower (so you don't have to face a robed expedition down the hall each morning, manhauling your toiletries) is called Ice Time. Primitive in conception, the more Ice Time you accumulate, the better housing you can expect. The Ice Time system rewards returning employees, an inexpensive carrot for retaining experience in The Program. But the official algorithm used to allocate housing considers not only one's Ice Time, calculated in months (minus Ice Time before 1990, which has expired), but also one's "job points," calculated from a hierarchical system that measures one's professional status in town. (For example, a Nurse, the Hairstylist, and the Meteorologist each receive two points, while a Quality Assurance Representative receives 12.) Those with fewer than 36 months of Ice Time add up their months and divide by eight. Those with more than 36 months divide by four. Adding job points to this quotient gives Ice Time.

A good way to avoid all these messy calculations is to have friends in the right places. Anyone with a friend in NSF ("the customer") is eligible for Housing policy exemptions, as are those having sex with managers. Managers are also quick to point out that Ice Time includes time "in the Program" and not just time on the ice, meaning that full-time workers in suburban Denver who receive Christmas bonuses, health benefits, who work standard 40-hour weeks, and who go home to their dogs each evening to eat fresh fruits and vegetables, have accrued lucrative Ice Time should they come down to McMurdo for any reason at all.

In practice, the value of one's Ice Time changes according to current conditions, but no matter what, in the summer, from October to February, everyone has a roommate.

When my friend Señor X flew down in mid-October, I rode his coattails across the tracks to Upper Case[1] housing. With only ten months of Ice Time, I had barely squeaked into Dorm 208. Now our room was bigger. We had a sink in the room and we shared a shower with only the neighbors rather than the whole floor. These were the fruits of Ice Time.

Señor X and I had been roommates in Lower Case the previous summer, when he was in Fuels and I was in Waste. Our room smelled like diesel and garbage. I would sit captivated as he explained to me how Fuels would "pig the lines" by blasting an oblong projectile through the hose to expel standing fuel. I would explain to him the latest methods of handling urine. (The task's greatest challenge was to forget the terrible havoc narrowly averted each time a u-barrel was successfully hauled down a steep and bumpy road above any cluster of buildings.) The relative ease of modern McMurdo urine processing impressed us because when Señor X had worked in Waste years ago, the u-barrels were taken to the Old Incinerator Building to thaw. Warmed as if by a mother hen, the hot piss was then poured into the sea at the hands of Waste Technicians who for the dark splashing foam kept lips clenched while observing firsthand the shades of mass dehydration in Antarctica's extremely dry climate.

Señor X was now on his sixth summer, but his first as an AGO groomer. AGO (Automated Geophysical Observatory) is a program of automated data collection sites on the plateau. Each summer the gadgets must be maintained and the generators that power them refueled with propane, which is converted to electricity using special on-site converters. For accommodations, two science techs stay inside the AGO box, a small shed with a heater, while two groomers sleep in tents. The crew is dropped off by a Twin Otter aircraft which leaves immediately because flight time is in high demand. For the next several days, while the science techs adjust the AGO units, the groomers prepare an ice runway for the larger LC-130 Hercules aircraft that will soon deliver all the supplies that the automated site requires to continue its clicking and whirring for the upcoming year of data collection. The groomers forge the runway on the ice by dragging heavy blades behind snowmobiles at high speed. Because some of the AGO sites have sastrugi—wind-formed ice ridges—as tall as a copy machine, groomers are frequently thrown from the machines. Groomers can break arms or crash through windshields. Their field kits include Vicodin. On the payroll Señor X was listed as a "Carpenter."

Señor X was to go to AGO 1 in a few weeks with a science tech named Jordan. Jordan was from a prestigious university. Señor X's boss was a little worried about Jordan going into the field because Jordan had recently asked at a preparatory meeting if there were showers at the remote AGO sites. Of course there weren't. The sites were out in the middle of nowhere. Besides that, all the women were buzzing about his eerie stare, and he was barred from one work center for loitering only to ogle them. Also, he had been telling people he came to Antarctica to meet aliens.

Now, settling into our shared room after work one evening, Señor X taped three photos of a field of flowers on the outside of our door. Beneath the flowers I taped a picture of the Norwegian black metal band Gorgoroth slathered in fiendish facepaints and wielding broadswords. One's door decorations are an innocuous but not entirely unnoticed representation of one's civic identity, much like at a boarding school. Identification with one's door decorations in McMurdo increases with abundance or with particularly obsessive themes, such as top to bottom Christmas decorations, or more than ten Peanuts cartoons, or more than one cross or other unmistakable Christian symbol, at which point one might be referred to as "the Snoopy freak" or "the Jesus guy." If someone were to describe Señor X to someone who didn't know him by name, the order of clues would be broadcast roughly as follows:

> by department or division ("You know that science support guy?"),
> by past or present sexmates ("…went out with that Fuels gal?"),
> by job title or function ("…is grooming runways at AGO sites?"),
> by physical characteristics ("…tall, has glasses?"),
> by roommate ("…lives with Nick Johnson?"),
> by past department ("…used to work in Fuels?"),

by office location ("...works up at 191 or MEC if he's in town?"),
by famous antics ("...the one who had his hat stolen by a skua?"),
then, in the unlikely event familiarity has not yet registered,
by door decorations ("...field of flowers on his door?").

As I had winced regarding his door decoration, Señor X urged me to examine the flower photos more closely, and said something about landscape and consciousness. In turn I reminded him that Gorgoroth were countrymen of Roald Amundsen, who had defeated Robert Scott in the 1911–12 race to reach the South Pole, and that they had authored such contemplative songs as "Crushing the Scepter" and "(Under) the Pagan Megalith."

Though my roommate and I were dissimilar in many ways, we were unified in our tireless enthusiasm for all things Antarctic. We were armchair strategists who argued over the complex logistics of the industrial caravans that traversed to the Black Island communications outpost 60 miles south of Ross Island. We regarded as superheroes obscure Antarctic figures such as Rozo, the baker on one of the French expeditions who did nothing but wear slippers around the hut and bake croissants, or Anton the Russian Pony Boy, who entertained everyone with his national dances.

Señor X had invited people over tonight for Thai food. He emptied tiny jars and festive packets into a prized wok procured from a departed winter-over, while I futzed around the narrow room, arranging the moth-brown Eastern Bloc furniture with grave deliberation, and running extension cords for our many appliances. I shrieked when I zapped my video camera with static electricity, forgetting to first reach for something grounded—this would become habit after a month or so in the dry air. On the walls I hung some Robert Scott masks and a map of the Tucker Glacier Area. I attached a tally counter, like bouncers use at nightclubs, to a new bulletin board, both of which I had recently found in a skua pile.

A skua (rhymes with "Kahlúa") is an Antarctic gull that feeds on baby penguins, seal placenta, McMurdo Food Waste, and is prone to cannibalism. Skuas are tough and aggressive. They occasionally appear at Pole, 800 miles away, and a skua was once spotted on a beach in Florida, gobbling corn dogs and sandy ice cream cones. Skuas sometimes molest people carrying trays of food on the short walk from 155 to their dorms. A bagel or danish may be plucked from someone's hand, and a screaming skua once swooped down and stole Señor X's hat from his head. The tasseled knit cap was found two years later across town near the Helo Pad.

Though the penguin image pervades McMurdo via work order forms, the mail flag, t-shirts, hats, bumperstickers, postcards, and cheap shotglasses, it contributes little to the language. As far as anyone knows, penguins don't really do anything, they're just darling and funny. Skuas, on the other hand, steal food from each other, prey on stray penguin chicks who move too far from the group, and try to eat each other's heads. The skua's workaday sensibilities have found it a significant place in the McMurdo vernacular.

Each of the dorms has at least one "skua pile," where people dump potentially reusable goods they no longer want, useful things like clothing, books, coffee mugs, and temporary tattoos of dinosaurs[2], as well as more optimistic items like broken pencils, packets of ketchup, and near-empty shampoo bottles. Skua piles are first-come-first-serve and free for all.

The early summer skua frenzy is often so vigorous that at times it might be called a mass pillage. Furniture raids on dorm lounges are planned, and information about a coveted loveseat is closely guarded to foil any preemptive strike. Anything left in the hall, when moving between rooms for instance, should be marked "Not Skua." This will protect the owner, not against clear-headed theft, but against rationalized theft. An adventurous woman once left a pile of food in the hall for less than one minute and returned to find a bag of avocados missing. "No one skuas[3] a bag of avocados," she said angrily. This incident recurs, but the objects change, from hot pots to bundles of clothes hangers. Despite problems of liberal interpretation, skuaing is a treasured community practice, convenient and practical for some, and for others a fond hobby, like rooting through thrift stores, but where everything is free[4].

Aside from the tally counter, I had recently skuaed a functional light bulb (an item sometimes scarce for those who don't know anyone in Housing), a bag of seaweed, a bottle of cumin, the sheet music for *Rocky Horror Picture Show*, and a reference book of bone fractures and their treatments, with photos and X-rays.

"What can we count with this thing?" I asked Señor X as I fiddled with the tally counter. "I think we should click it whenever someone says 'plane'."

"Each conversation involving planes? Or each use of 'plane'?"

"Yeah, that's a problem," I said. I imagined Ben repeating, "plane" as fast as he could. (Ben and I had become friends our first year when he was a blaster and I was a dishwasher. He told me how to use explosives to move ice and rock and I told him how factions evolve in a kitchen. Ben had introduced me to the beauty of the high-quality Hawaiian shirt.)

"Let's count the number of times someone clicks the counter," Señor X said. "Then we'll always be accurate." We agreed this was the best idea so far.

Kath arrived with a halfrack of Export Gold (a New Zealand beer). She was working Waste at Pole, but would be in McMurdo yet for a week or two.

"Hey Kath," I said, "look at our new counter. No, on the bulletin board."

She clicked it. "What are you keepin' track of?"

"None of your goddamn business. Where'd they put you?"

She began stocking our fridge. "155," she said. "But I got the whole room to myself, so I'm open for business." Kath had spent the last few months sewing fleece hats that she would now sell for $15–$20 apiece to her co-workers, who had plenty of money and nothing to spend it on. "I had five people come up during dinner. I already got a list of people who forgot to bring cash. That's the thing about this place. It's easy to trust people because they can't go anywhere and you always know where to find 'em."

We drank beer and talked while Señor X conjured steam at the desk.

Kath had first applied to work in The Program for the summer of 1996–97 when all Galley and Janitorial services were subcontracted to International American Products of Charleston, South Carolina. IAP's bread and butter was prison contracts, but they were branching out.

For a call to their office, Kath was rewarded with the position of nightshift Janitor Supervisor. She and the other IAP employees were flown to Charleston with contracts they had received in the mail, for lower wages than they had agreed to by phone. In the office, a secretary was collating stacks of documents by hand from the floor. They filed into a conference room for Orientation and the manager told them to rip up their contracts, then he passed out new ones with accurate wages. People who had worked in The Program before asked why they were only receiving $290 instead of the usual $300 for travel expenses. The manager told them ten dollars each was deducted for the pizza and Cokes they would have after the meeting.

One of Kath's new co-workers asked her where Antarctica was, and if there were cats there. The unemployment office had rung him one day to offer him a position as a cook, and said if he didn't take the job his benefits would be cut. "Is it cold there?" he asked.

When they got to the ice, they found that the IAP manager wore alligator shoes and a suit and tie to work each day. Wearing a suit and tie in McMurdo is like wearing a spacesuit to a bullfight. Even though he was a manager, Housing had dumped him in Lower Case, and Kath watched him from her window as he commuted to work through the wind in his parka and alligator shoes, clutching his briefcase.

Alligator held a meeting with the janitors. He set up his laptop on the Galley table and handed out graphs charting the season's performance. He introduced them to something called the managerial module, and asked the toilet-scrubbing crew for their input on measurement tools to chart performance efficiency. Nearby, a DA wiped tables with a wet cloth.

The meeting adjourned, Kath asked him where he was from, and what he had done before this. He rattled off a résumé. When he told Kath to attend weekly supervisor meetings at 2 p.m.—in the middle of her nightshift sleep schedule—she said no. He insisted, but she demanded to know how he would like to wake up for a meeting in the middle of the night. He relented, but was thereafter wary of her team spirit.

Meanwhile, the Galley staff was at odds with Alligator because he ordered that each day fresh fruit be decoratively cut and placed on top of the serving islands in the Galley, for the touch of class it added. "We're in Antarctica," they complained, "Fresh fruit is scarce and valuable." He demanded that the practice continue, so the top of the food warmers sported halved oranges with triangular ridges and sprigs of grapes that were hot and mushy by the end of the day. Finally, when murmurs percolated up through management that the new subcontractor wasted fruit, plastic fruit was flown down.

After a few months it became obvious that payroll problems among the janitors and Galley workers were not isolated mistakes. Some were receiving half pay and others had not been paid for as long as two months. Those who did receive checks noticed that these were handwritten and drawn from an offshore account in the Cayman Islands. Those who reexamined their contracts noticed an article prohibiting employees from discussing their salaries with NSF or with ASA (the support contractor at the time), punishable by termination.

Unrest in the rank and file was evident, so Alligator held a meeting with all IAP employees and told everyone to sign a statement promising not to discuss their salaries with NSF or ASA; anyone who did not sign would be fired and required to pay for their own plane tickets back to the U.S., and thus pay straight into IAP's pocket, since their contract with NSF guaranteed them the cost of employee travel expenses. No one signed the paper, and a few brought their contracts to NSF and ASA managers for consultation. The contract was illegal, and NSF demanded that IAP provide the employees with a new contract. Because of their previous troubles, 15 or so people no longer wanted anything to do with The Program and refused to sign the new contract. But because Alligator had previously fired a number of people to emphasize a no-nonsense work environment, the Galley and janitorial staffs were already running on skeleton crews. NSF and ASA had an emergency meeting and determined that the only way to keep those 15 people from leaving was to keep them bound to the original contract, meaning that they would have to pay for their own plane tickets should they decide to leave.

Now they had to pay to leave Antarctica. A few people told Alligator quietly that he wouldn't make it through Christchurch without a beating. Alligator, now afraid, held employee parties in the Coffeehouse and paid for oceans of wine from his own pocket, but the threats lingered in meaningful looks and gestures. At the end of the season he tried to leave on an early flight but ASA rebuffed him because, after all, he was a manager and supposed to oversee things until the end. As the end of the season closed in, he panicked and finally, wanting to make it through Christchurch before his disgruntled underlings got there, declared that he had a "family emergency" at home. "Family emergency" is a potent phrase, like "safety concerns" and "inappropriate behavior." It worked; a woman was bumped from her flight so he could leave.

No one knows whether Alligator made it through Christchurch scot-free. But some still remember the day one of Alligator's bags was run over multiple times with a loader, cologne seeping from smashed vials within, seams bursting, so that the entire mess had to be tied together with twine before resuming its place on the pallet of cargo.

Laz and Jeannie arrived for Thai food. Bulky red parkas slumped in a pile by the door. Boot treads relinquished filaments of snow onto the worn carpet. "The wind is loud in these corner rooms," someone said.

Señor X distributed bowls of rice covered in spicy gray sauce, spiked with carrots and peppers. If you had just awoken from years of sleep and walked into the room, the carrots and peppers would tell you a plane had recently visited. The white shreds of snow on the carpet turned clear before they melted. To the bulletin board I pinned a note that I had found tucked inside a cheap novel at a Seattle thrift store. I read it aloud to the feeding throng:

> Meg,
> Take this money to use toward your dress. I just wish I had more. You are just the best daughter I could ever have asked for. I love you dearly, Meg. There is some soup on the stove on "warm."

Can you stir it and turn it off when you get up. Wake me up before you go so we can visit a little.

    Love you, Mom.

"Awww," Jeannie cooed. "That's nice."

Señor X nodded.

"That's sweet," Kath said.

"Isn't it?" I said.

Laz remained silent, his mouth contorted like a toppled parenthesis.

"What the hell are you smirking about?" I demanded.

 "I don't want to spoil your tidy illusion," he said.

"Oh please."

"Obviously they had some sort of fight. They had an argument and now the mom's trying to make up for it. 'Hey, here's some cash. Sorry I yelled at you.' She might have hit her. The daughter came in drunk or all messed up on cocaine. She'd been out sucking a bushel of dicks. This is clearly the aftermath of some grievous turmoil."

"You're all fucked up."

"Sir, you may adjust your blinders as you see fit."

One morning near the end of October, settled and adjusted to my rounds as a town garbageman, I took a loader down to check the Wood and Construction Debris dumpsters that needed constant attention at the Playhouse demolition project. The Playhouse was a large Quonset hut in the center of town, located between the Coffeehouse and Southern Exposure, the smoking bar. The Playhouse had been constructed by the Navy many years ago, and was being demo'd to make room for an office building called JSOC.

It was Condition 2, the windiest day of the season so far, and the sheets of metal at the apex of the Playhouse arches were acting as a wind-catch. The whole structure was very unstable and leaning about 45 degrees, like a crumpling covered wagon. The workers had chained the bucket of a Caterpillar loader to the end of the Playhouse to stabilize it.

The new Safety Guy was there to watch. He had recently emailed emphatic demands that people on the construction projects wear hardhats and eye protection. He had braved the wind to visit the Playhouse to ensure strict compliance with Safety procedures. With one hand gripping his own clean hardhat to keep it from flying away, and the other clutching a clipboard, he watched a group of men wearing hardhats and eye protection run into the quaking Playhouse to collect the tools and scaffolding before the structure collapsed in the wind.

This brand of playacting, in which rigorously enforcing minutiae (such as hardhats) symbolically defends against larger dangers (such as a collapsing building), pervades The Program. The act requires a straight-faced zeal that favors the ignorant or the ambitious, simply because it is avoided by everyone else as a contagious brain-eating disease. One time, with winter temperatures hovering around −80°F, the South Pole Safety Representative, running out of topics for the mandatory daily meetings, instructed workers on first aid for heatstroke.

This new McMurdo Safety Guy had made his first public appearance a few weeks before, at the Driver's Safety Course in the upstairs lounge of the Crary Lab. The course was mandatory for most employees. Unlike most of us, who were dressed in insulated brown Carhartt overalls for working outside, the Safety Guy wore jeans and a Denver Broncos t-shirt.

"Well, let's get started," he said finally, once the room had filled. "Welcome to Driver's Safety Training."

He told us that conditions in McMurdo were treacherous because we'd often be driving on ice; that the speed limit through town was 15 miles per hour; and that it was mandatory for us to wear seatbelts at all times. We must make full stops at all stop signs.

"Just like in the U.S.," he said, "driving here is not a right. It's a privilege." He stretched a pause, pregnant with omen. "What that means is that if you're caught breaking the speed limit, you can have your driving privileges revoked. Now, if your job requires your use of a vehicle, and you can't drive…" he smiled and held up his hands palms out, as if to show that he wasn't holding a weapon, "…then that means you might not be able to fulfill your contract and may be sent home."

There was another pause, a sinking in of consequences.

"Okay? So let's just be safe out there and drive slowly. I'm here for your benefit. My job here is to make sure that you have a good season and go back safely to your families."

One moment he said that all vehicles were government vehicles and that we could never use them for non-work purposes. The next moment he said that we were taxpayers and that tax money bought these vehicles, so we should take care of them as if they were our own. Each of these messages he delivered as if explaining something as natural as a tide chart. He ended by saying that if we ever had any safety-related concerns, we should just stop by his office. And that if we ever had any questions, we should feel free to ask.

Then he told us to come up and show him our U.S. driver's licenses. We rose and shifted in a haphazard queue to have our names checked on a list he kept on his clipboard. When I handed him my driver's license, he reviewed it meticulously before checking me off. I cracked some little joke that made him smile so over the next few weeks we politely acknowledged each other in the hallways.

When I had finished my work at the Playhouse, I drove up to Building 140 to fork a White Paper that was on my collection list. I saw Nero outside strapping something to a pallet, so I climbed out of my loader to say hi.

I first met Nero one morning during my first summer when I dropped by the food freezer to investigate the legendary supply of hot dogs I had heard about. McMurdo had enough hot dogs, if they were laid end to end, to stretch to Pole. Years ago, when a Galley manager had set up a 24/7 self-help hot dog warmer in the Galley to alleviate the swollen inventory, the food purchaser back in The States compounded the problem by ordering even more hot dogs to keep up with the spike in consumption. With a forklift in the warehouse, Nero raised me to the ceiling so I could photograph the few accessible pallets of wieners, the bulk of them buried beneath a thick plateau of frozen jalapeño poppers and cocktail smokies. He also moved a cabinet from an office wall to show me various graffiti commemorating the hot dogs. McMurdo's legacy as having the world's southernmost obscene supply of hot dogs ended at the turn of the century, when most of the franks were retro'd from the continent to an unknown fate.

Nero had many stories from his time in The Program. He had been coming down since '94. His first year some guys abducted a penguin and took pictures of it stuffed in bed with someone who had passed out drunk. The irritated bird made a mess and ran around squawking until someone finally let it outside. He had taken part in the first live video feed from Pole, and he was around for some of McMurdo's most classic events, such as the drug-infested winter airdrop in the mid-'90s, and the Hammer Attack incident of winter '96. Actually, he has been at the center of strange events his entire life. One time when he was a child, Nero's father had taken him along in the car to kill grandpa, but Nero's uncle pulled up alongside them, and his father and his uncle screamed at each other through the wind, weaving neck and neck at 70 miles an hour, until the errand was aborted. As a child, Nero had a pet raccoon. When Nero matured, his parents asked him to burn down the house for the insurance money. He had once taken a strange woman home, where she bit off a chunk of his scrotum. Nero often says, "It's all good."

Briefly he was a clothed extra in a porn movie. The atmosphere on the set was jovial. One time the men dipped their cocks in some bitter solution as a practical joke before a blowjob scene. The women joked about biting off their dicks, and the men joked that the only way to shut them up was to blow loads down their throats. Between scenes, the other men would stand together naked in the bathroom drinking vitamin potions and joking as they absentmindedly tugged at their cocks. One of the guys wore a gold medallion depicting the fingers of a hand encircling the earth.

Around the time of his film stint, Nero was on a Los Angeles freeway driving to work in an expensive car. The seat was adjusted to accommodate his tree-like height, his long hair bunched in a ponytail, and his muscled arm stretched to the steering wheel; he wore sunglasses and was talking on a cellphone. As traffic slowed, he looked at the people in the other cars and some of them looked exactly like him. "What the fuck am I doing here?" he thought. Then he got a job stacking hot dogs in a freezer in Antarctica.

"Nero, what's up, dude."

We stood out of the wind next to my idling machine. Dry wisps of snow snaked over the roads as though the entire town were being dusted for fingerprints.

"Hey, man, did you hear about the janitors?" he asked.

"Uh-uh."

"I guess they were watchin' TV in one of the lounges during work. The guy told me they missed their break and so took a late break, but whatever. Some NSF Reps were giving a tour to some DVs and caught them watching whatever-the-fuck in the lounge. One of the Upper Case dorms. He fired 'em on the spot. One of them was a supervisor, too."

"So NSF is going to start cleaning toilets or what? Looks like we're going to be a community pretty soon."

"Looks that way. I gotta run."

USAP history is rife with exciting tales of termination and exile, the bulk of them low-level firings early in the summer. It's easy to understand why some people are fired. In the summer of 1998, Sean was fired for throwing rocks at Ron, who was trying to run him over with a loader. Their rivalry stemmed from a disagreement over which was the best techno club in Christchurch. In many cases, though, firings are largely understood to be a matter of slaying sacrificial lambs, as people in higher positions, or those who have seniors with clout to protect them, aren't fired for greater infractions. Common are the stories of uncorrected blunder and negligence by someone with allies in the inner sanctum of Denver or NSF, such as the station manager who once rolled a truck, or the System Administrator who made lascivious commentaries to a woman on his favorite of her boyfriend's emails to her, or the managers who broke into the bar, or the doctor who canceled his office hours so he could take Swing Dance lessons, or the other doctor who emailed a patient's medical information to her entire supervisor list, or the three doctors who all prescribed different antibiotics that failed to cure a patient's ear infection because, as the patient later learned, each of them was a different venereal treatment. In none of these cases was anyone fired, because it is tricky to instantly find a housebroken manager, an experienced System Administrator, or a competent doctor without a stateside practice and who is ready to work for peanuts, so most of those fired are like the janitors watching TV, or the woman in the Galley who came to work topless one holiday, or the fingee who fell asleep in the shower after a party, his naked butt cheek covering the drain, flooding the bathroom. After such a termination comes an appeal to the community for volunteers to help the short-staffed janitors, for example, by cleaning in the evenings. Warnings of disciplinary action are addressed to "employees." Exhortations to chip in are addressed to "the community."

In 1939, the German vessel *Schwabenland* spent two weeks off the coast of Queen Maud Land launching long-range seaplanes into the Antarctic skies with a catapult. As the Nazi planes flew over the Antarctic interior in a photo-survey of Eastern Antarctica, each flight carried 500 pounds of swastika-engraved javelins, one of which was dropped every 18 miles as they flew over the surface to mark "Neu-Schwabenland." They collected five emperor penguins for a zoo and planted a Nazi flag in the snow near the coast. The German press announced their scientific interests in meteorology and oceanography.

The night of the Halloween party, Laz came to my room dressed like a Nazi soldier with a trenchcoat, a helmet, and a Hitleresque moustache.

"I always suspected you of harboring some nationalist warchest," I ranted. "I suppose your pockets are full of swastika-emblazoned thumbtacks? On which scrap of frozen waste do you plan to scatter them, hmm?" Laz smiled patiently as I continued. "The frost-pocked bank of mud behind 165?

A patch of abandoned gloom between the beige ribs of Crary? I have always felt that that thin scratch of a snow-clogged ditch behind the Haz Yard was a ravishing bit of property best claimed by some august patriot."

"Sir, once again you have leapt to ignorant conclusions—though I suppose that is befitting your education. I am the Fun Nazi! I intend to make sure no one has fun this evening." He produced some implement to corroborate his claim. A whistle or something. "And you, I see, have labored intensely in the small hours, on the rim of imagination, sparing no expense to rise to the occasion." I wore a dirty white sheet, a hole cut for my head.

We walked down the Crary Road to the Halloween party at the gym. The firetruck was parked outside. Men were blazing steaming incisions into the snow behind the gym. There was a line of women waiting for the u-barrel. Inside, lit only by spinning and flashing colored stage lights, the gym was dark, and packed.

Hundreds of nearly indistinguishable red or brown parkas clogged the entryway. I stuffed my own into the back of the pile and pushed it to the bottom because I didn't want it taken by mistake. The next day Highway 1 would have "Lost Coat" signs, listing the contents of the pockets and the nametag on the front. It is usually a matter of mistaken identity, but some coats end up in surplus stores or as souvenirs in someone's closet in the U.S.

The Rec department was selling cans of Canterbury Draft and Steinlager for $2. I bought a Steinlager and tipped the Rec guy a buck. He would make about $300 in tips tonight, because opportunities to throw money around are few.

Occasionally someone at one of these parties has Pole moonshine or some concoction of peppermint schnapps and JATO from one of the station's many secreted barrels of pure grain alcohol, thought to have once fueled Jet-Assisted-Take-Offs when overloaded planes needed a boost on short runways. JATO tastes horrible, but since the community fate depends upon planes, there is a pleasure in drinking jet fuel, as an agrarian society eating dirt or a warrior culture drinking blood.

Through breaks in the mostly '80s music, an emcee urged people to sign up for the costume competition, which highlighted McMurdo's vast skua reservoir. Costumes have included a Caterpillar loader, Robert Scott and his ponies, a pee flag (yellow flag planted at camps to consolidate the ugly snow in one area), a black flag (planted to signal danger by crevasses or thin ice), the South Pole, an Aluminum Queen, a u-barrel, a Construction Debris[5] bin, the

Greenwave supply vessel, and someone dressed in his workclothes who said he was a drunk ironworker. The year the support contract was rebid, two guys came to the Halloween party as blind men with canes. One wore an ASA sign, the other a Raytheon sign, and they were connected by a rope labeled NSF.

"What are you?" a pirate yelled as I maneuvered through the dancing crowd in my white sheet. I handed him a pair of glasses with white paper taped inside the lenses and he put them on.

"Condition 1," I yelled.

McMurdo officially has three kinds of weather, or Conditions. Condition 3 involves wind speed of less than 48 knots, visibility greater than a quarter mile, or wind chill as cold as −75°F. Condition 3 is ordinary weather in which those so authorized may drive to the runway and those off the clock may enjoy outdoor recreation. Condition 2 involves wind speed as high as 55 knots, visibility of more than 100 feet, or wind chill as cold as −100°F. If Condition 2 is called, even those authorized to drive out of town must first check out with Mac Ops, so that when you disappear someone will know to look for you. Outdoor work is permitted in Condition 2, but not outdoor recreation. Condition 1 involves wind speed of more than 55 knots, visibility of less than 100 feet, or wind chill colder than −100°F. In this weather everyone must stay in whatever building he is in, as winds toss milvans into the road and send loose plywood into the air like a platoon of wooden blades in some unnerving *Fantasia*. Everyone except the Galley workers sits around drinking coffee, and the managers fret over delays to The Program.

Though the Condition System is theoretically based on observable scientific criteria, there are other unofficial considerations. For example, Condition 1 may be narrowly avoided because declaring it would necessitate having a Search and Rescue Team escort workers home. Since work schedules and other practical matters constrain the official severity of the weather, one must dress carefully and with forethought, no matter the Condition. Sometimes Condition 1 weather afflicts every location but McMurdo, which remains at Condition 2. Sometimes Willy Field and the road to it are in Condition 2, allowing Fleet-Ops to go to work there, but ten feet off the road, where Condition 1 prevails, is officially too dangerous to set foot. Among the legendary weather events is a Condition 1 storm that raged all day and night on Sunday but abruptly eased to Condition 2 at 7:15 on Monday morning. Once a fueling team, stuck on the road between two runways by an overly optimistic official pronouncement of Condition 2, negotiated a declaration of Condition 1 applying to the road they were on. This exonerated them for the delay, but to avoid the costly inconvenience of turning the plane around, everywhere else remained in Condition 2. This was like having tolerable weather everywhere on the gridiron but the storm-battered 50-yard-line.

Wandering around in a gymnasium dark but for disco lights, sipping a tepid beer, dressed as weather, watching administrative coordinators grinding to "Funkytown" and "Love Shack," I decided I was done for the evening. I retrieved my coat which had floated to the top of the pile, and returned to my room to read *Gulliver's Travels*.

The Halloween party, my first supervisor once told me, ends the introductory stage of summer. The couples that form at the party eat breakfast together in the Galley the next day, which announces to town their new mating status. Nearly everyone who's summering has come in from Christchurch, and the roommate and initial housing issues are settled. The people who latched onto each other at Orientation have joined separate cliques and now they have strained conversations when they see each other in the halls. New people are starting to understand how things work, and returning people, thrust back into the action, the jargon, the politics, and the stories, are starting to remember why they keep coming back. Some claimed they would never return again, but that was last season.

Just after Halloween, the National Science Foundation confiscated a shower curtain. Some women hung it in the bathroom of Hotel California for more privacy while men visited the nearby co-ed sauna. The NSF Station Services Manager seized it because it was unauthorized. After the women in the dorm petitioned NSF and filled out a work order, the shower curtain was reinstalled, and their revoked privacy reinstated.

Such skirmishes are a daily occurrence. They are the natural result of a teetering bureaucracy stuffed into a small town of people improvising in an unusual environment. The "by the book" mandates of management are eroded daily by the slippery traditions of a shifting mass of seasonal contract workers whose innovation—useful for jerry-rigging an engine or concocting some out-of-stock tool—does not dry up at the end of the work day, when residents sneak work tools to build lofts in their rooms, barter goods between departments (without all the messy paperwork), and find nice warm places to grow marijuana. Management's ceaseless campaign to harness this ingenuity only for the power of work is one of the primary themes of The Program, and incidents that illustrate this theme are popular gossip when they occur.

A few weeks after the shower curtain was confiscated, an NSF Representative went into Daybar looking for someone. Daybar—held in the smoking bar, Southern Exposure—is open three or four times a week in the morning for nightshift workers who, because the sun doesn't set in the summer, keep the bar as dark as possible. Often the only source of light is the glow from the screen on the cash register and the periodic flame of a cigarette lighter. The NSF Rep came to Southern and stood peering in through the doorway, remaining there longer than the standard time required for entry or exit. The glare from outside pained the Daybar golems, who let out a clamor to shut the goddamn door for chrissake.

She was not subject to the etiquette of a caveful of slouching grumps—she worked for NSF. She became furious and stormed into the bar, demanding the lights on. The next day the National Science Foundation sent an email to staff insisting that the bars must at all times have adequate lighting. Due to "safety concerns."

These weird little eruptions occur more frequently in the summer, when more big fish are around. Big fish in Antarctica are little fish in Denver and Washington, trying to impress by bringing big pond ways to the tiny backwater pool. So shower curtains are impounded, and sitting in darkness becomes dangerous overnight. But the workers know that they can redecorate and click off the lights the minute the bureaucrat creeps onto her plane. Despite the administrative sophistication that impounding a shower curtain reveals, the lesser inhabitants of the murky puddle resist the bureaucrat's refinement, not so much from a firmness of character as from a lack of interest in the bureaucrat's goals, like that of reptiles ignoring gameshow incentives that urge them to reach for the bigger prize.

One night in early November, the summer season in full swing, AGO Jordan gave a lecture called *The Reality of Dreams*. The lecture packed the Coffeehouse. The rumor of his rendezvous with aliens had brought the curious out of their rooms on a school night. Jordan was tall and had bright eyes, with dainty gestures and a perfectly groomed goatee. He wore a smart scarf around his neck.

The lecture was a fascinating mishmash of Southern Californian nonsense. After he reminded us that we live in a physical reality, he said that humans could transmit radio waves that are imperceptible to the human ear, because we have made transmitters and receivers, but that we have entered a digital age where data are reduced to ones and zeros. He said that dreams are just as real as our measurable external world and that humans transmit and receive streams of digital data via our minds and that these data streams are not measurable with current scientific apparatus, and that we do so at all times over great distances.

This explained that Jordan was not giving women creepy stares; he was actually transmitting messages to them via digital data streams. I wondered if his digital message was creepy too, or if it was more romantic. I wondered if he could hack into people's brains and look through their eyes or make them eat corn chips when they weren't hungry.

After his lecture he invited questions. Some people asked questions so they could argue a point here, a point there, get involved, and join in the freedom of intellectual debate with a horny mystic. I had seen this kind of excitement-murdering filibuster before at a lecture by four people with Romulan haircuts and infomercial sweaters who claimed that the human race was an experiment by a race of extra-dimensional Scientists who had given us life but urged us to recognize our true nature and join them on "the next level" where we would drive bio-organic space-time vehicles and live in harmony with our masters. Their cult drove around to colleges in a van trying to recruit people to join their "Astronaut Training Program" which involved computer programming and fasting. Even at that exciting lecture, the niggling pedants squawked about points of logic, drowning out the few in the crowd who tried to find out what the Scientists' space-time vehicles looked like.

Finally, someone delicately asked Jordan about the aliens:

"Many of us came here to verify something we've heard: Did you come here to meet someone? What do you expect to see out on the plateau? Why did you come here?"

Jordan replied: "I'm here to do maintenance on data collection devices for the AGO sites."

As was polite and proper, no further questions about aliens were asked, and people began to leave.

The new town psychologist was facilitating several community support groups, including a Women's Group, a Men's Group, and a Diversity Issues Group[6]. The psychologist had put flyers around town that read, "Need a place to talk? Support Groups starting soon..." The flyer was a soothing green with puffy bright yellow lettering. In its center smiled a beady-eyed clown made of primary-colored plastic. Its face, hands, and feet were agreeably rounded and smooth, as if to be safely gnawed by toddlers. When the support groups drew low turnout, she sent out an all-station email assuring employees that the group discussions, though sponsored by the company, were confidential.

The psychologist worked for Nicoletti-Flater Associates, a company hired to administer psychological screening for wintering Antarctic personnel. Winter-overs' employment packets included a handout, "Bypass the Winter Blues" by company co-founder John Nicoletti. The article outlined tips for minimizing "depression, irritability, apathy" and other psychological problems brought on by the disruption of the "body's circadian rhythms" by prolonged darkness, extreme cold weather, and "trying to co-exist with a small group of people."

Besides his stated expertise in cold weather psychology, John Nicoletti had been a police psychologist in Denver for over 25 years, and was an expert in crowd control. At a conference on campus riots held at the University of Northern Colorado, Nicoletti told a group of law enforcement and university workers, "The earlier you intervene, the higher the probability you can prevent a riot," suggesting that a riot is what happens without professional intervention. Nicoletti said, "When you decide to assault, assault with enough intensity that they know you're serious. You've got to look mean and quick and foreboding. This is not a touchy-feely time. You've got to come in as one big scary thing." He also suggested that water cannons are very effective but look bad on videotape. "We have to assume that rioting will occur," he said, "–that's where we have to come from, so then we're prepared."

The McMurdo psychologist came up to the Waste Barn one day to speak with the Waste Department about Stress Management. It was the end of a long week with heavy trash flow from Pole. We sat in the breakshack in our dirty Carhartts that had been ripped on metal from climbing in the CD flatracks, our gloves smelling of Food Waste, our sleeves sticky with beer from sorting Glass.

She described to us tunnel vision—when most of the world turns black and closes in on you—and told us that stress alone can give a person tunnel vision, and it can happen in an instant.

An instant? I fretted. I suddenly remembered all the clanking and crashing and rattling that I had grown accustomed to. I thought of how the details of each day are obscured by familiar patterns. I worried that all of life's sleepwalking moments would one day simultaneously demand accounting. The psychologist was an expert. I began to pay close attention. I did not want to suddenly get tunnel vision.

The psychologist was upbeat. Ready to make a million friends. She told us that we could talk to her in her office in the library anytime, and that she was hired to help the community and thus would have nothing to do with employees' winter psychological evaluations. She had powers of confidentiality. She told us that things were not easy here in this environment. But there are things you could do to recognize and relieve stress.

I was gripped as if by a thriller. The psychologist appeared to recognize how weird were all the little moments, even when just trying to relax. For example, each day before work I would drag myself out of bed in time for a cup of coffee and a cigarette in the 155 smoking lounge beside the barbershop. The stale chamber was outfitted only with couches, ashtrays, and a television. Few talked in the smoking lounge, because when we heard people talking they sounded stupid, saying things to each other like they were talking only to each other, even though the rest of us could hear them too. So we smoked and watched television, usually in silence. One day in particular I remember about a dozen of us, all haggard men in torn and filthy polar clothing, solemnly chain-smoking in the dark until the start of our shifts, silently watching a gardening show. It was not that anyone wanted to watch the gardening show, but that's what was on. The channel had most likely been selected an hour before by an early riser. Those who filed in later had watched whatever he was watching. Perhaps *Bonanza.* But once the early riser had left and *Bonanza* was over, each person who arrived believed the current channel had been selected by someone in the room, or possibly by everyone in the room. There was a sense that the channel was intended. Very rarely, someone would enter the filthy den and say, after a few minutes of watching *The Flintstones,* "What the fuck is this? Anyone watching this shit?" We were all watching it, but everyone shook their heads. The channel-changer would be fortunate if there was a ball game on another channel, which would be greeted by a murmur of approval. But if the other channels were no better, like a soap opera or the news, then sometimes the channel-changer would murmur, "Shit, nothing on…" but now he was in a pinch. In the warm ashtray smell of the lounge, he was to blame for whatever stupid show we watched, even if he returned to the original channel.

I listened to the psychologist carefully. As a backstage participant in the field of behavior modification, perhaps she would explain the indistinct variable ratio schedule of approval and negative reinforcement that rained down in daily emails. Maybe she would translate in which cases the artificial and material reinforcers in our contracts were authentic and in which cases they were just part of the shtick, to be later revoked. The psychologist might even reveal the Solomon's wisdom behind it all, and a design for frontier social control, thoughtful and well-executed, would clearly emerge from the smeared napkin-plan of The Program. I was on the edge of my seat.

The psychologist suggested that we go to bed early, quit drinking coffee, and quit smoking.

On Thanksgiving[7] weekend we had two days off instead of one. The Galley made an extravagant meal and people dressed in their finest. Many men bring down one suit and tie for these occasions, and women often pack at least one dress. On the tables were cards sent by kind people, such as the members of the Covenant Congregational Church in Elkhorn, Wisconsin, who wrote: "...we hope the important research you are accomplishing more than makes up for all the hardships you encounter."

Speed, an Equipment Operator from Pole, stuck in McMurdo by weather after a winter at Pole, had met AGO Jordan, and invited him to eat with us.

When someone asked Jordan what he did at home, he said he was studying lightning and then, in order to describe the fundamentals of his research, went into a detailed description of how a radio works.

I was focused on the cheese and salmon on my plate, and was pondering scenes from the previous evening in my room where I insisted on playing Brujeria all night, and maybe it was the dark metal vibe that led the editor of the NSF-sponsored *Antarctic Sun* to demand that Ben stab him in the arm with a fork. Ben made a practice stab on the cutting board, leaving four deep gouges from the prongs. Ben said, "You probably won't be able to use your hand afterward," but the editor didn't care. He was drunk. We were all drunk. It was a two-day weekend. I wouldn't allow the transaction in my room because I knew Ben would do it, just as he had once attacked me with a vacuum cleaner outside in the snow, and there was no reason for the editor to lose a hand if I could halt the game of chicken with a spontaneous policy prohibiting blood on the carpet, though I would have loved to see it.

I lost track of what Jordan was saying about radios and lightning, but I appreciated his thoroughness, and he was sincerely curious about local operations. We told him about the ice pier in Winter Quarters Bay that is formed like a cake with alternating layers of ice and dirt and attached with cables to the shore. We told him about the year the ice pier had outworn its useful life, and the Coast Guard was charged with towing it out to sea, but it broke into fragments that they surrounded in dinghies, scratching their heads in the middle of the bay, and how the replacement ice pier split in half last summer and had to be stitched together with cables. We told him how the hill above town is scraped by dozers to collect dirt for spreading on the icy roads, and how buried beneath the town's surface are deposits of scrapped wood, metal cables and barrels and charred debris from the trashburnings at Fortress Rocks, and how the entire town is saturated with fuel, and how the Navy in the winter used to push barrels of bad fuel onto the ice where they would disappear into the bay come the summer thaw. We told him that Laz's ass was likewise a repository for piss, but Laz argued that he was good for no more than two liters.

An NSF Rep was walking around to the tables serving pumpkin pie. The time-honored tradition of a head honcho adapting a servile role on a holiday was performed gracefully, and people laughed nervously and snapped their fingers for more pie, which he obeyed amidst a chorus of mitigating thank-yous.

The week after Thanksgiving, Jordan began approaching lunch tables and telling people that aliens would arrive at noon on Thursday, November 30. The aliens would come down from the sky to meet Jordan in the open lot between Medical and 155.

A local prankster made signs showing the spaceship from the movie *Independence Day* with the caption "We Are Coming." Someone else made pictures of the top of nearby Ob Hill and various landmarks in town exploding from laser blasts. These were posted on the I-Drive[8], communal space for photos on the local network.

On Thursday, November 30th, a co-worker and I were banding flatracks all morning at Fortress Rocks. Absorbed by the task, we lost track of time and came down late to lunch.

As we hung our coats in Highway 1, people were filing in from outside and a male and female NSF Representative were pacing the hallway. She said, "What should we do?" He said, "Well, I know what I'm going to do…" and he began ripping down the "We Are Coming" posters while his colleague stood in the hallway menacing those who toted alien paraphernalia. "What are you doing with that?" she asked a woman who walked by with an alien mask in her hand.

At noon Jordan had been outside waiting for the aliens. 50 people that Jordan had met at the lunchtables came to meet him. They were wearing alien masks and glittery bobbing antennae from the Rec Office costume closet. They had showed up to see what would happen, and stood in a group nearby, watching as Jordan wandered the dusty lot looking to the sky.

The NSF Representatives and some other higher-ups had heard about the gathering crowd and showed up to keep things in line, one of them taking video. They surrounded Jordan. Then someone wearing an alien mask raced up on a four-wheeled Polaris, did a few circles in the lot while the crowd of aliens laughed and cheered, and sped off. Recovering from their temporary confusion, the bigwigs corralled Jordan into Medical.

Later that evening Jordan was still in Medical; the word "lockdown" was used. He was manifested immediately and flown out the next day. A memo to the Commander of Operation Deep Freeze (CODF) described the evacuation of Jordan: "…a civilian patient began exhibiting erratic behavior. He described events about 'aliens' coming to McMurdo. He had been previously examined in Christchurch by a psychiatrist and deemed not acutely psychotic. However, due to his increasingly bizarre behavior, it was decided to transport him back to CONUS."

The abduction was hot on the grapevine and would certainly be talked about for years.

That Saturday, after work, lounging with the Fuelies on some cargo in the sun, an administrator told us she had seen the Photoshopped pictures of destruction on the I-Drive and was scared that Jordan was going to blow up the town. Before noon on Thursday, while Jordan was waiting for the aliens, she had driven her work truck down to Scott's Hut to avoid the explosions.

"Are you joking?" I asked.

"I'm not joking," she said severely. "At home I'm a grade school teacher. We're trained to pay attention to these things."

———

CHAPTER 2
NOTES

[1] The bottom of the barrel are Hotel California and MMI (Mammoth Mountain Inn) because they are far from the Galley next to the thundering Helo Pads and the walls are so thin that the neighbors can be heard humping or vomiting in the trash can. If you live here, everyone else's room is bigger than yours.

The Lower Case dorms are nearly identical except for 210 and 211, which were designed by a Hawaiian architect. They have high ceilings and uneven heating. Recently, Lower Case dorms 204 and 205 were renamed 203B and 203C, circumventing an arcane code concerning the number of simultaneous building renovations. Now there are three dorm 203s. If you live in the Lower Case dorms, everyone else's room is not really bigger than yours, but it appears so because their furniture is arranged differently.

The most desirable rooms are in the Upper Case dorms, 206–209, the large brown dorms with three stories. Dorm 209 is special in that 209 Bayside rooms have a view of the sea ice and the Transantarctic Mountains. 209 Bayside is full of managers and old salt. Some people with enough Ice Time to live in 209 choose another dorm instead, because 209 is considered stuffy and the walls have ears. If you live in Upper Case, your room is bigger than everyone else's.

[2] Forty million years ago, Antarctica was home to a giant carnivorous bird called Titanis, nicknamed the "Terror Bird." *The New York Times* ("Fossil 'Terror Bird' Offers Clues to Evolution," by Walter Sullivan, Jan. 31, 1989) wrote, "The bird's head was longer than that of a horse, and it presumably used its massive, hooked beak to tear apart its prey, after striking it down with one of its huge clawed feet." Crazed and insatiable, the feathered beasts slaughtered giant armadillo-like mammals for their brutal birdie feasts. A researcher from the Institute of Human Origins in Berkeley, CA, said it was "probably the most dangerous bird ever to have existed."

[3] Standard usage, though less common, allows "skua" to mean "contribute to the skua pile," such as, "I figured someone would want these sponges shaped like human organs that expand when placed in water, so I skuaed them."

[4] The Housing Coordinator who had received the death threat had, amongst her other achievements, made a new policy that skua piles were off-limits to winter-overs, who had formed the skua piles to begin with. This policy ended with her covert departure at Winfly.

[5] Though most people are very conscientious about sorting their trash, Construction Debris nonetheless remains a community favorite. CD is the category where one should put mixed floor sweepings, an inseparable chair made of metal and plastic and cloth, or a broken mirror, but when no one's looking it means "anything goes," and is where people sometimes like to throw bags of trash from their room that they don't feel like separating.

[6] "Diversity" is mentioned just often enough to scratch some statistical itch. The Program is overwhelmingly white.

[7] From K at Pole: "We have had a helluva Thanksgiving. The beakers supplied all the wine; so you know where the night went...hell in a handbasket. It was awesome. Last week this chick got busted giving a blowjob in the upstairs bathroom...not once, but twice in the same night. This past weekend she was making out with any woman that would. Wow, I tell you. She propositioned Speed and I one night in the bar; and she continues propositioning me. Oy."

[8] I-Drive might commonly be heard in contexts such as "Did you see your picture on the I-Drive? Why were you carrying a mop at that party?" or "I went to Cape Royds last week and took 42 pictures of penguins. I put them all on the I-Drive."

CHAPTER THREE

LITTLE AMERICA

We are anticipating that our expectations will become yours as well.

— Welcome to Raytheon memo

Someone has been trying to influence my mind.

— True/False winter-over psych eval

FROM THE FIELD CAMP come many of the greatest Antarctic stories. Here early explorers scrubbed their eyes with cocaine to ease the pain of snowblindness and then went to bed with bellies full of pony meat. At the field camp, paper-thin tents shudder beneath katabatic blasts of freezing wind, stoves sputter a stingy flame, and a few trudging specks haul shovels through a cold world where extra food and equipment cannot be bought at any price. The compilation of infinite suffering of those so isolated from society is an entrancing lesson that seems never to wear thin. The field camp—remote, minimal, and inconvenient—is the underlying image on which other Antarctic images are built.

Fingees arrive ready to work at remote field camps. When they instead find themselves beneath 155 chipping away at a glacier of frozen urine[1] deposited by staggering Naval ancestors, or shoveling on a snowy hillside looking for a load of buried pipe lost in the shuffling of expendable supervisors, that's when they realize that they have been tricked, and they begin to pine for the rugged field camp, where they can show what they are made of. Volunteering for what they imagine to be a daunting task, eager fingees are soon told by the old warhorses to get in line.

Field camps are desirable destinations. Given the chance, most people would work in the wind and cold surrounded by glaciers and nunataks at Lake Fryxell rather than work in the wind and cold surrounded by ditches and buildings at McMurdo Station. The stakes are as high as they have always been, but risk of death in the frozen wilderness has been reduced by the airplane, the radio, the emergency-homing beacon, the GPS unit, the satellite-tracking Orbcomm device, and improvements in clothing. Field camps have stereos and laptops. Abundant field camp provisions include New Zealand white cheddar, smoked meats, and lots of chocolate. The McMurdo field support Food Room dispenses dozens of beaten copies of *The Joy of Cooking*. Field camps are established only during the summer, and few scientists or employees stay at a field camp for more than a few weeks at a time. But field camps lack running water and may be cut off from communication by solar flares, so they provide the caliber of inconvenience that makes for an attractive struggle against nature, where mortality is as apparent as the tent and the radio. Nonetheless, in modern USAP history, most Antarctic fatalities have been related to transport or industry.

Fatalities are rare now, but in the bloodiest years, the first 30 years or so after World War II, an NSF safety report records that only three deaths were related to field activities: a scientist at Byrd Station disappeared, a research diver died from an accident beneath the ice, and a man died of a fall at Asgard Range. The other 40 or so American deaths during that period were more run-of-the-mill. Most were from plane or helicopter crashes, as when an aircraft cartwheeled during landing in 1956, or when, as recorded in an NSF report, an "aircraft landed in poor visibility conditions, and a few seconds later exploded." Many deaths were from tractors falling through the sea ice, and one went into a crevasse. People have been killed offloading ships and planes, crushed in loaders and trucks, scorched by an exploding fuel drum, and electrocuted in a ship's engine room.

But it is not risk in the face of industrial mishap that brings to the continent legions of people who wear Teva sandals over wool socks. When I asked people why they first came to Antarctica, they said they wanted to climb mountains, ski glaciers, hike, and see wildlife. At first I was shocked, not by the particular answers, but by their unanimity. Surrounded by people talking about climbing, skiing, paragliding, kayaking, or rafting, I suddenly wondered what the hell I was doing down here.

The main draw for many who go to Antarctica is a love of nature.[2] I find nature creepy and disturbing. No matter how staggering the horizon, wilderness only reminds me that I must eventually return to the colony. The great outdoors is at best a sideshow curiosity, and at worst an unreliable informant. For example, working at a fish cannery in the Aleutian Islands, I admired the austere hills and the white bulbs of cloud that could grow above them in an instant, as if the hills had ideas, but the natural image seemed a treacherous deceit. I preferred those more honest times inside the cannery at a meaningless task among the decaying machines and the vast architecture of technology. I preferred the aggressive hiss of a high-pressure hose echoing through a yellow-lighted room of stainless steel bins, with drains thoughtfully placed for the chemicals and the blood. I preferred those times when the tranquilizer of cosmic perspective could not reach me.

In contrast to the sobs of praise that accompany any barren stretch of dead backdrop, McMurdo Station is often called ugly by those who came down for sport. On his way to Pole from McMurdo by ski, Eric Philips, a member of the "Icetrek" expedition, stopped at Willy Field to talk with some grunts. They eventually went back into their job-shack, and Philips, who had a corporate sponsor, a huge insurance policy, and a satellite phone, wrote of them, "I pitied their restriction, bound to the confines of the Mactown environs by their work, by safety regulations, and by a general satisfaction with their experience of a civilised Antarctic wilderness. I was glad to see the door shut."

The resilience of mankind in Antarctica is inexorable; even the constant bleating of those who whine for permanent silence and infinite pristineness dissipates into an insignificant Buddhist drone beneath the soothing rumble of fleets of machines with pulsing hydraulics.

McMurdo is beautiful. A construction site exposed long enough to a rattling generator grows a building. Each growling machine drags a fumbled leash of diesel exhaust. A line-up of washing machines waits to be executed at the metal baler. In a janitor's closet in 155 a ladder leads to the attic, where a door opens into the sky. In the winter darkness, falling puffs of snow are bathed in the luminescent blue of a welding torch. A contingent of cylindrical acetylene tanks watches over a pile of inventoried triangles. In McMurdo one can warm up from the cold by a generous furnace, and fuck to the sound of helicopters.

A week into December I went out to the ice shelf with the women of the Remediation crew to dig garbage out of the ice, a rare trip for me away from station. The sea ice beneath us was over 100 feet thick. Beneath it was the Ross Sea. The Ross Ice Shelf continued for hundreds of miles to the south, a lot of nothing. We scratched and pried at the surface of the hard blue ice to extract wire, conduit, food, machine parts, and other debris near Pegasus Airfield, named for a plane that crashed in a blizzard in 1970. The plane remains buried in snow and ice, and is a popular landmark for NSF to show to DVs (Distinguished Visitors). The unsightly debris we were to remove was too near the plane.

Today it wasn't too cold or windy. The sunlit views of Black Island, White Island, and the Transantarctics were clear. From this distance McMurdo was an insignificant drab smudge swallowed by smoking Erebus, its silent overseeing authority. Daily life in the hive washed over me with a shock of pointlessness. I need to start paying attention, I thought. Shit, I need to call my mom more often. I should really sit down with my friends and tell each of them what they mean to me and why. My God, I'm going to die. I need to stop smoking. Like the psychologist says. I should jog or ride the Exercycle, and drink green tea, with antioxidants.

As I blasted away at the ice shelf with a diesel jackhammer to retrieve a 40-year-old fuel barrel left by the Navy, I imagined laughing with co-workers at lunch over jokes about cows or leprechauns rather than jokes about asses full of piss. I imagined in the evenings writing to schoolchildren in the United States, describing to them the raw beauty of the Antarctic and the quirky ways of the penguin rather than the toxic hill by the ice pier and the fierce hunger of the skua. "Your youthful enthusiasms drive me to such mirth," I practiced, as I reexamined my strategy for breaking from the ice what had at first appeared to be a small broken mop handle, but had now revealed itself through my successes to be a large cabinet of some kind, encrusted with turds. The crashed airplane slumped nearby like a slain bull. This irreverent debris cluttered the tragedy.

When I shut off the jackhammer, only a few sounds remained. My co-workers chipped at the ice in crisp intervals with ice-axes that sparked tiny explosions of cold shrapnel. The Spryte idled nearby, gargling fuel. The wind spoke as cautiously as unseen vermin. Each sound was like a distinct boulder in a river of silence. This turbulent silence, the sprawling ice, and the occasional sharp gusts of wind warn that eventually you will make a mistake. The threat is babbled endlessly, as if Antarctica were a lunatic.

At four o'clock we loaded the picks and shovels onto the sleds, refueled the jackhammer, parked and plugged the Spryte at one of the job shacks, and tied down at a Pegasus cargo line the triwall we'd been filling with debris. Then, jerry cans secure on the back of the skidoos and masks snug, we bounced the 18 miles back to town over the ice shelf, weaving fast through the trenches and divots made in the snow by all the heavy equipment traffic. Small, bright canvas flags of orange, green, and red fluttered on the bamboo poles marking the route. Though the poles were five or six feet long, some of them had been there so long that the ceaseless accumulation of snow on the ice shelf had left only their tops as nubs, the tattered flags brushing the snow in the wind like the foliage of trees shrinking back into the ground.

This first week of December had been warm, so it had snowed constantly, and so the planes stopped arriving. When the week of bad weather broke and the temperature dropped, flights resumed immediately. The good weather had allowed us to come out and hack garbage from the ice. The good weather had taken my roommate away to the plateau, and had promised to bring the Hot GA back to town from Siple Dome camp, where she had been for over a week.[3] The Hot GA was comfortable in dirty Carhartt overalls, sunglasses hanging around her neck, her face slightly burned and her lips perpetually chapped from shoveling snow beneath the ozoneless sky, her leather work gloves with the little steer logo marked as hers by the rounded scrawl of her name written on the back with a Sharpie, and her unruly blond hair plotting a disorganized escape from the knit cap that threatened to fall over her eyes. Since my roommate had been sent out to the plateau to break his arms in the service of science, my room would now be a good place for the Hot GA and me to drink wine and have sex in the chair.

The Hot GA, whom I had met recently, was an accomplished white-water kayaker.

Despite Pope Leo XIII's urgent warnings in 1884 that Freemasonry "generates bad fruits mixed with great bitterness," Freemasonry remains a time-honored Antarctic tradition. I only discovered the creeping Masonic influence when one evening the Freemasons held a meeting in the Coffeehouse. The Coffeehouse is a Jamesway, a type of portable half-cylinder of wood and metal made famous during the Korean War. Adorning the curving wood-paneled walls are some old wooden skis and a Nansen sled that Señor X one season rescued from a Construction Debris flatrack. The Coffeehouse is warm and has a big plastic tree and various smaller fake houseplants. At square formica-topped tables people knit, play chess, and read Trivial Pursuit cards to each other.

I sat near the Freemasons with a book titled *Secret Societies* on the table in plain view, to be sporting. In the Outer Rituals of the Third Degree, Masons commonly keep a Junior Apprentice at the north wall to ward off any "Eaves-droppers." If one is caught, he is to be "plac'd under the eaves of the Houses (in rainy Weather) till the Water runs in at his Shoulders and out at his shoes." Perhaps because it is too cold to rain in McMurdo, the Masons there had retired this hallowed code; I sat nearby, curious and unmolested.

The ringleader of the Masonic Secret Society spoke of a bust of Richard Byrd that had been installed early in the USAP and had originally displayed a Masonic plaque, which someone removed.

"When was the bust put up?" asked one curious Mason.

"Well, we don't really know," said the leader.

"When was the plaque taken off?"

"Well, we don't know that either."

"Who took it off?"

"Well, we can only assume that NSF doesn't want to be affiliated with a philanthropic organization and so removed it."

The Masons didn't know anything, but they were ready for action, about par for Antarctic Freemasonry, which goes back to at least Scott's *Discovery* Expedition. Both Scott and Shackleton were Freemasons. Neither of them knew how to ski, and Shackleton had never pitched a tent before their first expedition. Before the *Discovery* left port in 1901, a pre-voyage ceremony aboard the vessel festered with Freemasons. King Edward VII, a notable figure in the occult fellowship, inspected the national investment and chuckled attaboys to Scott, who had been recently promoted at the recommendation of a Vice-Admiral who happened to be a Masonic Grand Master.

The idea was that loyal fraternity and Royal Navy discipline—rather than cold-weather experience—would pull the gallant Brits through polar setbacks such as scurvy, which killed sailors by the drove and was described by a man on one of Cook's southern voyages thus: "I pined away to a weak, helpless condition, with my teeth all loose, and my upper and lower gums swelled and clotted together like a jelly, and they bled to that degree, that I was obliged to lie with my mouth hanging over the side of my hammock, to let the blood run out, and to keep it from clotting so as to cloak me..." The sponsor of the *Discovery* expedition, Sir Clements Markham, wrote in 1875, "a contented state of mind is the best guard against scurvy." Robert Scott also felt that scurvy was to be prevented by running a tight ship and maintaining a positive attitude, and that avoiding scurvy's dementia, swollen limbs, loose teeth, putrid gums, and stringy green urine was largely a matter of character. Shackleton developed the disease on the way to the Pole, and thereafter Scott hated him, grumbling that Shackleton had spoiled their expedition.

Unbeknownst to Scott and Markham, in the 1600s Britain's East India Company had administered to sailors a spoonful of lemon juice a day to ward off scurvy, and in 1753 the Royal Navy surgeon Lind had proven that scurvy, now attributed to Vitamin C deficiency, could be prevented and cured with oranges and lemons. Because of Lind's studies, which were later successfully applied by Captain Cook, in 1795 the Royal Navy began supplying vessels with lemon juice, and scurvy became, after a few decades, a medical rarity. The respite lasted until lemons were replaced with limes, which were cheaper, but lower in Vitamin C, so that scurvy once again began decimating ships' crews. Lime juice was dropped as ineffective. With detail-oriented efficiency, the blackened and stinking flesh of scurvy had been managed back into existence, the cure forgotten by the time Scott and company went on their polar quest.

As the Masons in the Coffeehouse had discovered, American explorer Admiral Richard Byrd was also a Freemason. In 1929 Byrd led the first expedition to fly over the South Pole, thereby proving Antarctica's penetrability by plane and officially ending the dog-and-pony show of the Heroic Age of exploration. Byrd was particularly worried about the possibility of dissension infecting his winter-over crew, and had once written, "Of the thousand or more men who lost their lives in the attempt to conquer the Arctic, many of the deaths were caused by disloyalty or mutiny." Only 11 of the 42 men living at the remote polar base were Masons like him, so in the middle of winter he established his secret Loyal

Legion. He furtively approached each recruit, said that he had a proposal the recruit must swear never to reveal, then subjected the recruit to a five-page screed of makeshift Masonic inducements: ". . . join with me in trying to prevent the spirit of loyalty of the expedition from being lowered by disloyal, treacherous or mutinous conduct on the part of any disgruntled members," and "Until you agree and become a member of this fraternity it will be nameless, for its name must not be known by anyone but its members." Then Byrd administered an oath in which the initiate promised never to divulge the existence of the Loyal Legion, always to follow Byrd's command, and to "strive just as faithfully after the expedition ends to maintain its spirit of loyalty and... oppose any traitors to it then, as now." In return, Byrd swore his own loyalty to the initiate, and pledged, "in evoking through you the spirit of the expedition to help save it from malcontents, agitators or traitors, that I will at the same time do whatever is practicable to save these men from themselves and from ruining their own lives." Byrd spun his covert network of informants as a support group for those not invited to join—sure to boost camaraderie in a small crew isolated for the winter in Antarctica.

Like other famous Antarctic Masons, Byrd felt that public glory was the natural result of dispensing with the petty details. Though the Smithsonian Institute gave Byrd an award for aeronautics, the renowned aviator was said by one of his pilots to be little more than a distinguished passenger with questionable navigation skills. The American Humane Society commended Byrd for his treatment of the dogs he took to Antarctica, unaware that Byrd had decided not to fly dog food to a sledging party, who consequently built an execution wall of snow against which to shoot some of the huskies to butcher them as food for the others. Earlier in his career, Byrd had received a ticker-tape parade in New York City because he told the public he flew over the North Pole. The pilot who accompanied Byrd on the flight later revealed that they did not actually fly over the North Pole, but rather disappeared over the horizon, beyond range of the nearest base, and flew in circles for 14 hours before returning.[4]

Byrd considered himself to be in the "hero business." To help nudge the public in the right direction, he manicured the image of his expedition by censoring radio messages, and though he allowed a journalist on his first Antarctic expedition, he insisted that no story be released without his approval. He made the crew turn over all their photos and negatives to him so that his account of the expedition would be the primary one. (On one of Byrd's later expeditions, a similar order came down, but from President Roosevelt, requiring of each person "the surrender of all journals, diaries, memoranda, remarks, writings, charts, drawings, sketches, paintings, photographs, films, plates, as well as all specimens of every kind.") On the way back from Antarctica, when the Hearst papers offered Smith, one of the crew, $15,000 for his story of the expedition, Smith's diary was stolen from his locker. Byrd ordered the ship searched, and swore to Smith that he didn't know who took the diary, but one of the crew later confessed to Smith that he had stolen it on Byrd's orders.

Awed by his fantastic public image, some suggested naming the newly discovered ninth planet "Byrd."[5] Byrd's Antarctic expeditions were sponsored with lard from Crisco and money from John D. Rockefeller, Jr. and Edsel Ford. After flying over the South Pole, Byrd returned to a hero's welcome in the U.S., and began raising money to pay off the debts on his expedition. Charlie Bob, a friend who had given Byrd a good sum of money for the expedition, was indicted for fraud associated with his mining company and sued Byrd to get some of the money back, after which Byrd changed the names of Antarctic mountains that he had originally named for the shady sponsor. In McMurdo, behind the Chalet, overlooking the sea ice and the Royal Society Range, a bronze bust of Admiral Byrd donated by the National Geographic Society presides on a pedestal of black Norwegian marble. It bears no Masonic plaque.

Byrd named his first Antarctic base Little America. He had captured penguins on his expedition, but most of them died on the return voyage from drinking cleaning fluid.

At lunch, one day in mid-December, J.T. and I were discussing our plans for next week's movie, in which an emissary from Zordon would come to Earth to reclaim Antarctica, which is only a fragment blown from Zordon long ago in an intergalactic space battle with its nearby enemy, Planet Raytheon.

Several of us made a movie together every few weeks. We scripted as we went and shot linearly to avoid editing. The only hard rule was that the movie had to be done by the end of the day even if it meant throwing a very bad ending on it and calling it good.

Hank joined us at the table. Overhearing our plans for making movies, he asked, "Were you filming last night?"

"No, but we made a movie on Sunday night," I told him.

"Oh," said Hank, "I'm supposed to investigate some people who were down there last night."

Hank and I were friendly. I admired his ability to weave together disparate facts to evoke the great suffering of the miserable bags of blood that crewed doomed expeditions. He appreciated my comprehensive research on the same subjects, and was curious about the irreverent interpretations I drew from the histories he knew so well.

I first met Hank when I was a fingee and he had taken several of us to Cape Royds on a boondoggle. In Shackleton's gloomy hut he told us stories about the *Endurance* expedition, on which Shackleton's boat was crushed in sea ice and his crew spent two years camping on ice floes, devouring seals, and amputating each other's frozen extremities.

I was overwhelmed with the sensation that I was merely a ghost compared to old tins of lunch tongue and Savoy sauce and rations of pea flour left behind by Shackleton. I was annoyed by my new boots, my camera, my breath, and the patch on my parka that bore the mark of a government institution. I felt trapped in a cheap knock-off of some original meaty experience. I wandered around the hut with my notebook, cataloguing cans of plain gravy soup and liquid bottled fruit. The ink in my pen had frozen, so I scratched into the paper: curried rabbit, sweet midget gherkins, roasted mutton, and Moir's Gooseberries. While everyone else went outside to take pictures of penguins I stayed inside documenting dysentery medicine and concentrated egg powder. Hank, a fellow Stamp Collector, noticed this.

"Are you sure the filming you heard about wasn't on Sunday night?" I asked him, describing the plot of the movie we had made, and then asking if it sounded familiar.

He nodded, and explained to me that a low-level administrator in the Chalet was, at this very moment, in tears. She had begged Hank for help. She had given the key to Discovery Hut to someone who reported that there were drunk people dressed like devils inside the hut smearing blood on Robert Scott's artifacts from 1902.

The explanation was simple.

Our movie last Sunday had been called *Cape Hades*, about two fingee NSF Reps who see a sign-up sheet in the hall for a boondoggle to Cape Evans. They sign up, but when their guide arrives, it is not a certified trip leader from F-Stop, but the Devil, to whom they have unwittingly signed away their souls. The Devil takes them to Hell, played by local landmark Hut Point, and begins torturing them, but they scarcely notice because of their excitement about seeing penguins. NSF hears that two of its reps have been abducted by the Devil and sends a Quality Assurance Representative to rescue them. In the climactic scene the Devil pushes him off a ledge, and then NSF tricks the Devil into signing a contract to work as a GA. The movie ends with the Devil shoveling snow for science and humanity.

For the torture scene, Jeannie had pricked her finger so we could shoot a formulaic close-up of blood dripping on my pure-white bunny boot.[6] While our film crew gathered around this, three ANG crewmen came over to see what we were doing.

We were not inside the hut with Scott's antiques, but Emily was wearing a devil mask, and Jeannie was smearing her blood on my boot.

"Of course we were drunk," I said. "It was Sunday."

Hank laughed. Originally Robert Scott and his crew used Discovery Hut only as storage and to perform "amateur theatricals" that historian Roland Huntford notes "were an absolutely essential part of Victorian polar expeditions." For performances the hut was called the Royal Terror Theater, and the men—many of whom had military backgrounds—brought down wigs, dresses, and makeup for use in the dramatic exercises. The hut's use as a stage for amateur drama predates its use as a frozen historical shrine.

Hank knew of my roiling passion for the historic sites, and that the rumor was out of hand. He assured me he would calm the skittish bureaucrat.

Every year during the holidays, large plywood candy canes and two-dimensional gifts are hung along the main roads around station. A painted-plywood Grinch on a utility pole has been authorized. The Galley is decorated with tinsel.

A week before Christmas we received a holiday greeting from Dan Burnham, the CEO of Raytheon Company. He wanted us to understand how much Raytheon appreciated our "good work" and our "hard work" that year. He said that he and the Leadership Team would like to thank us for our many contributions to Raytheon during the year 2000, including an Integrated Product Development System and an Earned Value Management System, as well as advanced technology for missile defense, new tactical missiles like the AIM-9X, and the AESA radar for advanced fighters. He wished us the happiest of holiday seasons and a healthy New Year.

A few days after the email, we all shuffled into the Galley for an All-Hands Meeting. Tom Yelvington, RPSC President and Program Manager, had come to town to scope out the operation at the ground level. He had a goatee and wore a baseball cap and jeans.

I forgot that we had this All-Hands Meeting and otherwise I would have worn my full ECW gear to really look professional. Would that not have been appropriate? Does anybody wear that stuff? I see the red jackets, but other than that there's some pretty eclectic combination of outfits I see here. I saw a guy that had his big red jacket on, then he had some kind of paisley vest over it. Is this a throwback to the hippie generation, or—what do you do at a rave? Is that what you wear to a rave? To get your groove on?

Silence flooded the room.

The former president of Raytheon, and my old boss, was fond of saying that he had two kinds of people working for him. He had the people like the people in this room, that he called "the earners," and he had the people like me that he called "the burners." So we are here to support the earners, and that is you guys.

The juice dispenser hummed.

Last year there was a party and there were commemorative glasses, and just the people at the party got them. The full-timers who were here didn't get them. So they complained bitterly about that. So well heck… So what we'll do is have an end-of-season party and at that party we can celebrate the success supporting science this season… Last year we polled people for our first party and they preferred to dress down so we had a party at this place called "The Stampede" and everybody dressed up in Western gear and some people who had too much to drink made fools of themselves on the mechanical bull.

The snow melted from our boots.

Did I say why I was here? I did say why I was here?

Someone coughed.

The company has a very altruistic goal... How many people hear about Safety routinely from their Supervisor? Every hand in here ought to be raised. Two hands ought to be raised. You're going to hear about it until it makes you sick. And if those numbers come down and people quit being injured, then you're not going to hear about it as often, and then you'll feel a lot better.

Tom Yelvington continued to talk, and we continued to listen, trying not to move too much, and hoping that he would say something intentionally funny so that we could laugh.

"I can be a squeaky wheel," he said. "I can go to the boss and say, 'Hey, these people need to know, we need to know, I need to know. If I know I can let 'em know.'"

He told us, "There's very little that goes on in this company that we won't be completely open about," and that if there was something we wanted to know, then we should consult the management and "ask them, prod them, cajole them into letting you know what's going on." He joked that people at home thought he was walking off the face of the earth by coming down here, but that they didn't realize how accessible phones are and that "it's easier for them to call in than it is for us to get out."

The RPSC New Employee Assimilation Survey reads: "If you are a contract employee (not a full-time Raytheon employee), please disregard this survey." In other words, we would receive neither commemorative mugs nor incoming calls in Antarctica. We were not supposed to be squeaky wheels. It was ominous to consider what would happen if we "prodded" or "cajoled" management for information. We were contract workers. We did not receive health benefits, matching 401(k) plans, signing bonuses, or holiday bonuses as Denver employees did. We knew what we had signed on for, and no one cared, but it appeared to us that this man running the show did not know the difference between a full-time and a contract worker, a difference plain to all.

He opened the floor to questions ("Questions are important—I ask a lot of questions") and eased the strained silence with chatter.

"Now I've been part of the All-Hands Meeting! I like All-Hands Meetings. The term though—there's got to be a better term—it brings back bad memories for me. My sweetheart in the tenth grade fired me. She ran me off. What do you call it? She broke up with me. She said I was 'All hands.'"

At this there was a nervous tittering.

One of the fingee DAs raised his hand. He was a trickster. Some feared him. Many disliked him. When I met him at a party in MMI, he was making fun of everyone around him and lifting his legs and ass in the air to show them his "pussy." He had a tattoo that said "Tattoo." He had seizures on the floor of the bar, and no one could tell if he was faking or not, though there were reasons to suspect he wasn't.

Tom Yelvington called on him. The DA, with a controlled smirk, told the President of RPSC that there was no First Aid kit in his dorm, and that this was a safety concern. The powerful man with the goatee became excited, like a circus strongman asked to prove himself by crushing a grape.

"We'll take care of that right away," he said. The next day, we received this email:

> All,
>   In response to yesterday's RPSC's all-hands meeting....First Aid kits have been installed in every dorm's laundry room.
>   Regards,
>   Jim Scott
>   Raytheon Polar Services Co.
>   McMurdo Area Manager

About mid-December, the buildings from the Ice Runway are moved to Willy Field on the permanent ice shelf. The larger wheeled aircraft can't land at Willy, so everything arrives on smaller ski-equipped aircraft. Mail slows to a trickle. For most of December, package mail piles up in Christchurch and people temporarily whine about the mail rather than the food.

Then, sometime just before Christmas weekend, NSF gives a thumbs-up, the planes are stuffed with pallets of mail, and the mailroom stays open late with the help of volunteers to distribute thousands of pounds of packages. People eating barbecued ribs and sipping cans of Canterbury Draft next to a hydraulic lift at the Heavy Shop Christmas party spread the word that the mailroom is still open. Hurry up, the mailroom is full! They need you to get your packages out of the way! It's about time, because people were almost out of decent coffee, had been making it weaker in the last few weeks, and now there would be new CDs and stylish ski apparel. People lug the boxes to their rooms, then return to the Christmas party, for which the mechanics have degreased the concrete floor with a high-pressure sprayer and hung tinsel and cardboard candy canes around the garage to host the eating of meat and the drinking of beer while the bands play classic rock covers.[7]

On Christmas, Ben and I met after brunch in the lounge of 210. We huddled over a soldering iron that I had checked out from the tool room in Ben's name, in case it got lost, and we built insectoid solar-powered robots that I had ordered on the Internet. People walked through the lounge all afternoon, and we fed them Bailey's and good coffee while we tested our robots on the table and Laz expounded on the merits of the gleaming red asses of baboons.

In 1826, when Antarctica had been poked and prodded around the edges but was still thought to be a smattering of islands, John Cleves Symmes revealed his theory that there was a giant hole at the South Pole through which one could enter the earth and find balmy weather, abundant reindeer, lush gardens, and a race of humanoids eager to open a new trade route to the surface world. Symmes sought funds for an expedition to prove his theory, and enlisted charismatic disciple Jeremiah Reynolds to give lectures, which Symmes hoped would increase the public's receptiveness to his theory, thereby eventually coaxing official support. Unfortunately for Symmes, Reynolds fluttered away once boosted into the limelight. Reynolds had discovered that more people cheered, and more politicians sniffed about curiously, when he broadened the goals of the expedition. He no longer stirred interest by hypothesizing on the gaping cavities at the Poles, or the subterranean world with its "salubrious climates," or the deranged troglodytes thus far deprived of humanity's friendship. Now he promoted a scientific expedition that would benefit the "human family" and "add something to the common stock of general improvement" that would bring the "thanks of the human race." Eventually, Reynolds broke with Symmes completely and became a key proponent of and lobbyist for the United States Exploring Expedition, commanded by Charles Wilkes, who, according to some, was the first to prove that Antarctica was a continent, not a collection of islands.

130 years after John Cleves Symmes published *Symmes' Theory of Concentric Spheres: Demonstrating that the Earth is Hollow, Habitable Within, and Widely Open About the Poles*, Antarctica had largely been mapped and probed. No vast recesses hiding gardens of earthly delights were likely to

be found. No unexpected tribes would emerge with strange spices or new species of meat. Putting an industrial station at the South Pole effectively rolled a boulder over the hole in the Pole, forever entombing hopes of new subterranean frontiers. All the real estate had now been parceled and X-rayed. There were no more remote corners promising vast riches and unmolested virgin lands to keep us marching when we became tired, at least for most of us. In 1969, when Pole had already been inhabited for over a decade, Raymond Bernard published *The Hollow Earth: The Greatest Geographical Discovery in History Made by Admiral Richard E. Byrd in the Mysterious Land Beyond the Poles: The True Origin of the Flying Saucers*, suggesting that UFOs came from within the earth rather than from the stars, and that Richard Byrd had actually flown into the earth's interior in 1947. Enthusiasts such as Bernard, against all reason, pursue fantastic frontiers, unsatisfied with the second-rate real ones, such as the muddy ocean depths, where fish don't have eyes, and the darkest reaches of space, which are very exciting, but where payoffs are small for huge efforts and long waits.

In 1605, 200 years before Symmes published his hollow earth theory, Bishop Joseph Hall wrote a fictional account of travels in the southern polar lands. Written under a pseudonym to avoid persecution by the grumping magistrates he criticized, the book satirized Hall's own country and the church that dominated it. No one had seen Antarctica or set foot there; it hid in a great blank space at the bottom of the map. Hall's book appeared long before the Pole had a hole, and before the hollow Earth was a hive of alien spacecraft. It appeared before Antarctica was the most pristine and dangerous land in the world, and long before it contained the secrets of peace and hope for future generations. His book, written when Antarctica had hardly been invented yet, was *Another World Yet the Same*.

A few days before New Year's, while we were all energized by Christmas and giddy from the anticipation of another upcoming two-day holiday, Tom Yelvington and Erick Chiang, NSF head of the Polar Research Support Section of the Office of Polar Programs, met the Waste crew in the break shack on a rare visit to learn about our jobs, The Program, what we liked, and what we thought should be done differently. A few days earlier our manager had emailed us reminding us to talk with him first before bringing up anything new at the meeting.

Chairs were brought for them from the office, we introduced ourselves one by one, and said where we were from and how long we had been in The Program. Erick Chiang took notes on a pad of paper, and Tom Yelvington used a Palm Pilot. Erick asked what we thought would improve the Waste Operation. Suggestions abounded, most of them involving the replacement or improvement of capital equipment, which would probably be the proposal of many departments; budgets must be met, and none of us expected that Waste would take priority, since our equipment was adequate for the most part.

The subject of an entirely new Waste facility was brought up. This idea had been kicking around for years, Erick said, but was unlikely to be realized anytime soon. Still, he humored us by reflecting on the plan.

"Where would we put it?" he asked.

Because the Waste Barn is on the edge of town, we spend a lot of time transporting waste, and our department would be more efficient if it were central to the work centers we most often service. Someone suggested the Ballpark. Someone else suggested the empty area next to FEMC. These were the only options, really, without displacing some other facility.

"We could knock down the Crary Lab and put it there," I said.

"I don't think that will happen," he said.

The Crary Lab, with its three-phase architecture, one-pass air exchanges, and deep freeze chambers, was very expensive to build and construction was a lengthy process. In order to remove it, a new lab facility would need to first be built so as not to disrupt scientific activities. That would take a few years. He had quickly assessed the input and found it was not feasible, so he did not write the idea on his notepad.

Someone asked why Raytheon had mistakenly ordered a costly amount of redundant ductwork for the Galley remodel. Tom Yelvington said this was embarrassing and that he was working hard to get rid of such kinks.

Tom Yelvington told us that in making these worksite visits, he discovered that we employees seemed to be concerned with wages. He said that a third-party consultant had been hired, and their task was to make sure that wages were the same as market wages in CONUS for equivalent job descriptions.

Someone asked him, "Will they take into account that we work a 54-hour week instead of a 40-hour week?"

"Now that's a good question. To tell you the truth—I don't know. I don't know. But I'm going to find out. And I'm going to get back to you on that."

He scribbled on his Palm Pilot.

About a year later, when the "compensation structure" review was completed, we received an email from Tom Yelvington in Denver saying that no significant changes to wages were needed in order to attract and retain talented employees.

I sent a query up the chain of command asking again whether the compensation structure survey was based on a 40- or 54-hour workweek. The Operations Manager, after two weeks of no response from Denver, wrote back saying, "Must be a good question if the answer is so elusive."

NSF is eager to bring to Antarctica anyone who can further the funding of science, such as the House of Representatives Subcommittee on Basic Research:

> Dr. Erb (NSF): Well, it is a wonderful place to do science, and it is a fascinating place to see. And I do hope members of the Committee will be able to find time, Mr. Chairman, yourself included, to see it firsthand.
>
> Chairman Smith: Thank you.

So late December through the end of January is high season for politicians, journalists, tourists, and other USAP special guests. At special banquets in the Galley they are fed creamy feta and red pepper roulade and stuffed chicken breast with rum-lemon glaze and green beans amandine, with fresh shrimp flown from New Zealand. DAs are yanked from the dishroom to serve them.

In the summer of 1998, NSF invited a group of Republican senators led by the Senate Appropriations Committee Chairman for a Pole boondoggle so NSF could beg for $125 million to build the new Pole station. One of the Senators was from my home state, and has been referred to in one of the Seattle papers as Skeletor, an alarmingly accurate portrayal. H.L. Mencken once wrote: "Observing a Congressman, one sees only a gross and revolting shape, with dull eyes and prehensile hands." I'm certain Mencken was referring to one of the Senator's ancestors. When I was a kid I had first seen the Senator at a groundbreaking for a shopping mall in my small hometown. For a while, the Senator had even sent me Christmas cards each year with a picture of him and his family. I had never contributed money to him but, in a political studies class in high school, our teacher had told us to volunteer for a political campaign, and

I didn't hesitate in my choice to work for the Senator: I had been haunted for years by the Senator's vein-hewn skull, the half-lidded roving tumors that dwelled within cavernous eye sockets that seemed big enough to receive endless buckets of golf balls, and by his smile, which looked like a compound fracture.

In a house-basement in the suburbs I stuffed envelopes for the Senator's campaign with a friendly woman who openly hated Democrats and carefully disliked Mexicans. A young professional guy with a white shirt and tie came in occasionally to stuff a few envelopes, but mainly just to soak up the action. His shirtsleeves were rolled up and the smell of wet envelope glue seemed to excite him. Our little campaign outpost was furnished only with tables and chairs and phones, the bare essentials of groveling for funding. But though we were small, we were part of a large and noble organism; there were thousands of us all over the state, huddled in basements like this one, doing our part to plead for money for the ghoulish Senator. After the school project, other students surprised me with revelations that they had volunteered for their chosen candidates, not from morbid curiosity, but from strong political beliefs.

I never did get to meet the Senator on the ice to reciprocate his Christmas greetings, but I liked to think that my efforts long ago helped get the Senator his million-dollar boondoggle to the South Pole to watch an NSF Rep wearing a hardhat and a smile grovel for $125 million, and that we were square.

One summer, during January's high tide of politicians, as Kath and I were driving the Haz Waste truck back to town after checking trash at Willy Field, we picked up two red parkas outside Scott Base who were waiting for a shuttle back to McMurdo. One of our passengers was Dr. John Berry, Assistant Secretary of the Department of Interior of the U.S. He asked why we came down here.

"For the money," said Kath. "Plus there's no bugs here, so it's probably the best place in the world to be a garbageman."

"Yes," I agreed. "Antarctica is 100% maggot-free." I asked what the Dept. of Interior was doing down here.

Part of NSF's program is Antarctic mapping projects, which involves a great deal of time and money. In the U.S., the Department of Interior pays for mapping projects. NSF brought him down to convince him to further open the DI purse for Antarctic mapping projects so that NSF could spend that money on other projects.

"How long are you going to be down here?" asked Kath.

"Oh, just a short time, but we went to the Dry Valleys yesterday and we're going to the South Pole when the weather clears," he said, and we're having the time of our lives, he exuded, clutching an armload of Scott Base souvenirs purchased from their gift shop.

We dropped him off at Bldg. 125, the lush apartment where only DVs stay.

A year later, I found the guest log from Bldg. 125 in the trash. John Berry had written:

> The words in this book focus on the awesome beauty and power of this special place. However, I am struck more by its fragility and its ability to signal to the rest of the world the vulnerability of our planet home. The science here shines as a beacon—both warning us of rocks ahead, as well as lighting our way to a safer homecoming. The people here are as dedicated and courageous as any who have gave [sic] so nobly before—and their mission is far more important than national or personal glory. With you, and the work you do, lies the hope for future generations: people united in peace, united in talent, to better understand and protect the handiwork of God's creation. As one privileged to stand both at the North and South Pole, I am happy to be part of such a fair-hearted clan and wonderful mission.

— John Berry, Asst. Sec. Dept. of Interior, Dec. 19, 1999

John Berry had not used the words "fruitbasket," "boondoggle," or even "money." These concepts were too crude to convey our awesome collective purpose. John Berry had not hitched a lift in the Haz Waste truck with a bag of souvenirs. Rather, he was riding the powerful wave of collective action, by which the fires of hope power the shining beacons that illuminate our planet home. Jesus, how exciting! If I had only known, I would have asked him whether hope matured like a treasury bond or whether it burned with a half-life like radiation. I tried to imagine actually applying the phrases "united in peace" or "this special place" to any experience I had ever had here. I tried to imagine for a moment that I believed that "the hope for future generations" lay with a seasonal swarm of scientists who squabbled over the specialized equipment in the Crary Lab as drunk workers squabble for their turn at the pool table. I imagined joking about appropriating funds as porn stars joke about blowing loads down each other's throats. I thought of the porn dude who wore a medallion of a hand gripping the Earth, and the NSF logo: people holding hands, encircling the Earth.

In January, as the town was crawling with DVs, the tourist ship *Khlebnikov* arrived. The *Khlebnikov* is a luxuriously refurbished former Russian whaling vessel. In little inflatable motorboats the crew brings the tourists to shore, where an NSF chaperone escorts them around town on a tight leash and keeps them out of the way. Dr. Karl Erb, Head of the Office of Polar Programs for NSF, had a different take on the role of the McMurdo chaperone when he was questioned at a Hearing before the Subcommittee on Basic Research in 1999:

> CONGRESSWOMAN CONNIE MORELLA: It is rare, indeed, though, that tourists get to go to McMurdo, is not that correct? Or has that changed? I mean, when you get your tour ships in and the planes, you do not let them go to McMurdo, do you?
>
> DR. ERB: The tour ships do come into McMurdo Sound each year... But when they arrive in McMurdo, they are, as Dr. [Donal] Manahan said, escorted around town. We have a fixed tour that we allow them to take, which keeps them from causing environmental trouble.

Besides putting trash in the wrong bin, or maybe throwing a cigarette on the ground and igniting McMurdo's fuel-soaked earth, it is hard to imagine what sort of "environmental trouble" Dr. Erb expects from the tourists who come to McMurdo.

Actually, just a few weeks before the tourist ship arrived, a few tons of sausage buried in the ground during a previous era had been discovered by a Fleet-Ops operator who was drilling into the earth in preparation for a new building down by the sea ice. With the drill he struck a noxious pocket of primeval sausage slime that squirted onto his face, searing his eye with a swift yellow infection that puffed up half his face and put him out of commission for about a week. The earth-sausage mixture was excavated from the frozen ground and dumped in piles beside the road, where a squad of GAs was dispatched into the feeding swarm of skuas to separate the meat from the rock and to throw it into triwalls that we banded up and loaded in milvans to be exported to the United States.

The activities at what became known as Sausage Point were not on Dr. Erb's tourist route, which is probably for the best, since the tourists were already too shocked by the machines thundering by and the skuas gorging on ruptured bags of spaghetti in the Galley bins to do anything but lope with dazed squints behind the chattering NSF emissary, who mercifully led them to the store to calm them with souvenirs.

One time I hopped out of my machine as I was making my rounds and asked one of the tourists a question about the ship. She laughed nervously and ran to catch up with the group as if I had asked her for spare change. I had approached her on my best behavior, but as I recovered from the sting of rejection, I realized I must look a mess, lurking in filthy clothes amid a terrific array of clanging metal and hydraulic voodoo at this lawless outpost on the lip of the world.

Where tourists are slain and their fat burned as fuel to heat our bowling alley.

All winter-overs have to take a psychological evaluation to determine their mental fitness to endure the long Antarctic night, when (because planes cannot fly in) they are trapped at the end of the planet on a continent made of ice with only a substantial video collection to keep them from polar madness.

The best method of selecting winter-over personnel has been a source of controversy since the earliest expeditions. Shackleton's interviews lasted only a few minutes, during which he asked questions such as "Can you sing?", "Do you know any good jokes?", or whether the applicant could recognize gold if he saw it. He selected one applicant because he looked funny.

One day in early January, while an equipment operator recovered from sausage infection, we packed into the back room of the Galley, where test booklets, pencils, and answer sheets were waiting for us on the tables. The overseeing psychologist was the same woman who, earlier in the summer, had told us she was here to counsel us confidentially and would have nothing to do with our winter evaluations.

We were taking this test for only one reason: Antarctic history is rich with grim tales of madness.

On December 14, 1912, Antarctic explorers Douglas Mawson and Xavier Mertz stood at the edge of a 200-foot-deep crevasse in the ice.

"We are in dire peril, Xavier."

"Yes," said Mertz, "We shall have to eat the dogs."

The third member of their expedition had just fallen into the crevasse—with most of their food. Their initial goal of surveying a 500-mile stretch of Adelie Land suddenly became impractical, and they set out for their base camp on the coast.

They fed their dogs with pieces of clothing until the dogs grew too weak, and then butchered one after another to feed the remaining dogs and themselves. They sawed the paws off with a knife and boiled them into soup, then took turns spooning out the brains and gnawing on the skulls, and frying the livers.

Unbeknownst to them, the dog livers contained toxic levels of Vitamin A. As a result, the men's flesh and hair began to litter the bottom of their tent at night. Pus-filled cracks opened on their faces. Their scrotums bled.

It was not long before Mertz went mad. He could no longer help pull the sledges and he would no longer eat. In his journal he wrote, "I cannot eat of the dogs any longer."

When Mawson tried to coax him to drink some "Beef Tea," Mertz screamed, "It is of the dogs! They make me ill because I eat their flesh!"

Mawson put Mertz on the sledge, which he pulled on his hands and knees through the twinkling white brutality. In their tent Mertz howled gibberish and filled his pants from dysentery. One morning Mertz screamed at Mawson, "Am I a man—or a dog? You think I have no courage because I cannot walk— but I show you, I show. . . " and bit off part of his little finger and spat it onto the floor of the tent.

Before he died, Mertz screamed, "Ears, ears! Earache!"

Mawson cleaned up. He was alone now and suffering from fingers black with frostbite, loose teeth, and snowblindness. The soles of his feet were falling off.

When Mawson finally made it back to camp, he had missed the rescue ship, so he and the remaining crew faced their second consecutive winter in Antarctica. The ship had brought some supplies and new support staff.

One of the new staff was a radio operator named Jeffryes who started "going off his base" a few weeks after Midwinter's Day, when he refused to do any work and began to suspect the others in the hut of being in league against him. Jeffryes secretly sent, in Mawson's name, radio transmissions to the outside world saying that the other members of the expedition were insane except for Mawson and Jeffryes. Mawson overheard him and sent a message the next day saying: "Censure all messages Jeffryes insane…"

22 November 1913

   Jeffryes is getting better. I spoke to him. He says he is helpless, that I have a spell upon him. I tell him that I put a spell upon him not to play monkey tricks when I am away.

— Mawson's Antarctic Diaries

Back in Australia, after a harrowing winter of dark lunacy, Jeffryes freaked out on a train, from which he was escorted to an asylum. He wrote letters to Mawson from the nuthouse, reminiscing about the special time they spent together: "We seven were chosen that scripture might be fulfilled... I am come as Christ in the Spirit of Prophecy, and the Wrath of God in the Flesh." Jeffryes suspected that his hospital had been infiltrated by Freemasons.

Stories of violent madness have flowed from Antarctic exploration since the beginning. In 1898, when the Belgian ship *Belgica* was stuck for 13 months in sea ice, one of the members of the multinational crew attacked whomever said "something" in French, because he believed the word meant "kill". More recently, the Associated Press wrote that "a violently deranged staffer" at Mawson Base had to be locked in a storage room for the winter, in the Australian tradition that has continued proudly there since Mawson Base was built in 1953 and, as recalled by station leader Philip Law, a man "had the habit, when heavily intoxicated, of piling papers on his bunk and setting fire to them." In 1983 the doctor at Argentina's Almirante Brown station burned the base down to force his own pre-winter evacuation. At a Soviet base, a man killed his chess opponent with an axe.

In the winter of 1996 a Galley worker in McMurdo clocked his supervisor on the head with a hammer while he was eating lunch. Someone who intervened got the claw-end in the face.[8] The red-parkaed assailant left the Galley and was intercepted in Highway 1 singing "Mary Had a Little Lamb" and taken into makeshift custody by firefighters. Carpenters made wooden bars for the windows on Hut 10, where the cook stayed in luxurious captivity until the FBI arrived to spend three days taking scenic pictures before escorting the attacker to Hawaii for processing. A new dining attendant arrived that evening for his first shift in McMurdo. He was excited to be on the seventh continent. His first task in Antarctica was to clean the human blood from the chairs in the Galley. The following Halloween, hammer-related costumes were in vogue.

The proctor told us to start the psychology test.

The first part of the test consisted of over 500 true-or-false questions, such as:

I see things or animals or people around me that others do not see.
Someone has it in for me.

There is something wrong with my mind.
Dirt frightens or disgusts me.
Often I feel as if there is a tight band around my head.
I like repairing a door latch.
I am sure I get a raw deal from life.
I sometimes tease animals.
I believe in law enforcement.
I believe I am being plotted against.
The top of my head sometimes feels tender.
I like science.
I believe I am a condemned person.
Everything tastes the same.
Most of the time I wish I were dead.
I would certainly enjoy beating criminals at their own game.
I like to drive a hard bargain.
and
I would like to be a florist.

I answered all questions on the test false if they mentioned "dread" or "worrying" or, in dealing with people, trying to "put them right," and I made a point of favoring "social engagements" over "alone time" because solitude is widely disapproved of and is favored only by criminals. In questions of authority I chose the most spineless possibility unless—when snitching on my fellow workers, for instance—a firm moral conviction impervious to peer pressure was called for. These methods of response brought me great success in passing the standardized psych eval.

A few of the questions had me stumped, such as:

I do not always tell the truth.

To answer "true" might imply deviousness. But to answer "false" would claim extraordinary rigidity about telling the truth. Who tells the truth about the money in his shoe to a thief? But how many other test-takers will make me look more devious by ignoring such obvious exceptions and answering "false"?

I was fond of excitement when I was young.

By saying this statement is true, does that mean I am no longer fond of excitement because I am no longer young, or just that I was fond of excitement at that time? By saying it's false, does that mean that my fondness for excitement has not been diminished through time, or that I have never been fond of excitement? What does it mean anyway to be "fond of excitement"?

I have had very peculiar and strange experiences.

One time in a city of ten million people in Asia I ran into a friend I had worked with on a fish-processor in Alaska. Was that peculiar and strange?

One time I went to the Grand Opening of a Supermall where a band played the National Geographic theme and a local TV celebrity used giant scissors that were insured for $10,000 to cut a ceremonial ribbon before the teeming throng rushed inside to buy Tupperware and eat yogurt cones. Was that peculiar and strange?

The psych eval itself was peculiar and strange. Disturbing, even troubling. I took an educated guess and answered "false."

After the written test we were each interviewed by one of a team of crack psychologists trained in riot prevention who had been flown to Antarctica to apply the last-chance tourniquet to stop the flow of dementia into our quiet village.[9] I wanted to get Grade-A marks that did not include authority issues, so about two minutes before my appointment I walked into the psychologist's office and immediately began blabbing like an idiot.

"Hi! Am I too early!"

"No! Come on in!" she said.

She shuffled some papers while I sat down and adjusted my backpack on the floor. Outside the window, loaders beeped and rumbled carrying frosty cargo. I had left work early for the interview.

"Did you get to spend any time in Christchurch!" I asked.

"I did! There were some weather delays!"

"Isn't Christchurch beautiful!"

"It's so gorgeous!"

"So, is this your first time down here!"

"Yes! And it is just great!"

"It's something, isn't it!"

With a single stroke of her pen, the psychologist could have me removed from Antarctica. The blue-collar worker therefore wished to make the white-collar subject comfortable in her new environment by introducing her to unique environmental and social phenomena that she may not have previously considered when temporarily adjusting to a new locale. His experiment consisted of relating geo-specific anecdotes, to facilitate her feeling of acceptance and thereby allowing her response to unfamiliar stimulus to be one of pleasure and nurturing rather than one of hostility and distance.

She would be full of glowing ideas about rough isolation and scientific progress and stark romantic beauty, so I did not tell her that Larryville, otherwise known as the pipe yard, is so named to honor a Navy guy who once managed to fly down a couple of prostitutes. I also did not tell her that Jeannie and Wilson had hosted "Eggs and Porn" Sunday in their dorm room, where we gathered in the morning to gobble watery scrambled eggs before a video pageant of drooling fur and squirting shanks. Nor that a Marine Tech on one of the science ships once ran up a bill of thousands of dollars by calling sex hotlines from Antarctica on NSF's expensive satellite phone.

I told her about penguins and weather. "Isn't that something!" she shrieked.

"Isn't it!" I screamed.

After the chitchat we got down to business, but I had already passed the test.

"Do you ever feel sad?" she asked.

"Not too often," I said.

"Well, sometimes there's this kind of, well, we all feel a little bit—it's not to the level of depression or anything—but what do you do?"

"This too shall pass," I said.

"So you just let it go?"

"Yeah."

"That's great. The winter is dark and cold and you'll be away from your friends and family for quite a while. If you start getting depressed, how do you think you'll handle it?"

"Well, I like to read a lot. I bought a ukulele. I'm going to learn how to play Hawaiian songs. I write. I like spending time alone. But I also have a lot of friends here. I talk openly with them. So either way, if I want to be alone, I have lots to do, if I want to talk to people, I have good friends."

"That's great."

"Yeah."

"Do you drink?"

"Yeah."

"How much?"

"Oh, a few beers after work."

"You know, in the winter some people get depressed and try to use alcohol to boost themselves out of depression, but it only makes it worse."

I nodded soberly.

"Have you ever taken drugs?"

I thought of the time in the parking lot of a Dead show when I had gotten drunk, smoked weed, snorted coke, drank a bottle of Robitussin DM, and finally, when I took a hit from a nitrous balloon, had a vision of the sun as a benevolent symbol of death, one day to explode but presently growing our food, a recurring reminder that death is not a far-off distant point, but a core component of life. The sun remarked on this little paradox by appearing before me in sunglasses.

"I'm not into that stuff," I said.

"Okay. What would you consider to be one of your strengths?"

I had to think about that one, and she stared at me while I looked off into the corner.

"I'm flexible. I try to adapt," I said, thinking primarily of how social codes change like weather when you cross borders.

"And what would you say is one of your weaknesses?"

"Uh. I try to adapt. I accept in order to understand. That makes me gullible."

"Okay. What is your greatest success?"

"I'm where I want to be."

"And your greatest disappointment?"

In 1974, psychologist Stanley Milgram published the results of a program of experiments at Yale University in which unwary subjects were recruited and paid a small sum to act as "teachers" in a "Study of Memory" that was actually an experiment in obedience. A learner-victim sat in a separate room and was to memorize word-pairs read by the teacher. The "teachers" were told by a scientist to administer electric shocks to the victim each time he failed to memorize the word pairs, with the shocks getting progressively stronger by 50 volts with each incorrect response. The victim was an actor and, after 150 (fake) volts, began protesting the shocks and asked to be released from his chair, and by 270 volts screamed in agony. These screams and protests continued until, at 330 volts, he became silent, as if unconscious. Whenever the "teacher" became hesitant to administer the shocks, the scientist made simple statements like, "The experiment requires that you continue," or "You have no other choice, you must go on." At the command of the scientist, most people went on to administer the highest shock of 450 volts.

"I don't know," I said after a long uncomfortable silence.

"Nothing? You've never experienced anything that really let you down?"

I wanted to tell her that even though I despised Elton John, I knew the words to dozens of his songs from hearing them in supermarkets and elevators.

"Sure, but there's not one incident that stands out," I said. I've been pretty lucky, I think. I've never been to war or had the plague, so I can't really complain."

Then she pulled out my test results.

"First of all, this part of the test"—she pointed to a line on a graph—"is where you answered the questions favorably because you knew you were taking the test for your employer."

I looked at the graph in astonishment. She knew I lied.

"Is that what those 'always tell the truth' questions are about?" I asked.

"I can't tell you how the test works."

"Okay, so how do you grade these things when everyone's a bunch of liars?"

We had a good laugh at my inappropriate terminology.

"Well, it's only natural for people to want to impress their employer, and there's a standard allowance for this," she said. She told me how different types of mental patients and prisoners show different results. "Yours is fairly normal. What that means is that these other areas of your personality"—she pointed to the graph—"are a little bit more extreme than they actually would be. So this spike over here isn't really that pronounced. We read it as if it were a little lower. And these low ones? We read them as a little higher."

I was excited. This was fun. Like going to a palm-reader, but zanier.

Since the test had compensated for my lies, she explained, we could now read it with some accuracy.

"When I look at this"—she pointed to the graph—"you're not someone who tends to somaticize stress. You probably don't get a lot of physical complaints: headaches, bellyaches, backaches. Some people get a headache whenever they feel stress. You're not going to do that."

That's true, I thought.

"That's true!" I said.

"And here"—she pointed to the graph—"it shows you're not familiar with depression. You may not have a language for depression. That's good in that you're not prone to depression. But if you face depression you may not know what to do."

I thought of those periods, sometimes lasting days, sometimes weeks, when any crumb of joy I can muster seems sure to be the product of some internal delusion and must be discarded. When the world's fluctuations are a fragmented and absurd chaos. When the mere presence of any object in its space is one more word of vocabulary in a universal language of brutal occupation.

"Isn't that interesting?" I said.

She referred back to the test.

"Your anger is somewhat deflated. I don't see much expression of anger. When it comes up, you probably diffuse it quickly."

I recalled driving a taxi, the blur of screamed exchanges between myself and shithead drivers and cocksucking pedestrians who weren't paying attention until I made them pay attention you fucking assholes.

"Huh," I said.

She showed me a different graph whose center axis was vertical rather than horizontal. Down the sides were lists of opposing psychological traits. To one side was femininity and sensitivity, to the other masculinity and assertiveness. To one side was practicality and conventionality, to the other imagination and whim. She pointed out that I was in the median range for most traits. But in one category the line veered entirely to the left edge. The daggerlike vertex revealed that I am "Genuine, Forthright, and Artless."

After she'd finished explaining my psychology, she asked if I had any questions, and I did.

"We signed a consent form that allows Raytheon to distribute the results of this test. Are the results used only for jobs on the ice? Or if I apply to work for Raytheon somewhere else in the world will they have my psych results in the file whereas other employees vying for the same jobs won't be asked to show psych results?"

"That's a good question," she said. "I don't know about that. I'll find out and get back to you."

She took down my email address.

"Also, could I get a copy of the test results?"

"Huh, that's interesting," she said. "I'm not sure. I'm pretty sure that's against policy."

"If the consent form allows anyone in the world to have the results, it's funny if the people who are being evaluated can't have a copy."

"Okay, I'll look into that. I have your email address right here."

We chatted for a while informally. She was very nice, though she does not always tell the truth. She never got back to me.

After the psych eval I went to Ben and Laz's room. Jeannie and Ivan were there. Psych eval debriefing was in progress. Someone handed me a drink. I was the last person to finish my interview.

Laz's mouth began to form the tight-lipped downward curl indicating he was about to ridicule me.

"Well, it appears to me, sir, that you were the first one in and the last one out. I do believe"—his faux-Victorian diction grew more pronounced—"it took approximately an hour for the good doctor to wade through the murk that inhabits your delirium-riddled cranium, whilst most of us were discharged promptly with high marks."

"Dude, she liked me," I laughed. "We were talking. Her kid plays the guitar. She was nice."

"I suppose to one as desperate as yourself, the interest of an inquisitor would seem as friendship."

"Yeah yeah…"

CHAPTER 3
NOTES

[1] The frozen piss chipped from beneath 155 was scattered to melt in the yard, a few weeks later the site of Winstock, an outdoor concert, with dancing and a chili cook-off.

[2] A squinting survey of American Antarctic workers turns up several prominent character types and reveals some of what brings people here:

Outdoorsies like to hike and witness profound natural beauty. They want to see the truly immense and baffling wonders of Antarctica. When they get there they find out they have to work most of the time in dirty buildings or outside in the cold surrounded by dirty buildings. Nearly everything they want to do is prohibited. They have to check out with the Firehouse before they go anywhere. They stay only one season, because they can do all the things they love elsewhere. It makes more sense for them to leave than to stay.

Crazy Outdoorsies are the same as Outdoorsies, but they keep coming back. They find that glimpses of the immense and profound natural beauty of Antarctica are worth the toil and mindless drudgery, and they are often savvy enough to do what they like regardless of prohibitions. Some of these people are legendary. One guy silently borrowed a skidoo on a long weekend and climbed Mount Erebus and made it back into town by Monday with no one the wiser. Another waited until the last Winfly flight left in August and quit his job, thereby freeing himself from the control of local authorities. Though he probably lost over five thousand dollars in pay and bonus, he spent the next six weeks going wherever he liked, camping out at Castle Rock, and skiing and hiking all over before he was kicked out on the first plane at Mainbody. One worker at Pole, who may or may not fit in this category, hoarded food, got his hands on a sledge, and set out skiing to McMurdo, over 800 miles away. A team of people on skidoos went after him and brought him back.

Stamp Collectors derive their pleasure in Antarctica almost exclusively from historic associations. They want to walk where Robert Scott walked, they try to see the mountains as if Shackleton were peeking over their shoulder, and they get all worked up about IGY. Antarctica is not a work-in-progress, but a museum. They like to show slide shows and videos of the great explorers in the Coffeehouse. Nothing is valid until it is historic. Stamp Collectors, if given a ride to the moon, would run around looking for Neil Armstrong's footprints.

Mercenaries have no interest in Antarctica itself, as a place, as an idea, or as an experience. Like migrating herds of marine mammals, they follow the warm waters of cash flow. Antarctic pay is substandard for foreign contract wages. Food and rent are covered, however, so all money goes in the bank. It's a good deal if certain conditions are unimportant. These people, if they think about him at all, think Ernest Shackleton probably had a set of balls, but what of it? They do not attend the lectures put on by the Stamp Collectors. They are not interested in local affairs unless they interfere with the television programming or their paychecks. They are quick to roll their eyes about the way things are run in their department, but also quick to defend rules and order even if they run contrary to their interests, because they are protective of the hand that feeds them.

Mercenaries' Foremen are like Mercenaries, but interested in titles and positions rather than paychecks. Also, they are more likely than Mercenaries to have streaks of the Stamp Collector or the Penguin Hunter.

Penguin Hunters want excitement and adventure, so they buy a lot of souvenirs at the store. They came to Antarctica to see penguins. Antarctica is rough for them. They bemoan the absence of their favorite shampoo, diet soda, and hand lotion. They send down ten boxes of stuff for their four-month stay. Their walls are full of photographs of family. They hang Christmas cards and wreaths on their door during the holidays. They buy phone cards more than one at a time, and they check email ceaselessly. They try to bring their friends down the next season, but their friends hate it and leave, and so do they eventually, unless they're one of a married couple.

Quicksanders also appear in all the other categories. The more time you have spent on the ice, the less time you have spent elsewhere; your orbit can shift before you know it, and it seems you have nowhere to go but back to the ice. All your things are in a storage unit, or at a friend's or a parent's. Better to go back to the ice than deal with all that shit just now. Just one more season. Maybe another winter. Then that's it. You'll live in a town or a city where you don't know who founded it or when, and where every day there are more people you've never seen or heard of than all the people you've ever known in your life. Where you'll wait at traffic lights with all those people. Maybe just one more season. Then that's it.

[3] Good weather allows boondoggles. By its strictest definition, a boondoggle is a recreational trip out of town, but it has been blurred by threadbare jokes to mean any trip that is desirable, whether for work or not. The most common authorized boondoggle in the summer is to Cape Evans, where Robert Scott built a hut in 1911 for his fatal expedition to the Pole. To enroll for the trip, one must find an empty slot on a signup sheet on the Rec board in Highway One. The signup sheet appears sporadically and may fill up minutes after being posted. Fingees learn quickly that this first-come-first-serve opportunity passes quickly and learn, rightly enough, that one should sign up whenever one can. And since old-timers know this about fingees, and know that fingees aren't yet aware of how restrictive their new environment is, occasionally other boondoggle signup sheets appear, such as the one for the "Russian Submarine Ride," or the "Mt. Erebus Ski Trip," or the "Swim with the Antarctic Cod" boondoggle. Times and meeting places are given to add credibility, and these lists fill up quickly with the full names of fingees who can later be humiliated in person before a jeering crowd.

[4] Honored with framed photos hanging on the wall in Bio-Med at Pole are Edward Wilson, the first doctor to reach the South Pole, and Frederick Cook, the first doctor to winter over in Antarctica. Besides his historic Antarctic involvement in the *Belgica* expedition of 1898–99, Dr. Cook in 1903 claimed to be the first person to reach the summit of Mount McKinley, a claim that was debunked when one of Cook's party later confessed that they had never come close to the summit, verified by two climbers who duplicated Cook's photo of "the summit" at a point 14,000 feet below. In the later years of his life, Dr. Cook spent five years in prison for securities fraud.

[5] "They might as well have named the North Pole 'Pluto' then, since Byrd didn't fly there either."
– Señor X

[6] Bunny boots are white insulated cold weather boots. They have a valve on the side, left open during plane flights, but otherwise closed to keep a layer of air trapped in the boot. Boots with valves on them are somewhat peculiar, and this oddity was put to good use once to convince a fingee Waste manager that he had to have his boots filled with glycol, an antifreeze, before he could use them outside. He questioned that because he hadn't heard it before, but what more evidence did he need? Look at the valve on the boot! Why else would a boot have a valve? They dropped him off in front of the Heavy Shop and he took his boots inside. Unfortunately, it was just a few minutes after breaktime, and all the mechanics were lingering around the front desk. "Is this the Heavy Shop? I was told to come to the Heavy Shop and have my boots filled with glycol." No one knows whether the laughter burst from their throats or spewed irrepressibly through their noses.

[7] The soundtrack of any American-sponsored frontier is less likely to feature the haunting orchestral strings of *2001* than the tinny strains of Bad Company and CCR and Steve Miller.

[8] Because of a personal conflict with his supervisor in the Galley, the cook had tried to leave on the earliest possible flight, but management had denied his request.

[9] A psychologist once told a winter-over, after scoring his test, that he was either schizophrenic or an artist. She later purchased three of his paintings.

CHAPTER FOUR

The South Pole

Antarctica is cold and forbidding.

— NSF brochure

There is no ATM at South Pole.

— South Pole Station Guide, 1999–2000

Two days after my psych interview I was sent to Pole to fill in for its Waste Supervisor, who was taking R&R. R&R (insistently renamed "Preparatory Leave" by Denver) is an enticement to sign contracts when the company is desperate to fill winter positions. The Pole Waste Supervisor had signed a winter contract on-ice, so she was given a week of R&R in McMurdo. McMurdoites are flown to Christchurch for R&R.

That morning I packed my orange bags and caught the airport shuttle to Willy Field. On our way across the ice shelf the radio emitted soothing static and the chatter of Mac Ops and Mac Weather operators orchestrating the morning's events. There were four PAX on the flight, including a writer sponsored by NSF. She was chatting to two of the other passengers about her research on the early Pole station and how "Paul Siple did as much shoveling as the grunts."

In 1957, Siple was among the first to winter at Pole. He devised the windchill factor and is the namesake of Siple Dome camp. Few have matched his extended time in the Antarctic, and he had been popular with the public ever since he tagged along on Byrd's first expedition as an accomplished Boy Scout. His application included an essay on why he wanted to join the expedition.

Here is the first paragraph of Siple's essay:

> From my first observation of Commander Byrd I have highly admired him and his work. Because of the scientific training and experience that I would receive from association with him and his companions I hope to be the fortunate Scout to go on the polar expedition. If there were no other merits to be derived except the close relationship with Commander Byrd I would feel highly honored, if chosen, and while that is one of the foremost reasons why I would like to go there are others of great importance to me.

Elsewhere in his application he described himself as "mentally awake and morally straight." During the winter at Little America, Siple was a member of Byrd's secret Loyal Legion.[1] After the expedition, while everyone else was out banging whores and getting loaded in New Zealand, young Siple wrote, "I spied some late summer [flower] varieties blossoming on the other side of a fence and I leaned over to inhale their fragrance deeply. Then I hurried to a field where I flung myself on the ground and lay daydreaming in the soft warm breezes until my body cried out for a glass of milk and some fruit." Siple's wholesome appetites continued throughout his career. He was chief scientist-observer for the U.S. Army in 1946 during Operation Highjump, which historian David Burke described as "the most massive military force ever sent to Antarctica," including helicopters, landing-assault vehicles, 13 ships including a submarine, 23 aircraft, and 4,700 troops. The goals of Operation Highjump were covert until 1955, when one of the directives was found to be "consolidating and extending U.S. sovereignty over the largest practicable area of the continent." Afterwards, while planning Highjump II (later canceled), Paul Siple mused: "Success [of Highjump II] would establish a preeminent American claim over the entire continent...the U.S. could be in a unique position to claim Antarctica for its own should it so desire."

The NSF-sponsored writer was three-quarters finished with her book, she said, and excited to visit Pole to augment her research. Her clothes were very clean. She said she had just talked to the Colonel, who had told her Pole was only 40 flights behind on fuel from McMurdo. This surprised me because I had heard otherwise from Polies, and I told her so.

"Well, I'm not going to question the Colonel," she laughed.

"Why not?" I asked.

She laughed.

Waiting in the Galley building at Willy for the call to board the plane, I drank coffee and stepped outside occasionally to smoke. In the Galley I met a woman just back from Vostok, where the U.S. was setting up a new summer camp, East Camp, just across the runway from the Russians, to study an enormous lake below the ice. The lake is of immense interest because it has been sealed off from the rest of the world for millions of years, and the bacteria in it will contribute to the progress of humanity.

I asked her about the recent "international incident" at Vostok that had reverberated all the way up to Washington. The rumor around town was that a drunk Russian had stormed into the American camp waving a gun. The woman just back from Vostok said the incident occurred during their solstice celebration.[2] A drunk Russian, hooting and hollering, had fired a flare harmlessly into the snow in the middle of nowhere. Instead of seeing the flare as a makeshift firework, such as Americans use to celebrate Independence Day or as Admiral Richard Byrd's men fired to celebrate the return of a sledging party, the manager at East Camp saw the flare as a threat and reported the incident to his superiors, who took it to "the next level," as they say in McMurdo. Dr. Karl Erb, Director of NSF's Office of Polar Programs, wrote a severe email to Valery Lukin, Director of the Russian Antarctic Expedition, concerning the "absolutely unacceptable" behavior of the two Russian tractor drivers involved. "Sometime during their visit," wrote Dr. Erb, "one of them discharged a firearm. Fortunately, no one was injured...I strongly protest not only the behavior of the Vostok drivers, but also the fact that members of the Russian Antarctic Expedition are allowed to carry guns." He wrote that this was a security threat not only to residents at East Camp, but also to everyone at McMurdo Station and to the residents of Vostok itself. Vostok Station, with its drunk Russians and flare pistols, had been there since 1957. The Americans had just moved in next door. During the Cold War, such proximity would have been unlikely, but these days it is welcomed. The Russian Antarctic program is very poor. American visitors to Vostok have said that the food supply for the year appears to be little more than a pile of frozen potatoes, sacks of flour, and cases of vodka. The U.S. has earned warm Russian cooperation with expensive gifts of fuel and cargo transport. "Your immediate attention to this matter is necessary," continued Dr. Erb, "to prevent any further deterioration in our relations and to allow our partnership to continue."

This typifies the American understanding of "peaceful cooperation."

The linchpin of international peaceful cooperation is the Antarctic Treaty, first signed by 12 nations in 1959, which established an internationally recognized legal framework for activities in Antarctica. "More than any other nation, the United States benefits from the Antarctic Treaty," wrote William J. Burns in a 1996 Department of State Memorandum to the National Security Council. The U.S. likes the Treaty because, unless a nation is an original signatory, the privilege of exerting influence by voting at Treaty meetings requires that the nation in question perform substantial scientific research in Antarctica. Countries who do not have that kind of cash may join in the peaceful international cooperation, but only as observers at the meetings; thus smaller nations tend to view the Treaty as a rich man's club.

Before the Treaty was signed, seven nations had divided most of Antarctica into wedge-shaped claims based on their early explorations. These claims have been deferred for the life of the Treaty. The United States, which did not get in the Antarctic game early enough, was left a miserable slice of the pie, which it rejected in favor of a tactic of non-recognition that dates back to 1924, when Secretary of State Charles Evans Hughes wrote that discovery by exploration "does not support a valid claim of sovereignty unless the discovery is followed by an actual settlement of the discovered country."

The U.S., with three year-round stations, is maneuvering into position for the dispute that will inevitably arise when Antarctic hydrocarbons or mineral reserves are confirmed and the technology to extract them cost-effectively has been invented, at which point cooperating nations with good claims will find the Treaty cumbersome. The current state of affairs was best summed up by Eisenhower in 1958 when he said, "The U.S. is dedicated to the principle that the vast uninhabited wastes of Antarctica shall be used only for peaceful purposes..." Vast uninhabited wastes are much easier to share than a billion barrels of oil or veins plump with ore, and neither the U.S. nor any other nation wants to be left in the lurch when the Antarctic bauble has finally been appraised.

International law typically finds "fictional occupation"—planting flags, mounting plaques, or dropping swastika markers from an airplane as the Nazis did—less convincing than effective occupation, best illustrated by Chile, which an NSF report says has "placed whole families in residence at its Antarctic stations, with schools, banks, and other evidence of 'effective occupation.'" Chile is not the only country playing house in Antarctica; Argentina has reportedly established a hotel on the continent, and a woman at Esperanza Station in 1978 gave birth to the first native Antarctican, which Argentine President Jorge Gonzáles Videla said "reaffirms not only the role of the family in our society but also the inalienable role of Argentines in those far lands." Homesteading like Chile's and Argentina's is not recognized by the U.S, which has instead, as publicized by the CIA in 1978, "stressed its neutrality by placing its Amundsen-Scott Station at the South Pole where six of the claims converge." This curious definition of "neutrality" was restated in 1996 by Undersecretary of State Tim Wirth when he said, "If we weren't at the South Pole, there would be a mad scramble for territory... We're the only country that can manage the logistics in that extraordinary place. We have to maintain this presence to maintain the continent's neutrality."

In other words, if it weren't for American station managers taming the Russians with safety concerns, or for U.S. "proactive leadership" in squatting on the Pole, the world's stray dogs would no doubt lapse into a frenzy of bloodshed. "Our proposal," said Eisenhower, "is directed at insuring that this same kind of cooperation for the benefit of all mankind shall be perpetuated."

By 9:15 we were in the air, strapped to our canvas seats and clutching brown-bag flight lunches (a couple of sandwiches, a box of juice, and some candy). I had been to Pole the summer before with Jane. One of the Pole Wastees, Chernobyl—nicknamed for his manic and messy work style—had met us at the plane. *People* magazine once ran a full-page photo-story on him. The story consisted of a few paragraphs about the snow and cold at the "international scientific base," and a few details about Chernobyl's upbringing. The photo showed him with the Dome in the background, shoveling snow in a photogenic area that typically doesn't need shoveling. Chernobyl gave us a tour when we arrived, including his room.

"Why do you have all these tape measures?" Jane asked, indicating the several dozen tailor-variety tape measures in his small room, hanging from makeshift racks and curled on shelves.

"I keep them and give them to people if they ever need one," he said.

Chernobyl used to perform as the Wheelie King, driving around the floors of arenas packed with motocross fans howling as he rode an everlasting wheelie. He once went to Mexico to find Juan Valdez of the Colombian coffee TV commercials in the 1970s. He located Juan Valdez's small hometown, then loitered there until he bumped into the celebrity, who invited him to dinner at his house. Chernobyl always carries with him a picture of himself and Juan Valdez, and people often encourage him to repeat the story.

I nibbled on my flight lunch as the plane streaked over the plateau. My bunny boots still wore the dried smear of Jeannie's blood from our filming of *Cape Hades*. The previous night while I slept Señor X had written "Work me" on the back of my left boot and "to death" on the right. Laz and Señor X, I later found out, had emailed Kath the libel that I had been boasting of my upcoming "vacation to Pole." On the toes Señor X wrote, "Hi Kath, we miss you," with a drawing of an arrow-pierced heart.

Kath greeted me as I came off the plane. I threw my bags in the back of the van; the driver would deliver them to Summer Camp. We walked toward the Dome. I stopped to show Kath my boots with the messages from her friends in McMurdo.

"Tsk," she said, "I'm afraid I'm gonna have to work you until you collapse in a heap."

"Don't forget: I'm replacing your boss. That means I shall find some warm and comfortable nook in which to shuffle the papers while you tend to the tasking. I need a fucking smoke." We entered the Dome through one of the arches.

South Pole Station looks like an elf village overrun by a blue-collar tribe that worships Martian gods. Inside the Dome, red buildings are stacked like walk-in Christmas presents and surrounded by boxes of Cocoa Krispies and cartons of ice cream. Only buildings are heated, so the Dome and tunnels are cold like the outside, but enclosed for an aesthetic like Disney rides and childhood forts. Unlike the coastal stations, Pole has no animals, so simulation is more apparent there. Plastic flowers are planted in the snow outside some buildings. On a desk a magnetic fish lurches in its fishbowl, and in the Galley a plastic potted smiling flower dances to loud noises. A snow bike with miniature tractor tires leans against a drift as if waiting for a leprechaun.

Leading out from the Dome are tunnels lined with thick fairyland frost and crammed with shelves of spare machine parts, tools, and conduit. Barrels and shovels and sleds always stand along the bootprinted path. The snow around the Dome is patterned with equipment tracks, and the patterns of perpetual machine sound occasionally dominated by planes coming or going are its soundtrack. A beaten boombox regurgitates classic rock in the garage, where the snow is streaked with oil.

The Martian aesthetic is enshrined in the Dark Sector, the Viper Telescope, Seismic Vault, the ground shield moon door, and the elevated blue dorm that looks like a cross between a McDonald's Playland module and a spaceship. A building across the ice was pointed out to me through a window in a lounge called Skylab: "That's where they're using telescopes to find out how fast the universe is expanding."

Kath and I went to the smoking bar, passing a group of people in unfamiliar clothes who were talking excitedly in the upper Galley at a table by the shelves of board games.

"Who are the heroes?" I asked her as I lit up.

"They flew down to 89 degrees and then skied the last degree to the Pole."

"Wow. That's a good one. How far's that?"

"About 60 k." Kath finished rolling a Drum, and I lit it.

The bar is small, but because of the crowded Polies' advanced understanding of unattainable privacy, Kath and I could inoffensively have a conversation that excluded and all but ignored friends coming in to smoke. I was acutely aware that I didn't know anything about the bearded men in dirty and blackened Carhartts smoking silently in the lounge, but they, at the very least, knew I wasn't a Polie, though, by my own ratty overalls, that I wasn't a beaker or a manager.

"So they paid to ski across a piece of map?" I asked.

"You got it. Then they get a free cup of coffee, a hero shot at the Pole, and a boot in the ass to get out."

The expeditioners were alone in their excitement over this accomplishment. Tourists aglow from having arrived at the South Pole are met by management with a unique official courtesy that borders on scorn, and with indifference by Pole citizens more concerned with who's screwing his or her way to power and the technical problems of the power plant. People talk about tourists when they come, but with less interest than about construction projects or the Galley menu.

Members of one expedition were hanging out one morning in the warm bathrooms in Summer Camp after their long flight to camp beside Pole. When our friend Quill came into the bathroom barely awake that morning to brush his teeth before work, he met an enthusiastic crowd who asked, "So, it must be exciting to live here, eh?" Quill had once been afflicted with high-altitude pulmonary edema; his lungs had filled with thick black fluids, endangering his life and requiring an immediate medevac to a lower elevation. He grunted at their simplification and drooled in the sink.

In 1997 three men were the first in history to die while skydiving at the South Pole. When they fell, two Polies were watching the Hollywood blockbuster *The Rock,* in which terrorists overtake Alcatraz for evil aims. The terrorists make their move during a tour of Alcatraz, and one of the tourists murmurs, "What kind of fucked-up tour is this?" This scene reminded the two Polies that the skydivers were to jump soon. They went outside to watch as three black dots in the distance met the horizon, as silent as falling fleas. "What kind of fucked-up tour is this?" said one of the Polies. "We're going to have to make a new Waste category," said the other. The skydivers had paid $22,000 each for the honor of having their wrecked bodies excavated from the plateau by overworked Polies, put in body bags, and sent back to where they came from. The well-outfitted bodies were said to rattle like bags of crystals when pulled from the ice. Later some people were offended when someone partially buried a pair of boots upside down in the snow, but others solemnly hung their heads to veil the giggles, and the next Halloween, skydiver costumes were in vogue.

Madcap antics such as those of the skydivers have contributed to an official attitude summed up by Dr. Karl Erb of NSF: "They cause us difficulties in different ways. They get into trouble, and we have to go rescue them." The official cold shoulder is meant to discourage people from coming to Pole and requires the compliance of employees, who have been warned, as in this email from the McMurdo NSF Rep, that "private expedition personnel will not be allowed in any USAP facilities (to include vehicles) without the approval of the NSFREP. Additionally, USAP personnel will not perform any services for private expeditions, to include sending or delivering messages or mail/email." This means that if you rowed a boat down past 80 degrees south, crossed an ice shelf, climbed glaciers, crossed mountain ranges, avoided crevasses, didn't die of frostbite, hypothermia, infected wounds, starvation, or suicide, finally made it to approximately the coldest, most hellishly isolated spot on the globe, and asked for a dish of tater tots, you might be told no. Employees are usually too busy to pay much attention to expeditioners, but NSF's barely restrained contempt for tourists is not shared by the workers, who prefer to deride or praise on a case-by-case basis. Most people seem to understand that a nation building a station beside a global landmark that has attracted tourists since Earth became round is more or less begging to play park ranger.

New Year's Eve 2000 brought crowds of tourists. A television crew seized the Pole at midnight to shoot their live footage while one of them pushed Polies out of the way. Earlier that day, the Pole Station Manager had sent out an All-Station email: "Please DO NOT invite [the expeditioners] into the station, including the party tonight, for any reason except for emergency medical assistance." Rex, who, in defiance of black-tie convention, had assumed the alter ego of a caped and helmeted superhero named "Dash Fantasy," befriended the Singaporean expedition who'd skied from the coast and tried to sneak them into the party that night by dressing them in makeshift costumes, but the managers kept kicking them out.

Jim Lovell, American astronaut of *Apollo 13* fame, came down for New Year's. He was extended the extraordinary official courtesy of being allowed to sleep in the gym. He and his entourage were also allowed to eat meals in the Galley. Rex volunteered to work in the Galley one night, where he served three types of pizza: meat, supreme, and spam and cheese, labeled respectively as the "New Jersey Meathook," the "Cleveland Steamer," and the "Dirty Sanchez." (These labels are more commonly applied to hooking a finger up a woman's ass while fucking her from behind, shitting on someone's chest, and wiping shit-covered finger or cock beneath a partner's nose, respectively.) "These all look good. What would you recommend?" Jim Lovell asked Rex, who suggested the Cleveland Steamer and asked the astronaut what it was like to go into space. Jim Lovell preferred talking about the Tom Hanks movie about him going into space.

About a week after New Year's, a strange expedition arrived in snowbugs. They included a Mir cosmonaut who planned to be the first to fly a hot air balloon over the South Pole, and a Russian orthodox priest who wanted to be the first to hold a mass at both Poles. A few weeks before they arrived, Rex and some friends had built a 12-foot-tall snow replica of an Easter Island head near the geographic pole. Rex wrote in an email: "The priest was very disturbed by the sculpture. He felt it was pagan in nature and did not want to hold a mass in its presence. We explained that it was only for fun and that we did not worship it. He was wary however."

While tourists on plane flights are generally either ignored or treated to hairt-rigger courtesy, Polies are more enthusiastic about cross-continent expeditioners who actually work for their glory. As we smoked, Kath told me about two Norwegian guys who had skied to Pole after working 14 months at the Norwegian base on the coast. [3] When they gave an informal presentation to the Polies in the gym, someone asked one of them what he missed most after all that time away from civilization, and he bashfully replied, "Women."

"Did they get any?" I asked.

"I don't think so," Kath said. "I would have heard about it by now."

But as the ragtag Norwegians were skiing away from Pole toward Ross Island, a woman ran from the Clean Air Facility and flashed her tits, to which one of the polite Scandinavians called out, "Thank you. Thank you very much."

I agreed to meet Kath at work, then left to attend my South Pole

Orientation. When I got to the library, Abby was there with a meek young graduate student. Because of her position, her public role in Antarctica, I knew of Abby. I had heard stories about her and had seen the nice little emails she sent out.[4] Abby gave us each a South Pole handbook of rules and facilities with a map on the back. She emphasized that we were not to cross the skiway when planes were coming. We were not to do laundry on weekends because, unlike McMurdo's, some of Pole's water is distributed by vehicle, and if the water runs out on the weekend, someone will have to fill up the tanks on his or her day off.

Here's how they get water at Pole: Pole Station stands on a gargantuan ice plateau. The ice is so thick that to even consider it reminds you how scrawny and weak you are compared to the massive violent patience of the universe. Into this ice, masterminds drill a hole about 400 feet deep near the station and pump in heat, then pump out the resulting liquid water. This creates a huge subsurface cavern, and when the cavern begins to grow too large, they start a new one somewhere else.

Abby, about to adjourn the Orientation, asked if we had any questions. I asked if the store took credit cards. I wanted to buy booze and smokes and postcards and perhaps a South Pole souvenir from the store, and I was cash-poor at the moment. Abby said the store didn't take credit cards because of the poor satellite link.

Jesus fucking Christ, I thought, what kind of place is this?

Later, when I was borrowing 50 bucks from Kath, who had piles of money from cornering the fleece-hat market at the South Pole, she told me the credit card question was a sore topic. It was one of Abby's goals to modernize Pole to McMurdo standards. Her main emphasis this summer, said Kath, was the store, and some thought it strange that steel for the new station was stuck in McMurdo while Pole was getting huge shipments of t-shirts and caps and sweatshirts weekly.

If the store has a particularly good season financially, those funds will bring a better selection of goods the next season, which is good for morale. One winter an electrician had spent close to $7,000 on alcohol, and when the plane flew in to pick up the winter-overs, the pilots came out to take pictures of him lying sprawled drunk in the snow before loading him onto the plane with a makeshift stretcher. The next summer everyone was pleased that the store had so many new gift items.

That was a banner year at Pole.

The store quit selling liquor to a scientist that winter because he enjoyed cutting himself about the arms. When winter began, another scientist revealed after all the planes had left that he was afraid of the dark. He always slept with the lights on, and after the sun went down for the winter, someone had to walk or drive him to and from his lab each day. At the end of that winter it came to light that the station doctor had cleaned out the entire supply of painkillers and muscle relaxants. He took a cut from each prescription he wrote, and could sometimes be found in the bar with a fruitbowl of pills.

During one of the violent tequila parties that summer, a Muslim scientist accidentally partook of the liquor because all the juice dispensers had been spiked. He angrily shrieked, "The fires of hell are burning on my tongue!"

"Why are the tequila parties always violent?" I had asked my friend who related this incident.

"I don't know," my friend said. "They're always violent. I got violent. I woke up with my clothes shredded and I didn't know where I was. One guy broke his leg."

Violent parties are a time-honored American Antarctic tradition, going back at least to Byrd's Little America, when some of the expedition's unpaid volunteers fueled their parties with drums of medicinal alcohol. Roused by a heated argument, one of the crew attacked and didn't stop punching the mechanic in the mouth until knocked unconscious from behind by someone with a heavy ski boot. One of the men's diaries described one party at Little America as "a spectacular and riotous drunken orgy." And when at another party someone named Mulroy punched someone in the mouth, "the group, enraged, their pent-up hostilities exploding, converged on Mulroy like caged animals released, pummeling him viciously until Gould pulled them off."

After my Orientation I walked out to Summer Camp, collected my bags, then went to my Jamesway.[5] The Jamesways are very dark and very quiet, because at Pole there are three well-populated shifts, and it's always someone's bedtime. The Jamesways are so quiet that discreet couples who want to have sex wait for the furnace fan to kick on before mounting each other in eight-minute increments.

The space is small (about ten feet by six), but warm and comfortable, with extra insulation on the walls provided by Unicor blankets. I plugged in my video camera to recharge, made my bed with the linen provided, and unpacked a few things, including two huge bags of presents sent with me by Kath's admirers in McMurdo, containing Jim Beam, fruit, and rewriteable CDs. I also had to deliver a wrapped gift from Jeannie to one of the McMurdo Fuelies who was working a three-week shift at Pole.

I remembered to put my water bottle on the bed instead of the floor, where, Polies had told me, piss cans freeze. The bathrooms are separate from the Jamesways, so, to avoid dressing up just to run to the bathroom, people pee in coffee cans kept under their beds. A former janitor at Pole told me that many short-term scientists left their piss cans on the floor when they departed. In one case she found a lid for the can, leakproofed it with tape, found the researcher's address in the States, and sent his piss back to him.

Before I left McMurdo, Nero told me about his two weeks at Pole. He didn't know anyone, and no one talked to him except one Polie who was avoided by the others. Nero's disheartening Pole experience climaxed one day with him knocking over his recently-used pee can. He watched with horror as the golden puddle flowed across the corridor into someone else's cubicle, whose occupant was present and quickly remarked, "That better not be what I think it is." Nero, mortified, sprang with his towel to mop and grovel.

I went to work and found Kath at the Polar Haven, an unheated Quonset hut covered with what looks like colored rice paper. She introduced me to *Sundog*, one of the Cat 953s, and we spent the rest of the warm sunny evening (-15°F or -20°F) banding triwalls and loading trash onto air force pallets.[6] After work we went to the smoking lounge at Summer Camp to catch up. The wooden walls were carved with names and dates. I saw Sid's name and those of a few other people from McMurdo and Polies I had met in previous seasons.

At midnight we went to meet Quill from Cargo who was just getting off work. We took a sauna in the Dome, then sat on the floor in an office cubicle downstairs. A seismograph in the corner was measuring seismic activity all over the globe. Handbooks for hazardous chemicals and instruction manuals for gas chromatographs and reference books on database management filled the shelves. Tucked in scant spaces between books were fuel testing kits and spare cartridges for respirators. We munched on cheese and crackers that I had brought from McMurdo while Kath and Quill updated me on Pole news.

South Pole was unofficially on the edge of fuel crisis. It was January, and Pole did not have enough fuel to make it through the winter. For the rest of the season fuel flights would take top priority, which meant materials for winter construction on the new station would be left in McMurdo, which meant a bunch of winter contracts would be canceled, and no one knew whether they would be paid out or not.

The NSF Station Rep, singled out by the white hardhat he wore everywhere, repeated at every All-Hands Meeting that construction was currently "on schedule and under budget." He said this without irony, so everyone laughed at him behind his back. The ceiling of the new Power Plant was melting from the heat of the exhaust pipes a few inches below, fuel was at a premium, and construction on the new station was facing a year delay. The NSF Rep was funny, Kath said. He never said hello to her unless he was showing DVs around the station, in which case he always waved an enthusiastic greeting.

At first, Quill said, five planes a day minimum were scheduled until the end of season, with only fuel as cargo, but recently the number had gone down to four. Some days only three came in, for various reasons, including weather and Air National Guard crew rest days. Kath hid a few triwalls of wood on a distant cargo line for her friends so they could build fires in case things went to hell when winter came.

I left them sitting on the floor in the dim office space and returned to my Jamesway, where I slept like marble. The next morning I threw on my long underwear and a shirt, and my fleece and my boots, and my sunglasses and a hat, to go to the Ice Palace 100 yards away from the Jamesway.[7] I sat on the shitter and examined the collage on the stall door, a scene of nebulous space dust and distant galaxies pulled from a science digest. Floating in the center, cut from a financial magazine, was a chubby banker with plain tie and eyeglasses and great gleaming watery eyes, the vast expanse of the cosmos flanking him on all sides. The only other distraction of interest in the stall was a sign above the toilet instructing, "If it's yellow, let it mellow; if it's brown, flush it down."

Shit has a rich history in Antarctica. Some stations or camps have primitive outhouses built over snowpits, where "shit trees" grow quickly because the turds do not slide down the sides as they might in steamier climates. The shit freezes into stalagmites of which each new turd is the pinnacle. Explosives have been used to demolish these. In McMurdo, before the recent completion of the waste treatment plant, shit from the dorms was flushed into Winter Quarters Bay, while only shit from field camps was packaged up and sent back to the United States. Nevertheless, NSF long asserted that human waste was entirely removed from the continent. At Pole, shit is pumped into the huge subsurface caverns created by extracting water, where it freezes into great bulbs. By the time one cavern is full, a new one is ready to go. Since the ice sheet is moving toward the Weddell Sea at 2.7 cm per day, it may millions of years from now squeeze frozen superturds into the waters off the Antarctic coast. Mollusks will feast.

Someone at Pole once took a shit in the tunnel that runs from the Dome to Skylab. The astonishingly thick loaf, though immediately frozen and easily disposed of, so impressed and mystified the rank and file that Pole management felt compelled to quell the disturbance by attributing the turd to an unnamed tourist.[8] The mystery may never be solved, but few believed an ecstatic tourist would be more likely than a disgruntled local to dump a load there.

Uncertain what I'd be working on today, I donned all my gear in the Jamesway and then went to the Dome to drink coffee in the Galley and wait for Kath. We were on swing shift, so though I'd just woken up, people were filing in for lunch. Someone was playing Jane's Addiction in the kitchen. Kath showed up looking tired, with hair that defied gravity but would settle down after a few hours under a hat. We ate and went to work. Planes flew in and out all day as I minced huge wooden spools with a chainsaw and ground with a demolition saw through the metal supports and loaded the wood onto pallets to be flown to McMurdo.

Every humidifier or washing machine bound for Pole goes through McMurdo, and Pole's trash is flown to McMurdo for processing. With their different cultures and linked logistics, McMurdo, the center of the action, and Pole, the famous capital, are like two squabbling but inseparable brothers. Polies are issued green and black parkas; McMurdoites, red. When visiting Pole from McMurdo, it is good to have a reference. If one is introduced by a Polie, Pole is generally a friendlier, less cliquish, and more inclusive community than McMurdo. Otherwise, who knows. As one Polie put it, "When Polies see the red coats come off the plane, we think they're not real Antarctic workers. We see McMurdo as a luxury resort. We think we're tougher and want the people from McMurdo to see how cold it is and how much ice we have in our beards."

Few McMurdoites have as advanced an understanding of cold as does the Polie, because most intense cold at McMurdo is windchill. Pole gets little wind, so the cold is ambient and cannot be mitigated by a layer of windscreen. I once asked Speed whether he could really feel the difference between minus 60 and minus 90, and terror crossed his face as he nodded and said, "Oh shit yeah." Polies have told of pissing a blend of steam and crystals, and cold so annoying that even a cigarette won't work properly because the slightest moisture freezes and blocks the filter. A metal machine brought into a warm building sucks up heat so fast that it emanates cold as a fire emanates heat. Fuel gets so cold that a lit match thrown in it won't ignite it. Pole workers get used to frostnip as McMurdo workers get used to scrapes and bruises. And Polies are also used to scrapes and bruises.

This cold, which often depresses Polies to post-work catatonic slothfulness, is without financial compensation. Denver pays by job description, so Polies make no more money than if they worked in McMurdo. Furthermore, Pole has no boondoggles. There is nowhere to go. No trips to ice caves. No trips to see penguins at Cape Royds. No lucky opportunities to help out at Siple Dome or Black Island. South Pole Station sits on a bulge of ice two miles thick at the center and thinning gradually toward the coasts. There is nothing around but ice under empty space. The place is a visual Alcatraz where the surrounding nothingness bends one's attention inward, back to the station. Speed told me that he and some other Polies once gathered to admire a rare clump of dirt stuck to a piece of cargo.

At Pole, any administrative blunders (such as canceling the subscription to the daily *New York Times* faxsheet to save money) are seen as the result of either kinked local powers or of McMurdo meddling. "Denver doesn't exist at Pole," one Polie said.[9] Pole's contempt for McMurdo is fueled by the stacks of McMurdo's weekly *Antarctic Sun* that are flown to Pole in the summer. In the McMurdo paper, announcements about bowling tournaments and peppy stories of marine logistics accompany the explorer trivia questions and pictures of penguins. (Similarly, Denver's office newsletter *Polar Services News* fuels McMurdo's contempt for suburban Denver. In the Denver paper, announcements for the company golf tournament and the family BBQ accompany explorer trivia questions and pictures of penguins.)

To many people around the world, "the South Pole" is synonymous with "Antarctica." Grumbling workers in McMurdo receive well-intentioned cards from relatives who remind them to bundle up down there at the "South Pole." Polies are conscious of and enjoy their status at the most famous location on the continent. But because the location itself generates the fame, more than anyone working there or anything that happens there, the fame is hard to enjoy. In 2002, management scheduled the New Year's party two days earlier than New Year's so that it would fall on a weekend rather than a workday. Polies reported a dismal general inability to feign excitement about New Year's at the party on December 29, and on New Year's Eve people celebrated in separate groups because there was no main party. People at McMurdo and Pole work even on Labor Day (which is observed in Denver and Washington), so Polies went to work on New Year's Day without surprise or complaint. But the sting of Pole's fame, and their place in the shadows, was worsened by a New Year's greeting from an outsider. A Writer's and Artist's Grantee that summer was friends with Matt Groening, the creator of *The Simpsons*. The cartoonist had been kept abreast of the novelties of the polar station, and for

New Year's had sent down a signed poster that showed the famous cartoon family greeting the Polies with a cheery reminder: "South Pole, the only place on earth to celebrate New Year's twice!"

Though Polies probably do have the most lucrative bragging rights in The Program, swaggering one-upmanship is common at every level of The Program. If you've only done one summer, you are a fingee. If you do multiple summers, you haven't done a winter. When you do a winter and find out that winter is actually easier than summer, then you haven't done multiple winters. If you've done multiple winters, you haven't been to Pole. If you've done a summer at Pole, you haven't done a winter at Pole. If you've done a winter at Pole, you haven't done multiple winters at Pole. And, finally, once you've done multiple winters at Pole, you are afraid to leave Antarctica because you'll have to pay for food and look both ways before crossing the street.

Occasionally I paused from sawing to look at the horizon, flat but for the nearby buildings and clutter, as if planed and glued to the sky uniformly by an unimaginative but exacting craftsman. Somewhere out there buried in the ice were barrels of fuel, tool chests, and bundles of lumber, all lost during airdrops the first year at Pole, traveling since then at a glacial pace away from the Pole as naturally as we are drawn to it. There are tomato juice and caustic soda, sausages, a bag of mail that broke open in mid-air and rained down like a confetti of names and dates over a half-mile area. A whole set of encyclopedias was out there somewhere, making a break for it.

A few days after I arrived, the scientists at the Atmospheric Research Laboratory hosted their monthly slushy party in which they use a cooler of "the cleanest snow in the world" to ice various liquors. I talked to a Galley worker about soccer hooligans for a while, then went upstairs to see the laser that flashed purple in the dark while the engineer explained that it needed more power, which she hoped would be provided once the new power plant was completed and the emergency plant got a rest.

Full of snow and Kentucky whisky, I walked to the South Pole. There was a shark crafted from snow, as if emerging through the surface of a white ocean, contender in a recent ice sculpture contest. Nearby was the tent of some Danes who had skied from the coast.

In 1997 a United States Antarctic Program External Panel evaluated U.S. activities in the Antarctic. The 11-member panel was chaired by Norman Augustine, CEO of Lockheed-Martin. It found that "the geopolitical importance heretofore assigned to a permanent U.S. presence in Antarctica, particularly at the South Pole, appears fully warranted. This consideration, *in itself,* justifies a year-round presence at several locations, including a moderate-sized facility at the Pole, along with necessary supporting infrastructure." The panel chairman called Pole a "crown jewel."

Usually only such musty logs as External Panel reports, Unclassified Memoranda to the National Security Council, and Congressional Hearing Records mention "geopolitical and stewardship considerations," or recognize that "strategic and foreign policy objectives" are "anchored at the South Pole," or that "this vital experiment in the governance of a non-sovereign territory has been so successful." If we relied only on these dust-caked tomes to fuel the flames of our charitable pursuits, we would soon feel the chill of self-interest, so we are lucky to have newspapers.

Robert Lee Hotz from the *Los Angeles Times* got his Pole boondoggle in January 2001 and wrote an article describing "a community struggling at the limit of what the human body can endure and civilization can sustain." He described the skiers who "walked the ice like the maze on a cathedral floor, seeking the one true journey concealed in every labyrinth. It brought them here, where nothing can grow or survive except the spirit." Construction of the new station at Pole was called "a labor of grace and renewal at the last place on Earth." When his plane landed back at McMurdo and the cargo door opened, he was "born again into the white." The article ends: "If we can, we repeat certain journeys, each a voyage to something true in us, to all who will listen."

When the *Los Angeles Times* ran the story "Last Journey to The Last Place on Earth: At the South Pole, Nothing Can Grow Except the Spirit," it was forwarded to all Antarctic staff by the RPSC Communications Manager: "Below is a piece written by Robert Lee Hotz who visited South Pole as a media event last season. It's a 'make you proud' article. Please distribute to your staff."

Robert Lee Hotz is a science writer for the *Los Angeles Times.* Journalists who come to Antarctica are hand-selected by a USAP committee including media officers from NSF's Office of Legislative and Public Affairs. Journalists apply, and NSF decides which ones are allowed on the plane. "I would like to quantify in some way our support of media visitors," wrote an NSF publicist to her colleagues. "It will help me to analzye [*sic*] whether or not the return is sufficient, and to more obviously make the point to journalists—when required— that they are 'guests' of NSF. (Which *might* in turn increase sensitivity to giving NSF credit.)"

By the time the "guests" arrive in Christchurch, an NSF scout has sniffed them out for trouble, alerting on-ice NSF Reps to what kinds of questions they've been asking ("Kelly asked about coordination among nations. Marta asked about role of State Dept."); or their moods ("He slept comfortably on the plane and is feeling fine. He bowed out of lunch in favor of shower and shave..."); or any other notable or useful traits ("Pam has avoided computers. She reports a pleasant train trip to Greymouth (a potential point of conversation for you).")

Arriving in Antarctica, they are busied with field training and boondoggles to the huts or the ice edge or the snow caves. They have a day or two in town before they are flown to the South Pole or the Dry Valleys or Siple Dome. They're understandably excited. "Even though we're doing a piece for '60 Minutes' (among other shows)," wrote a CBS producer who deployed in January of 1999, "we're not Mike Wallace ;-) No ambushes, no tricks; we want to work with everyone to help tell a series of great science stories as clearly, accurately, and colorfully as possible!" If such professionalism is maintained, the journalist may be invited back, or even hired to help with NSF Public Relations.

It is more professional for a journalist writing a story about the polyethylene weather balloons going up not to ask where they come down.[10] And as an adventurer, the journalist's Antarctica card is bolder, brighter, and more dazzling if his eyes scurry away from the old leaking machines and big screen TVs. Describing American journalists who cover presidential campaigns, Joan Didion wrote: "They are willing, in exchange for 'access,' to transmit the images their sources wish transmitted." Similarly, we read in the paper that science in Antarctica is the end rather than the means, and because of this generous pursuit, everything, very soon, is going to be even better than it is now.[11] When the NSF-sponsored journalists step from the plane, Antarctica's beauty speaks for itself, and the psychedelic vastness hobbles the critical faculties. Their stories recount the "howling wilderness" and the "gale-force winds" on "the highest, driest, coldest" and most "desolate" continent, which is "pristine" and "remote" and "isolated."

"I just got back from Antarctica," they're saying.

We are like a broken record still playing classic hits from the days of Captain Cook and Columbus. The reported particulars are not always untrue, but the consensus fellowship of professional journalism keeps things simple and catchy, so that Antarctica always brims with scientists and researchers just as wooded clumps next to the freeway brim with wildlife.

When the ad agency representing Hostess became interested in McMurdo's eccentric Twinkie Club, whose members launched Twinkies into the winter night against monotony with pressurized airguns, a draft of a Hostess press release described the enthusiastic participants as "scientists." When the Twinkie Club President clarified that none of them were scientists, the agency asked if the word "researcher" would be better. A New Zealand paper once wrote that an aircraft was "flying back with scientists from Antarctica," but it was full of winter-overs, none of them scientists. Aviation Week and Space Technology calls Antarctica "a pristine frozen laboratory."

This notion is creatively incomplete. Science and science support play a large role in many people's workdays, but science is also the only way to expand by the letter of the Antarctic Treaty. In 1970 Richard Nixon said, "Science has provided a successful basis for international accord, and the Antarctic is the only continent where science serves as the principal expression of national policy and interest." As stated by the External Panel, the primary national interest is physical occupation, and science is the loophole through which the necessary infrastructure can emerge.[12] For every grant-funded American scientist on the ice, there are approximately five wage earners, most of them involved in building or maintaining infrastructure. As the External Panel wrote: "The U.S.'s scientific and environmental research in Antarctica give substance and relevance to the national presence." In other words, ironworkers don't support science; science supports ironworkers.

The perverted notion of science leading the brigade is nurtured by NSF and dispersed mainly through network television, newspapers, and magazines. But there are other information support staff for the American frontier. The NSF Artist's and Writer's Grant brings down a more sophisticated breed of bricklayer. Writer's and Artist's recipients are usually either naturalist writers like Barry Lopez or the genius Stephen Pyne, whose vast talents would be wasted writing about anything less than Antarctica's history as a cultural construct; or ex-schoolteachers who make children's books or paintings about seals and penguins, like Sandra Markle, who authored such books as *Pioneering Frozen Worlds* and *Science to the Rescue*, or Gretchen Legler, who wrote on her website: "... when we first entered the dive hut a mother seal and her baby (these are Weddell Seals) were in the dive hole in the hut, breathing hard, their black eyes and whiskers above the water line, curled around each other like a yin-yang symbol, that ancient Chinese symbol of balance." While the seals are engaged in a cosmic dance, winter-overs are bribed not to report work injuries. While science is on its way to save the day, a fuel spill is officially reported with great understatement as "over 200 gallons," and Lake Bonney in the Dry Valleys is tainted with glycol from a previous spill.

These daily unpleasantries are more common than meteorite-seeking robots, seals with cameras on their heads, the discovery of new microbes, and photos of the beginning of the universe. They are Antarctic facts, but distasteful, not suited to the pristine popular image of the continent. Accordingly, everyone who arrives at the last frontier is an explorer who throws caution aside and ventures to live a dream, conducting wholesome and tidy science. Antarctica is the pure white fatted calf that will yield a feast for all if tended thus.

This was the attitude of a man who one day came to the Waste Barn for a tour. For ten minutes he helped me throw bags of plastic in the baler. He had come down as part of NSF's program for schoolteachers (Teachers Experiencing Antarctica) to help scientists, and to promote education about Antarctica in the classrooms of America. (Later NSF brought down journalists from *Education Week* to write stories about the teachers they brought down.) The teacher had worked for NSF. Later I read on his website about how he had helped me for ten minutes: "I decided to give them a hand. After all, I helped produce the trash, I might as well help recycle it." I met the teacher again when I went to Sea Ice Training at F-Stop. The instructor asked us, in the course of introducing ourselves, to name our ideal Antarctic boondoggle. The teacher wanted to go to Pole. "It's not for me," he said. "There's five thousand kids back in Wisconsin who need me to go."

This recasting of self-interest as generosity was masterfully executed in the famous rescue of the doctor from Pole in 1999. The incident held the attention of the press around the world. The doctor, diagnosed with breast cancer, received an airdrop of medical supplies in the middle of winter. A *Baltimore Sun* headline read, "Mercy flight heads to end of the Earth." *USA Today* called it "a risky humanitarian mission." An Australian paper wrote: "The drop opened a new chapter in the dramatic record of Antarctic emergency aid." CBS called it an "unprecedented effort." These stories did not mention that winter airdrops to Pole were standard procedure until 1996, when they were stopped because of budget cuts.[13]

The doctor was finally flown from Pole on October 16, 1999, about ten days before Pole's first normally scheduled flight. One northern hemisphere journalist called it a "never-before-attempted feat of flying to the South Pole in deepest winter ..." It was so deep into winter, in fact, that it might have been called the beginning of summer.

Out with the doctor came a worker who had an undiagnosed broken hip. He had been in such pain that he couldn't work most of the winter and had to walk on crutches. When both he and the doctor were flown from Pole, he was dropped off in McMurdo to wait for the next plane, while she went on to Christchurch, where the media would be waiting. Some headlines from that time included the following: Mercy Dash to Antarctica; Antarctic Mercy Run: Dangerous Airlift for Ailing Doc; Rescue at the End of the Earth. At lunch, I talked to the guy with the busted hip who had been dumped in McMurdo. Though at the time he attributed his pain to kidney stones, he didn't mind waiting for the next, less publicity-arousing flight, and found the situation amusing. A feather in the cap of NSF's Office of Legislative and Public Affairs, the rescue story rephrased slight deviations from standard procedure as heroic goodwill. Public approval is a useful amulet against future budget cuts, such as the one that threatened The Program and eliminated the airdrops in 1996. The Rescue had all the elements for a good return on investment.[14]

In early 1999, while the doctor was still adjusting to her first months at the South Pole, a *Washington Post* journalist, Curt Suplee, was allowed on the continent by NSF. He already had a good history with NSF, and his interests that year revealed a perfect triangle of Antarctic media stories: climate, astrophysics, and a story on penguins. Two years after the South Pole rescue, Curt Suplee had left the *Washington Post* to work for NSF, where he offered suggestions on how to handle the famous South Pole doctor's appearance on the *Oprah Winfrey Show*, whose associate producer had approached NSF with requests for a special email hook-up to Pole, and for stock footage of Pole and the new station construction. "There is absolutely no way to predict what Dr. Nielsen will say in a forum such as the Oprah show, with an audience literally in the tens of millions," the ex-journalist cautioned his colleagues, citing her statement that her cancer was caused by stress. "One does not succeed on these shows by talking about the weather." He suggested that NSF not be involved in arranging an email hook-up to Pole for the show—"What question will be asked? What will the answer be? Is the modest amount of attention NSF will get conceivably worth the possible downside?"—but that NSF would provide stock footage "as long as it clearly emphasizes science and dedication to research."

Dr. Karl Erb agreed that the new station construction should not eclipse scientific activity. "We have to convey the message that science is driving the construction effort and not vice versa."

On a trip to Cape Evans the next summer, one of our group's nametags said "Peter West." I knew from the press releases I collected from the garbage that he was the NSF Representative for Public Affairs, the primary media contact for NSF. When the press had asked questions about a rescue, he had answered them. In the year 2000 edition of *Antarctic Press Clips* published by NSF, he had written in the introduction that the South Pole doctor had been flown from Antarctica, "stirring the sympathies of millions around the world." As we crossed the ice from an idling vehicle to Robert Scott's hut, where the ship's anchor from the *Aurora* expedition lies half-buried on the shore, I asked, "You must have been pretty busy during all that rescue hubbub, huh?"

He grimaced and sharply swept the air with the back of his hand.

"It was nothing," he said.

On Saturday, the day after the slushies at the Atmospheric Research Laboratory, Kath sent me to the Heavy Shop in the loader to pick up some triwalls of vermiculite. The Heavy Shop guys had staged the triwalls where I could reach them with the loader, and as I drove into the arch one of them came over to watch. Having never operated a tracked 953 before coming to Pole, I was still clumsy with the controls. One of the guys on the ground started giving me hand signals, as if I couldn't see. After a few minor fuckups, I had the triwall on my forks and was backing out of the arch. He walked to the door of the machine and yelled something to me. I stopped and yelled "What?" over the noise of the machine. He looked at me in disgust, dismissed me with a wave of his hand, and turned away.

Fuck that shit.

I quickly set the machine in neutral, set the brake, and leaned out the door with my forearms resting on my thighs, relaxed. "Hey!" I yelled. He turned around. "Do you have something to say?" I yelled. He smiled and waved, shaking his head.

Goddamn Polies.

When I returned for the next triwall I got out to ask him a question, a gesture of mild deference. He answered my question with unnecessary detail then told me he had a present for me and picked up from the ice an oily sock that had been used as a rag and threw it at me with a smile. I caught it as it bounced off my chest, and thanked him and told him I would treasure it forever as I stuffed it in the pocket beneath his chin, then ran to the loader as the sock hit my back.

Now we were good.

Since it was Saturday night, Kath and I took off work a little early and went to join Quill and some of the other cargo crew in the DNF (Do Not Freeze) building. Part of Cargo's responsibility is management of the DNF, a heated Quonset hut for cargo that would be damaged if stored outside. We drank beer and whisky in front of the Preway. An uncomplicated and reliable heat source, the Preway is pleasant to huddle around because it produces a flame and, with the door open, is more aesthetically enticing than a heat duct.

Quill told us about the action at the end of the day when he came into DNF and found that the Preway had been removed from the building. FEMC had fulfilled an old work order to fix the DNF furnace and, upon fixing it, decided that the Preway was no longer necessary. FEMC moved the Preway outside without asking Cargo, who would ultimately be responsible if the DNF became too cold. Quill had been outraged when he found out they removed the Preway without asking, and promptly found a friendly UT to reinstall it. One of the FEMC foremen saw the UT reinstalling the Preway and walked away fuming, "It's going to the next level."

We decided to make a movie dramatizing the Preway debacle, so I grabbed my video camera and, with an inflatable Dalmation as the star, we began shooting *Preway vs. Evil*, an utterly nonsensical and forgettable movie, except for the ending in which irrational forces snuff the flame.

On Sunday morning I went to Kath's room in the Hypertats by the runway and had coffee with her and Quill, then idled the day away in warm places watching movies and eating. Even though it was Sunday, Quill said the Preway incident was rumbling. FEMC hated Cargo for some long-forgotten discourtesy in years past, and it didn't matter that no one knew why. Neither did it matter that the DNF was listed in the Emergency Plan as a muster location in case of catastrophe, precisely because the Preway was independent of the power plant. Quill explained to me that reinstalling the Preway had challenged FEMC's authority, and FEMC presently ran Pole.

It had not always been so, but ever since NSF had received approval for and was currently building a new station to replace the Dome, construction had dominated logistics, and the number of people in FEMC at Pole had grown, dwarfing every other department. Senior coordinators and foremen in FEMC began to flex muscle and regard anyone outside FEMC as a "bottom-feeder," as one Polie put it. This political influence was visible in what is commonly known as the Power Table. The Power Table is next to the stairs that lead to the

upper Galley, and is occupied by the senior ranks of Pole FEMC and their sex
partners. One of the main players at the Power Table, a white-collar manager
once seen in his Jamesway making blue-collar rips in his overalls with a utility
knife, once had the plastic Christmas tree moved upstairs where no one could
see it because it restricted movement to one of the seats at the Power Table.
Several bottom-feeders have performed experiments by sitting at the Power
Table to see what would happen. The bottom-feeder is not explicitly told to
leave, but is actively ignored amidst general discomfort.

On Sunday Quill had decided to address the Preway matter in a

Once in McMurdo, as a planeload of Polies bound for the runway boarded
the big and loud Terra Bus and the smaller and quieter airport shuttle with tinted
windows, five figures from the Power Table stood aside talking. Soon the more
desirable airporter shuttle had filled, but there was still room for passengers on
the Terra Bus. The Air Services Rep, who coordinates PAX movement, stepped
onto the airporter and said that five people would have to move onto the Terra
Bus. No one moved. The Air Services Rep pointed at five people and told them
to move to the Terra Bus. After they got off, the five figures from the Power
Table stepped on and took their seats. On the trip to town, some of the Polies
hassled them for not standing in line like everyone else. "You'd better watch it if
you want to keep your bonus," one from the Power Table said.

On Sunday Quill had decided to address the Preway matter in a
preemptive late-night email to his department boss, in which he explained
the various reasons for keeping the Preway installed and commented on the
irrationality of the conflict over it: "That silly Preway has become a battle
flag of goofy power-trip from a couple of different directions. Our use and
reliance on the DNF Jamesway for day-to-day operations seems to dove-tail
with another departmental fiefdom . . . Last I checked, our friends in Facilities
had unhooked the outside connection and kinked the brass tubing from the
fuel tank leading to the Preway, an obvious sabotage. Kindergarten games."

Monday morning Kath and I found the Preway dumped out in the snow,
crushed to pieces by a loader.

CHAPTER 4
NOTES

[1] "[Byrd] has one grand idea and ideal which puts more pep into me for the expedition, and… if my opinion of the commander had not yet reached the sky it surely got there today." –from Paul Siple's diary the evening he was inducted into the Loyal Legion

[2] Vostok is set to Moscow time, while American camps, including East Camp across the runway from Vostok, go by New Zealand time for logistical purposes.

[3] This expedition got little press. After spending 14 months at Norway's Troll Base, they skied to Pole, arriving on December 20. Then, to the great consternation of local authorities, they continued on toward Ross Island. The Norwegian expeditioners had filled out all the right permits with their government, but some document had landed on the wrong desk, and all agencies concerned believed that the expeditioners would only ski to Pole. NSF sought answers from heads of the Norwegian Antarctic program, who replied, "They worked for us last season, and during the winter they did maintenance at Troll [Station], but once they left Troll they were in no way part of our programme." The Norwegian administrators washed their hands of the expeditioners, and NSF became agitated because a couple of punks were skiing the continent without authorization by any government. A Norwegian official told NSF that his organization didn't know whether the expeditioners were "actually doing what they said they would do in their application. They already seemed to have made major deviations, including lack of communication!" NSF administrators cast a web of email involving Norwegian administration, the NSF Cruise Ship Coordinator, the Scott Base manager, and the publisher of an Antarctic tourism newsletter. Amidst the fog of speculation came the information that their path would take them over the Alex Heiberg Glacier and that they hoped to catch one of three tourist vessels. "Hope their insurance is good," quipped a power player, considering that they would have to fly out if they didn't catch one of the boats. They finally arrived at Scott Base, camped nearby, and washed some dishes in exchange for the facilities and food they used.

[4] "This is a nice little reminder that rumors are not tolerated in Antarctica. For RPSC employees, you should have gotten a nice lecture on this at orientation."

[5] There are several housing options during the summer: Jamesways in Summer Camp, Hypertats by the runway, rooms in the Dome, rooms in the El Dorm, or rooms in the New Station.

[6] In McMurdo, "warm" is any temperature where people spend a few extra minutes talking to someone outside with whom they've crossed paths. Anything above zero is "tropical." "Cold," whether ambient or windchill, is where mere discomfort edges into pain, in which case at lunch

a simple "Cold today" is allowed, to be met with grunts or murmurs. When the machines start getting flat tires and the hydraulics slow, the occasional "It's fuckin' cold out" is fine, as long as it's not overdone.

[7] At Little America, the men would play poker games in which the losers were charged with duty of the "crystal palaces," breaking up the frozen spires of shit that threatened to poke up through the outhouse seats by the end of each week.

[8] In this same tunnel I found on the wall a cupcake hanging from a string.

[9] On the shelf of board games in the upper Galley is "Denver Monopoly."

[10] In 1997, an aquatic ecologist at Oak Ridge National Laboratory estimated that there were about 12,500 weather balloons scattered throughout Antarctica and the surrounding ocean. [*Knoxville News-Sentinel*, Sept. 8 1997, "Early warning from Oak Ridge: Downed weather balloons may pose threat to whales in the Antarctic"]

[11] The cover of an undated CD called *Antarctica: The Last Wilderness* by Med Goodall features four Adelie penguins in a snowy landscape. The artist bio reads: "Med Goodall is a successful artist who daily experiences nature's forces in Cornwall, England. His music is softly melodious, pleasant and slightly mysterious." Released in the Netherlands by Oreade Music, the "effectively relaxing" sounds of soft synthesizers, orchestral strings, and panpipes include the songs, "Ice Skating Penguin" and "Snow Kingdom Forever." Back cover: "The first two tracks reflect the sheer scale of Antarctica's untouched splendour. 3 gives a subtle change and is more haunting; the elements of the harsh environment. 4 has a shift and hints at a sadness that this is the Last Wilderness. 5 reflects the sense of struggle and hope for survival. The final 6 calms down and reflects back, coming full circle to a mood of positive hope."

[12] Speaking of loopholes: "[That all time zones converge on Pole] could have been a handy implement for our four Catholic Station crewmen, since they could have walked around the Pole and skipped Fridays in this fashion. However, the Vatican had ruled that since the Friday food rules could not be observed at the Pole, the men could forego them, thus removing temptation."
— Paul Siple from 90 South

[13] Before 1996 the risky "humanitarian" flights brought mail and freshies (fruits and vegetables), and much appreciated cocaine to a guy at McMurdo who liked to climb onto the roof shirtless wearing his cowboy hat, and acid to someone who said tripping on a snowmobile at Pole in the winter was about as good as things get anywhere.

[14] "Every effort shall be made to manage the program in a manner that maximizes cost effectiveness and return on investment." — Ronald Reagan, President's Memorandum Regarding Antarctica, 1982

CHAPTER FIVE

The Most Peaceful Spot
in This World

*Age by age, through gulfs of time at which imagination reels, life
has been growing from a mere stirring in the intertidal slime
towards freedom, power, and consciousness.*

– H.G. Wells, *A Short History of the World*

*Even during off-duty hours, events may occur that require swift,
intelligent action.*

– USAP Participant Guide, 1998–2000 Edition

BACK FROM POLE, I noticed in the shower that there were fewer shampoo
bottles than usual. Within hours, by then comfortable in Hawaiian shirt
and New Zealand wool booties, I learned that my suitemate had been fired
while I was away. He was the manager of the Galley and had been in The
Program for many years. When I was a DA he had gracefully dissolved petty
spats over whose turn it was to do pot-room duty, and he went out of his way
to get boondoggles for us.

He had hit on a man at the bar. The man went to the Human Resources
office and charged Lenny with sexual harassment. HR began an investigation.
They called in people who had been at the bar that night and questioned

them about the incident. No one saw or heard anything that constituted "out-of-place" or "inappropriate" behavior. HR told the victim that there wasn't enough evidence to warrant a sexual harassment charge. The harassed victim threatened litigation. Then Lenny was put on suspension without pay. The next day he was told to pack for the next flight.

NSF obliges the support contractor to subcontract portions of its operation, which it does by token gestures. Two managers in the Galley worked for Marriott, though the rest of the kitchen staff were RPSC personnel. Because Human Resources is a department of RPSC and Lenny worked for Marriott, he was not summoned during the investigation for his side of the story. HR's investigation consisted of passing the testimony of one of its own employees to Lenny's boss at Marriott, who fired him. The following season at the Raytheon orientation, someone in HR with a singsong voice would show videos about non-discrimination, tolerance, and diversity in the workplace. Thick-skinned women would remain the conventional recipients of ceaseless botched overtures at the McMurdo bars.

Residents generally accept without question that a dispersed committee of career administrators arbitrates town moral standards. Workers tacitly concede that there are no truly private spaces, and that one's personal affairs outside of work are to be regulated just as are one's work duties. A South Pole station manager once said at an All-Hands Meeting, "I am the area manager. I am the manager for 700 miles in every direction." He later told them, "Anyone who says anything bad about Raytheon is out of here." As easily as he assigns a crew to a special project or calls for a rush inventory, such an authority may make a vast array of decisions on personal matters, from the decency of door decorations, to sexual preferences and conduct, to the number of guests one may entertain in one's room at a time, to the type of language appropriate in conversation with those guests. It is uncomfortable for professional managers to exempt from control some sphere of life that might be made more efficient with a little tweaking. But governing such conduct is a headache of ceaseless maintenance, because inattentive employees continually violate NSF and company policies in their off-hours. So the work of Human Resources is never done. In the U.S., the realm of a low-level HR administrator might not extend beyond the walls of the office, but at a polar base the clerk finds himself with influence over an entire town. Because he is made of eyes and ears, a lull frequently follows the HR Person into a drunken party. Everything inappropriate is there in action. Throughout the night there will be confrontations, lechery, and displayed flesh. Any single person removed from the context of the party could be spotlighted and found in violation of a hundred written standards. "Watch out! HR's here!" someone says, and everyone laughs. "I quit working at 5:30!" says the HR Person, and everyone laughs. Inappropriate behavior resumes after the brief chill. The discomfort subsides as the HR Person joins in the sexual banter and the intoxication.

Human Resources is the primary interface between the employer, who praises loyalty, and the employees, a ceaseless stream of troublemakers asking about benefits. For the HR rep to humor this selfish current, to freely provide details to an employee about various mundane entitlements, would be to acknowledge that a business transaction is occurring. That each worker is in business, selling his labor to an employer, just as a defense contractor sells weapons to a government, is a repulsive thought. It is preferable to maintain that each of us is on the best side of a great and charitable enterprise, in which the employer and the employee are locked in a pledge of selfless loyalty. In a business transaction, on the other hand, it is best to avoid getting screwed. If, for example, a shipment of cluster bombs is to be delivered on Tuesday, the manufacturer of the munitions is likely, at some point, to inquire as to the date of payment for the weapons. If a senator from some backwater province insists that it is no business of the manufacturer when or how the payment is delivered, the alert weapons-maker is unlikely to agree. Likewise, if the neighborhood weapons dealer tells the senator that someone named Larry will be by on Tuesday in a blue Honda to drop off the lethal spiderbombs and asks if he may leave them at the door, then the senator is likely to consult his notes regarding the terms of delivery.

I inadvertently crossed the line from selfless sacrifice into business one summer when my intestine blurped through my abdominal muscles as I lifted a bulky HF radio. I thought I had pulled a muscle, but when the pain didn't recede I went to Medical. The doctor determined that it was a hernia, and told me to avoid lifting more than 50 pounds at work and to have surgery when I went home. Our transaction was complete. That afternoon, as I remembered the word "surgery," I went back to Medical to determine how this expensive process would unfold.

"Am I supposed to fill anything out for Worker's Comp?" I asked the Medical administrator after explaining my diagnosis.

"Sure," she said. "Here's an Injury Report Form."

I filled it out then gave it back to her.

"Okay!" she said, as she slipped the form into a folder.

"Okay," I said, standing in front of her desk awkwardly.

"You're all set," she said.

"Okay," I said.

Later I learned that you can't PQ (Physically Qualify) to be rehired if you've had surgery within six months of deployment. I went to HR to see if I could get the ball rolling. I explained my wish to be rehired next season to Missy, the friendly HR representative, who told me I should wait until I went home to take care of all this.

"Is there any paperwork I need to fill out?" I asked.

She didn't know.

I said that I didn't want to endanger future contracts by these events. If there was no paperwork, that was fine, I told her, but if there was paperwork, then I could fill it out in the meantime. She told me to call Jo, the HR rep in Denver.

Jo was very friendly. She told me that the work comp carrier dealt with all the claims, and that I should call them when I went home. "I'll be home in February," I said. "Is there any paperwork that could be sent to my PO Box in the meantime?"

"Why can't you wait until you get home?" she asked.

"Because I want to work next summer. If I get a summer contract, or a winter contract, or any contract, I don't want to be physically disqualified for it because of a delay in paperwork or whatever."

"You have a winter contract?"

"No. But if I did, then this would be even more important."

She said she would call the Work Comp insurer to find out what the process was and that I should call her the next day.

The next day she didn't sound as friendly. She had not called the Work Comp carrier. "I called Missy in McMurdo," she said. "She checked your file and you don't have a winter contract."

"I never said I had a winter contract," I told her.

"I thought you did," she said.

My supervisor told me later that HR had called him, his boss, and his boss' boss and had told each of them that I was trying to get out of my present contract. That's when I dropped the questions about medical insurance.

A few days after I returned from Pole, the field instructors at F-Stop invited the Wastees and the GAs to Room With a View, a Scott tent planted during the summer at the base of Mt. Erebus. After work we piled in the Hagglund and rode to the Scott Base Transition, where we mounted skidoos and sped over the sea ice and then back onto Ross Island until we reached the base of the volcano. We ate, peed in the snow by a yellow flag, and took photos. A dark cloud hung like a wool blanket draped over the sky. Inland the gray light purged sky and snow of contrasts; with eyes wide open nothing was visible but a uniform gray as pure as sleep. The ice shelf to the south was glowing. People complained that the clouds were blocking the view of Erebus.

One of the guys on the boondoggle, Arthur, was a cop in his other life. He was the one who had posted signs all over McMurdo selling phone cards featuring pictures of penguins and icebergs. He also had manufactured and brought down packaged CDs of the hundreds of pictures he'd taken throughout his seasons. Many of the photos were of a teddy bear named Spencer in different locations.

I told him I had always been curious about law enforcement and asked him about his job at home. He worked in a small town, he said. "And it's the communities themselves who decide the kind of law enforcement they receive. It depends on how much they're willing to take," he said. "If you don't like your local law enforcement and want to change it, you have to be active. It's the apathetic communities—"

The trip leader hollered for us to start our machines and follow him. We sped down the hill to a patch of snow scarred with skidoo tracks and footprints of recent visitors to IMAX Crevasse, so nicknamed because of its use in an IMAX movie called *Antarctica*. We roped together in groups of four in case one of us should fall into a cavity hidden by a snowbridge. We filed down the hill and then crept along the bottom of the colossal chasm. The crevasse walls were infused with a thousand blurred hues and covered with intricate striations. I thought of small objects, like boxes of envelopes and folding chairs, and then heavy machinery and airplanes and mobile homes. All these things could fit in here at the same time. But there were no handrails or counter space. This crack in the ice was indifferent to our dimensions. We were warm microbes infecting the frozen wound. It would have been enough to unhinge anyone from culture, were it not for the group, roped together and chattering within the monstrous gloom. Arthur, behind me, was asking J.T., behind him, about the weather of northern Wisconsin in April. When the line moved slowly Arthur pulled out the teddy bear and took pictures of it against the crevasse wall.

I was roped to the Hot GA in front of me. We didn't speak. Once only, in a twilight blue, walls of dark ice rising on either side, we kissed.

The far end of the crevasse opened into a cavern. I was gawking at the forms and patterns and fractures of the surfaces when Arthur edged over beside me. "Pressure, Ice, and Time," he said with gravity, like a National Geographic narrator, before sighing.

After we left the cavern we rested outside in a smaller grotto. People ate cookies. I noticed for the first time Arthur's amazing array of gear. His sleek black clothes matched his form-fitting backpack. They were cold weather clothes, but managed to look as thin as a sweatsuit. I remarked on his gear, and he showed me his watch that, if I understood correctly, would function as perfectly on the moon as at the bottom of the ocean. Unlike anyone else in our group, including the trip leader, he wore a bouquet of carbiners on his waist. We all wore connecting ropes clipped to harnesses, and each of us had an ice pick to grip the mild hummocks we had scrambled over.

"Have you been here before?" I asked.

"Many times," he said.

"What are all those carbiners for?"

"You can't be too safe," he said.

We inched slowly in formation through a serpentine gallery of archaic frost and then up a featureless rounded incline. When we got to the skidoos, I couldn't get mine started. Arthur came over to help, and started it on the second try. I thanked him.

Each year around New Year's the Coast Guard icecutter cleaves through miles of thick sea ice to get to McMurdo, where it docks at the ice pier and loiters off the coast until the end of the season, tending patches of open water and loosening the sea ice in hope that the wind will blow it all out to sea. The boat slices through ice that supported landing planes just a few weeks before. In this way it makes a path for the tanker that delivers the next year's fuel, followed by the supply vessel.

The arrival of the supply vessel begins Ship Offload of milvans full of cargo for the coming year's operations.[1] The cargo includes materials for construction projects, spare parts for machines, and janitorial supplies. It includes new videos, liquor, and penguin souvenirs. The ship deposits a mountain of liquid eggs and frozen chicken.

For some departments, and in terms of traffic around town, Offload is the busiest time of the year. A year's worth of stuff in milvans is unloaded in about eight days, and a year's worth of plastic, cardboard, piss, heavy metal, ground wood, and radioactive contaminant is loaded and exported to the United States. Some people work all season just preparing for Offload, which runs 24/7 until it's finished, requiring of most people 12-hour shifts with no day off. Crews split into day and night shifts if they don't have them already. Someone must man the scalehouse to weigh the trucks. The Galley must prepare extra snacks and hot food for workers at the ice pier. A hundred NAVCHAPs (Navy Cargo Handling and Port Group) are flown from the U.S. to help. (The bars are closed during Offload, and no alcohol is sold at the store, reportedly because one of the NAVCHAPs drank himself to death years ago.) A line of trucks is on the pier at all times, each one waiting for a "can." The Supply Department drags people from other departments to keep up with the mammoth workload. Bamboo, bundles of orange plastic road markers, construction steel, pallets of food, and thousands of mysterious crates are stacked around town, then disappear gradually, squirreled away to the cargo lines. Offload marks the end of the summer season, after which people will start flying to Christchurch.

This season the *Polar Star* icecutter arrived. Last season it was the *Polar Sea*. The first serves Starbucks coffee, and the other serves Seattle's Best Coffee, each from a small counter by the weight room, where we lined up as soon as we boarded for our seasonal Morale Cruise one Sunday at the end of January. As the boat plowed through the ice like a bullet through cake, widening the shipping lane to the ice edge, a few hundred of us wandered the decks in red parkas cooing at minke whales and sipping hot coffee from Seattle through petite oval holes in sculpted plastic lids. We were allowed on the bridge and almost anywhere on the upper decks.

The Coasties are gracious and courteous hosts, patiently conceding the right-of-way as McMurdoites lollygag in the gangways, oblivious to the most fundamental military protocol. They have creased pants and shiny footwear. We are hairy and soaked in filth. Their pins, stripes, and baubles of rank remind us that we have more freedom than they do. We snore sprawled on the deck in the helo hangar, our limp paws stuffed with souvenir t-shirts from the ship's store.

As the vessel cut the ice, squads of penguins sprang from the water and fled in terror on their bellies across the ice. Some of the seals took evasive action, but most just watched as we slid by. We have heard of them getting popped like grapes beneath the boat. Whales stitched the surface of the open sea with spray. Cracks emerged in sheets of ice like dark lightning on a clear white sky. The boat wedged the floes apart, each one disintegrating at the edges, sounding like crumpling styrofoam, but deep like a toothache. Clean tables of ice beside the ship were spattered with blue stains in the snow that vanished once washed with seawater. The boat maintained an even speed. The effects were mesmerizing and too numerous to watch.

In their wooden ships, the first people to enter McMurdo Sound were on the edge of the known world. Every mile south was a new mile of map previously unreleased to the public. No one had lived here before moving on, and no one had been here by accident on the way to somewhere else. The people who first sailed through these waters were in danger. Now as the hulking steel vessel crashed through the powerless terrain, I reflected that among my earliest memories were those of supermarkets and parking lots. I once spent six hours at a video game and got a million points. I had worked for Kits Cameras, Subway sandwiches, and as a valet at International House of Pancakes. I had once been an office manager. As I dawdled on the deck of the shuddering ship that chewed up 4,500 gallons of fuel per hour, I imagined that I was trapped under ice, clawing futilely to reach the surface. I imagined falling overboard, floating paralyzed with cold as a pod of killer whales nuzzled from below. Or being swept into the propellers, the meat of my body then bobbing peacefully in the ship's wake. One wrong move and my goose would be cooked, I thought. What's that asshole doing here?

Howard Dell stood nearby in his pristine red parka. He worked for the company that bought the recycled waste from the USAP. Last year in Denver he had tried to pep-talk the Waste crew into sorting plastic into 12 types, a process that would require roughly ten times the labor and processing space and would save his company a little money. His company also sold industrial equipment. His casual but tucked-in decorum pleased our managers. He was always trying to sell them something or other, and they enjoyed being tempted by his catalogue of Waste Management technologies that entailed certain improvement. When he had visited Pole, he had tried to pump up Kath's enthusiasm for a cardboard baler. "We don't have electricity running to the Waste building," she had reminded him.

I moved away from him and wandered up to the bridge. There were telephone handsets in the ceiling and a video monitor that showed the ice cracking in front of the ship. Below, employees clogged the railing in red parkas, flowing from one side to the other as the sights escalated in novelty. Seals were household objects by the second pod of whales. Delighted gasps had ceased a few dozen penguins earlier. After the icebergs, the front deck thinned out as if after the biggest firework. I went down to the rear deck and found Butch lounging on one of the nets at the perimeter. While we were talking, a McMurdoite in a red parka piped at him from nearby, "I think that's probably against the rules to sit on that."

I walked across the yard one night after dinner. The Hot GA and her friend Sonia were on nightshift for Offload and were strapping some cargo between dorms 210 and 211. I stopped for a minute to shoot the shit.

"We were just talking about your cock," the Hot GA explained.

"Is there anything I can do to help?"

"Sonia wants to see it."

"Not here," I said to Sonia. "Let me take you somewhere warm."

"That sounds kind of dirty," she said, and then the girls had to get back to work.

Though living so close to one's coworkers has many unwelcome aspects, a powerful motive behind chronic Antarctic recidivism is the polar community's opportunities and appetite for heedless fucking. This attraction, best in the summers, is never mentioned in employee handbooks or at the job fairs. People are thrown together for a finite time. No one lives in town permanently, and each will return, if at all, under different circumstances. Winter-overs have to take an HIV test to get their jobs. Each season is a clean slate that makes it easy to change partners or to hook up for kicks. Though the gender ratio is unbalanced, and many will go hungry for long periods, whatever sex does happen whips the mob into an expectant frenzy, as the sound of coins piling up in a nearby slot machine excites the other gamblers. Everyone has busybody roommates, so people have sex in the greenhouse, the library, the aquarium, and the Cosray Lab. Any warm little generator shack will do. The radio station, the record library, and the band room are premium, because there are only a few keys to them, and no one is likely to intrude. Sometimes you'd swear it was a full moon by the sweaty tension and people making out in Gallagher's on a Wednesday night for no particular reason. On these nights there are antics in the bar bathrooms, in the dorm lounges, and weird careful sex behind curtains while the roommate pretends not to notice.

There have been so many hail-Mary fucks that men learn never to say never, despite a woman's boyfriend, despite the fiancée back home, despite marriage. Men with wives at home turn to "ice-wives." Couples form who later marry—in the BFC is a wedding photo where both the bride and groom are ice folk, and about half of the guests are somehow involved with the ice—and long relationships, even marriages, are broken within months of exposure to the sexual free-for-all.

Classic tales are repeated, such as the one about the married couple who once worked on the same shift in the Galley. The woman had an affair with a Navy guy and would bring him back to the dorm room when her husband was out skiing. Everyone knew about it except the husband. Eventually the affair was revealed, and the married couple separated, but continued working in the Galley on the same shift.

A man who had sex with at least three gorgeous women at Pole one summer is a legendary figure whose name will be uttered with quiet reverence for a few seasons, and he may have a cargo berm or other industrial landmark named after him. A woman who manages to sleep with an NSF manager in McMurdo or an FEMC manager at Pole gains social power, an ambassador's immunity from the piddling hoops traversed by hoi polloi. The sneaking around of big players is of particular interest, for it affects tomorrow's interdepartmental leniencies. The doors in 209 in the early morning are those most carefully closed.

Here's a more clinical view from a psych report by Lawrence A. Palinkas:

> Temporary relationships between male and female crew-members are a common and accepted part of the winter-over experience. Although John's relationship was not widely approved by the winter-over crew as a whole because it violated the normative rule that this form of coping behavior should not be exercised by married men or women, it was tolerated because it met the individual's immediate need (to depend upon someone to cope with the isolation) and because it produced an improvement in John's performance at work. Thus, although the extra-marital affair may have been viewed as maladaptive back in the United States, it was seen as a pragmatic means for coping with the unique circumstances of the Antarctic physical and social environment.

As the female population (30% to 40%) is always smaller than the male population, a unique sexual culture forms. Women, whether they like it or not, have the pick of the litter. A woman there in the early '80s, when the female population was even lower, said that living at Pole was "like being a bone in a pack of dogs." One woman who has been down for many years said she enjoyed the attention for the first few seasons but tired of it, eventually finding it more of a hassle than anything else. She said some women treasured the ego boost of having a hundred suitors at their beck and call. A female friend reports that, as long as a woman maintains good standing with other women on station, there is not much damage to social status if she wants to sleep around, but that if someone avoids other women and only hangs out with guys, the other women will probably turn on her.

Men tend to informally size up the situation as early as possible, gauging at the start of a season, whether summer or winter, their chances of getting some. In rough order of increasing potential, the male network determines who is a lesbian, who has a long-term boyfriend, who is married, who has a short-term boyfriend, and who is looking for action. According to those who aren't getting any, the town is jammed with lesbians. A common resentful appraisal of an overly popular woman is that she is merely "a plane ride away from being ugly." A more constructive maxim suggests, "Go ugly early."

Despite these complications, few men long for the puzzling days when the Navy insisted that women in Antarctica would spoil their grand adventures, as when Richard Byrd suggested that his Antarctic base was "the most peaceful spot in this world, due to the absence of women." (By the end of his first expedition the crew was on the verge of mutiny.[2]) Admiral Reedy once called Antarctica "the womanless white continent of peace." Rear Admiral Dufek said, "I felt the men themselves didn't want women there. It was a pioneering job. I think the presence of women would wreck the illusion of the frontiersman—the illusion of being a hero."

At the end of the season, during Ship Offload, the entire Waste crew was given redeployment dates of around February 19. Margaret wanted to leave earlier to meet her boyfriend in Christchurch. She asked Saul, the full-time Waste manager, if she could leave earlier. He said no, because it is in all cases easier for managers to say no than yes. I told this to Margaret and mentioned to her informally that if she really wanted to leave early she should be persistent, to let Saul know that her desire was not whimsical but important to her. She said she didn't want to screw us by giving us extra work. "We're going to work ten-hour days and get everything done whether everyone's here or not," I told her. "In exactly two weeks no one is going to give a shit whether it was five people or six people who got everything done. Vacation in New Zealand sounds good, and since everyone else doesn't want to leave early, there's no reason you shouldn't."

A few days later I was doing a walk, checking the trash bins around town, when I ran into Margaret in front of Medical doing the other half of the walk.

"Hey," I said, "I heard you might be able to leave early? Is that true?"

"Yes, I wanted to talk to you about that," she said.

We halted in front of Medical and stood facing each other, holding our clipboards.

"I could handle another week of delay," she said, "but if I had to wait 'til the 19th then there would have to be some changes in the workplace."

Uh-oh.

The previous summer Margaret had come up to the Waste Barn a few times to work with the Waste crew, testing out the waters to see if she would like the job. That summer the crew was tight, we had fun all the time, and our breaktime conversations were always absurd. Margaret was a General Assistant and, like all GAs who are thinking of returning to the ice, was looking to move into a better job. Sizing up the Waste department as a casual and fun-loving crew, void of redneck machismo and intimidating vibes, she sought a position there.

During that short time she had established her preferred images of herself. Vermont. A desire for fresh organic vegetables. A love of the outdoors, trees, and sunshine. McMurdo is about loud machines that leak oil, and meals of ancient frozen chicken. Where a behemoth ozone hole makes the summer sun a relentless blazing sphere that will sear the eyes and plant tumors in exposed skin. Where most of the outdoors is a restricted area, and where the average lot is ceaseless toil interrupted only by dead sleep or stupefying intoxication.

Earlier in the summer, while we were clipping boards with a chainsaw, Margaret asked what my favorite children's book was. I said I liked Kit Williams' books and the Babar series. I asked what her favorite was.

"*The Giving Tree*," she said.

I was barely able to contain my horror.

The Giving Tree is a story of a tree and a boy. When the boy is very young he enjoys climbing in the branches of the tree. The tree is happy that the boy is happy climbing in the tree's branches. Later the boy no longer climbs the tree, but comes to take the apples from the tree. This makes the tree happy, because the boy is happy when he sells the apples. Finally, the boy slaughters the tree, chops it up, and sells it as timber.

This makes the tree happy.

Because the boy is happy.

The tree sacrifices. The boy profits from the sacrifice.

The tree represents people. The boy represents other people.

And the reader awards the dead tree a medal for its service to humanity.

The Giving Tree is a hideous tale, a blueprint for a society of parasites.

Now Margaret and I stood in the frigid wind looking at each other through sunglasses on a treeless continent with wooden clipboards in our gloved hands. Margaret told me that the work environment was unacceptable. She pointed out numerous obvious improprieties to me and said that, yes, she was leaving early. She had approached Butch and made it clear that if she couldn't leave early she would make an issue with HR. She was not angry, and was actually slightly apologetic, as if it were too bad it had come to this.

By any grab-bag standard, Margaret had a point. Our break conversations were filthy. We swore constantly. I had once explored the intricacies of mating large felines with real estate agents, and accused Butch of molesting me before asking him for a raise. A woman had once surveyed us all on our masturbation habits. There were no creepy advances like the ones in the orientation videos, nor was Margaret implying such, but there were a thousand examples of filthy talk. We were nasty, crude garbage grunts. Though there were five women and three men on the crew, an official investigation would certainly implicate our male supervisor, who was in a convenient position to add some weight to Margaret's request to leave early.

On the last day of Mainbody I ran my loader down to MCC, where the final group of summer people was checking in for last flight. The day before, they were reminded to wear their ECW gear, to have their passports ready, and not to show up intoxicated. Dressed to the nines in cold-weather gear and lugging their orange bags, people loaded onto the caravan of vehicles that would transport them to the runway.

The end of summer is unceremonious. People are working beside you, then suddenly they get on the plane to leave. Next season people would be promoted, or fired, or would change departments, or would not return. Buildings would rise or be torn down. Odd new equipment would be crawling around town. Saying goodbye to Kath and Señor X and Butch and the Hot GA was sad not only because they would be absent, but also because the concoction would never be duplicated even if they returned. The abrupt ending—one day is summer, the next is winter—only aggravated the melancholy.

As the Terra Bus and the vans and the shuttles drove in a line down the road toward Scott Base, it was a moment of finality, like placing a bet, or like hearing the verdict at the end of a trial.[3] My loader idled as I watched the vehicles disappear in the distance; its soothing industrial purr assured me that all this was much different from the early days, when the crews watched as the wooden ships that had dropped them off for the winter sailed over the horizon.

―――――――

CHAPTER 5
NOTES

[1] Also known as simply Offload, or Vessel, as in "Does the Galley have any more cajun shrimp left? No, but there's some coming at Vessel."

[2] After the booze-fueled near-mutiny of Byrd's first expedition, he insisted that no liquor be taken on the second expedition, except for medicinal purposes. Thomas C. Poulter, Senior Scientist, was put in charge of Little America I, and noted carefully where the sled of medicinal liquor was stored. As soon as the supply ship left, Poulter hid the liquor in an old disused tunnel behind a wall of snow. A few months into winter, he gave permission for some spiked punch to be served. That night one of the crew was found outside toppled on a snowbank. "Never again," wrote Poulter in his journal, and by the end of the month, people were "hunting for my liquor cache by probing through the snow with six foot long steel rods." Before they could get to it, he moved the liquor from the hidden tunnel to the shack that housed his meteor observation platform. To sate the thirsty mob he authorized another night of spiked punch. Poulter reports that one man passed out in a hole outside, and two others passed out in the dog tunnels, where it was minus 50°F. He decided to dump the liquor. He removed a board from the floor, drilled a hole, and began dumping the liquor into the snow through a funnel. During the procedure he burned wool to mask the odor of 500 bottles of Golden Wedding Whiskey, after which he was left with 500 empty glass bottles. He dug holes in the snow and crushed the bottles in the holes. "A wooden 4x4 worked very well for tamping," he wrote, as if recording a Standard Operating Procedure. He made sure to refill the top of the holes with lots of snow so that "exploratory digging" would not reveal the evidence. "Charlie Murphy was the only other person in camp that knew about this and it was never told until the movie of the Expedition was released by Paramount Studios after our return. Charlie Murphy wrote the script for that movie and he incorporated the story of the liquor in a conversation between two penguins in the picture." Meanwhile, the ship's crew on the New Zealand arm of the expedition was selling the ship supplies. The ship's cook had borrowed a thousand dollars from New Zealand citizens and then disappeared. "Authorities are hunting him," wrote Poulter. By May Poulter felt it was obvious that some of the crew had another source of alcohol, because one of the crew became "quite argumentative—to the extent that he is quite a nuisance." "Wish I knew where their supply was and I would take it," wrote Poulter, who began to fear that the crew was drinking vanilla extract. "I dumped 13 quarts of vanilla extract tonight," he wrote at the end of May. – Thomas C. Poulter, Senior Scientist, Little America I, "The Winter Trip to Advance Base: Byrd Antarctic Expedition II 1933–35." Typed and bound, P.J. Skellerup Antarctic Library, Christchurch, New Zealand.

[3] Someone wearing an alien mask and holding a sign that said "Jordan" stood by the side of the road as the procession went by.

CHAPTER SIX

THE GRINDER AND THE
PROJECTED MAYHEM INDEX

Their great physical suffering went deeper than their appearance. Their speech was jerky, at times semi-hysterical, almost unintelligible.... These events had rendered these hapless individuals as unlike ordinary human beings as any I have ever met. The Antarctic had given them the full treatment.

— Captain John King Davis,
rescuing the *Aurora* party at Cape Evans

My experience is that in general the members of expeditions do not get along very well with each other.

— Finn Ronne

T HE FIRST INTENTIONAL winter-over expedition in the Antarctic was a private British expedition managed by Norwegian Carsten Borchgrevink in 1899. Before they had even landed on the continent, Borchgrevink notified geomagnetician and physicist Louis Charles Bernacchi, who kept extensive journals, that he considered all crew diaries to be his property. When this was protested, Borchgrevink told the crew that he would allow them their diaries, but that all private notes significant enough to constitute books were his.

During a summer sledging expedition, camped on shore, they awoke one morning to find that huge waves threatened to carry away their sledges, supplies, dogs, and even the tents they slept in. While the rest of the crew rushed to pack the gear, Borchgrevink ran out of harm's way to the top of a slope and, after watching them struggle in the waves for a time, called for one of them to bring him a box of biscuits.

Months passed at their little hut on Cape Adare, cut off from the rest of the world, and by midwinter the spirit of the group had soured. Bernacchi wrote, "Such oppressive feelings is [sic] reigning within our four walls, that everyone looks as if he is half dead. If one of us should try and start some fun [to] enlive[n] the rest, he would be suspected of an attempt to break down the discipline, and under such circumstances the safest thing is to keep as quiet as possible so as not to make the discomfort greater than it is…"

The crew's disgust with Borchgrevink climaxed when he read aloud a letter supposedly signed by the expedition sponsor which asserted "That the following things would be considered mutiny: to oppose C.E.B[orchgrevink] or induce others to do so, to speak ill of C.E.B., to ridicule Mr C.E.B. or his work, to try and force C.E.B. to alter contracts etc." Bernacchi regarded the letter as a forgery; it was written on their ship's paper.

On the Queen's birthday they had a party, after which Borchgrevink told them all that he felt he had not been included in the spirit of celebration. A few weeks later, he dismissed one Colbeck, but said he would reinstate him and destroy evidence of disciplinary action against him if Colbeck admitted "his ingratitude towards him." Bernacchi wrote in his diary that Colbeck had "always done his duty willingly and to the best of his ability.…As Borchgrevink cannot prove a charge of misconduct or gross insubordination against Colbeck, and according to contract he is compelled to give him three months notice, Colbeck has a very good case of breach of contract."

This was the first winter human beings had lived on the continent.

Of penguins, Bernacchi wrote, "What impressed me greatly was the general appearance of madness prevailing amongst them. They appear to be under the shadow of some great trouble…"

In July, Borchgrevink went exploring for ten days (says Bernacchi) to three weeks (says Borchgrevink) and returned with a mineral sample of common iron pyrites that he said was worth £50,000 and said that he had discovered gold in such quantity as to indicate a second Klondike.

As winter turned to summer, the crew zoologist died and was buried. Borchgrevink informed the crew that he had taken possession of the dead man's private diary. On Christmas, the crew toasted Borchgrevink's health with empty glasses, so he withheld the Christmas cards that he had made for each of them.

When the last plane left, I was helping Thom dump a bin of carpet and tile and insulation. It would normally be a solitary task, but today was windy, and there was a lot of insulation in the dumpster, so it was useful to have someone on the ground to scramble for the larger pieces. The last plane buzzed the town and wagged its wings, the pilot telling us to have a good winter. Soon the mountains would sink into darkness and cold stars would appear.

After a few hours at my normal routine, while I was in a loader retrieving Contaminated Wood from the Carp Shop, I realized that each person I saw would be here at least until the first Winfly plane in August. Six months was not a long time, but I suddenly felt anxious.

I would be stuck in an outpost with all-you-can-eat desserts and an endless procession of theme parties. A small town where phone numbers are four digits but the budget is nine digits, where everyone had frequent flyer miles and no one had wisdom teeth. A town that courted ambassadors and senators with luxury accommodations in Building 125. A town with disco clothes and high-power microscopes. A town into which people have smuggled goldfish and where a pet snail from a head of lettuce faces execution by government mandate. A town where going outside requires authorization. A town responsible for divorces. A town where corpses have reportedly been stored in the food freezer and where it is illegal to collect rocks.

This was America, I realized, all in a tight little bundle.

And there were no more flights out.

After work that day, we had our first winter All-Hands Meeting. Because these meetings are public events where, if anyone were listening, a murmur theoretically could sweep through the crowd, the warnings are put softly: we are reminded that the sea ice is off-limits this time of year, or that we need to chock the tires when we get out of our vehicles. After the warnings, the muckety-muck thanks the aggravated and workstained mob for all the hard work we've done. The work thus far has met great success. But this is a tough time of year. We must continue to look forward. There are challenges ahead.

The Winter Station Manager, Larry C., renowned as a decent and unbureaucratic papa-like figure, opened the meeting and told us there were exactly 222 people wintering in McMurdo this year, and there were ten at Scott Base down the road. That's 232 humans on Ross Island until August, he said.

He introduced some key personnel and reminded us about some winter-over dangers. Insomnia and depression can occur. Alcohol will not help depression, it will worsen it; so, in order to facilitate a healthier environment, Raytheon Polar Services Company will sponsor more activities without alcohol this winter, so we can "experience ourselves," he said. Boredom is a problem. Phones, email, and TV have helped, but the routine nature of this environment is bound to give rise to such problems. We could also expect some loss of concentration and memory. This is an unexplained phenomenon of working in the Antarctic, he said.

All of us knew of the findings of winter-over psychology studies. On the wall in one of the Crary hallways is a tidy professional display of the results of one from 1996. Thom, my workmate, took part in the study. He said they had to periodically answer questions and take pills. Early in the study, the experimenter had told the participants how to determine if their capsules were placebo or not, which they did. At the end of the winter he and the other participants each received a medal for assisting the scientific study.

As the summer people had left their rooms, we were now free to move into our winter housing. I moved to dorm 207, where my new room smelled like vomit and bloody boogers streaked the wall. Most people moved simultaneously, so we visited each other in our new rooms and drank Steinlagers from warm refrigerators in half-decorated rooms filled with boxes. Ivan and I were suitemates. We kept the bathroom doors open and occasionally darted over to see the progress of the other's furniture arranging or to help hang posters or dismantle the beds. The skua piles were enormous, because a thousand people had just left, so we squirreled away mounds of crap.

I brought a pickle down from work, and from seven to midnight we heisted couches from massive furniture piles in the dorm lounges, each of us determined to create a lush cavern for solitary living for the next six months. Later that evening, driving along the north end of the brown dorms with a putrid-orange couch on my forks, I looked down at Robert Scott's hut across the bay at Hut Point and realized I hadn't been down there in a while. There, long ago, in that frozen outpost of exploration, I had received a fantastic blowjob.

Discovery Hut is described by historian Lennard Bickel as "little more than a wooden shell of planking tough enough to withstand the battering blizzards and gales of winter. It was used also for storing equipment and supplies, and by parties in transit, but later it was to be blessed sanctuary to a few debilitated wretches struggling back from one of the most harrowing sledge journeys of all time." Those debilitated wretches from the *Aurora* expedition had lived in the filthy hut for months at a time, where water froze within a foot of the stove and they had only three sleeping bags for six people, where they spent the winter flaying seal carcasses and lancing frostbite blisters.

But I knew only that as my girlfriend's frozen breath rolled across my stomach, the historic monument curled around me as if I were inside a hazy snowglobe of warm bounty. By my head was a mutilated seal that had been freezing and thawing since the Heroic Age. There was an old box of rocks off to the other side. Nearby was a mutton carcass that had been dripping goo for nearly a century. Though the soot-covered blubber stove had been abstinent since early in the century, the object, wedged in its context, still released history.

Robert Scott, who erected the hut in 1902, is the most famous man to have died in Antarctica. In 1912 he and his men set out to claim Pole as their prize. Ponies hauled their sleds of supplies and were shot and eaten along the way. One of them, good old Christopher, moved just as they shot him and, with a bullet lodged in his head, angrily stormed into camp before they could finish him off. When they ran out of ponies, they manhauled the sleds until they reached their miserable goal, which Norwegian explorer Roald Amundsen had already won, leaving behind a tent with a letter inside, and a note asking Scott to forward the letter to the King of Norway.[4] Someone once said that Scott went to the Pole an explorer and returned a postman. Scott's party—who would on the way back die one by one: one lapsed into a coma, another whose hands and feet were frozen meat walked into a blizzard so as not to hold back the others, and the rest froze and starved … miles from a cache of food and fuel—stood at their miserable goal and snapped a photo.

Scott and his men could never have predicted the events that would occur at this spot. As polar explorers with bellies full of pony meat, all familiar with the horrors of dysentery, they could never have imagined that by century's end a Human Resources Representative would be whisked to the South Pole in an urgent deployment to discipline two men for calling their assistant "Poopypants."

Poopypants was a General Assistant, meaning she had to do a lot of unsavory work for next to no pay. Some say that Poopypants liked to complain, and that she had a knack for politics, as she was fucking the Safety and Health Representative, who didn't mind too much when she bumped a pedestrian while driving the van. Some did not consider her a hard worker, and it was in this spirit that two workers chided the GA when she was slow returning from break: "C'mon, Poopypants, let's get with it."

Poopypants immediately reported the insult and, because the men were unapologetic during preliminary counseling showdowns, a Denver HR Specialist who had been cut loose for a McMurdo boondoggle rushed down on a disciplinary expedition to the South Pole, where she explained to the men the seriousness of their inappropriate behavior. When one of them asked, "Should I say 'fecal britches' instead?" he was fired.[5]

My boss asked how big my unit was, but I didn't know because I'd never measured it. I said I would give her a report, but that in order to measure the girth I would need one of those tailor's measuring tapes, like Chernobyl had. Jane said she would get me one. And I might need her help, I said. "Yeah right," she answered on cue.

The previous day I'd asked her if she knew where her G-spot was. She said she wasn't sure where it was, because it was hard for her to poke around in there. She explained to me the difference between a pad and a panty liner, and told me she had a very large canal. She told me she once had a boyfriend who liked to whack off with Neosporin, and that she had fucked a guy whose dick was so small that she couldn't even feel it. She had felt bad for him and didn't say anything. In contrast, she once fooled around with a guy on the beach in South Carolina who whipped out a femur-sized cock that she didn't want anywhere near her. The phrase "femur cock" would stay with us all winter.

On our ten o'clock break the winter Waste crew—Thom, Jane, and I— were settled comfortably in the break shack drinking hot beverages and leafing through *Vogue* and *Cosmopolitan* magazines we'd rescued from the trash. Jane—who had once spent two years in the Americorps Program, working in Africa to battle the deadly guinea worm—was excited by a *Vogue* article on palm-reading. It was a recent hobby, as it turned out, and she even had a palm-reading reference book in her room.

She began with Thom while I continued reading the *National Enquirer*. (Most of the magazines in Antarctica are over two years old. This does not seem important until the humiliating day when one joins a lunchtime discussion to find that celebrity gossip must be up-to-the-minute to be of interest to its connoisseurs.[6])

As I read the magazine, I overheard Jane telling Thom that, though he was very passionate, he would die soon.

This would be my second palm-reading of the year, as my friend Cyrus had read my palm about a week before I left for McMurdo. Cyrus is conservative, a genius programmer who worked for a certain software empire back when they had cocaine at the office parties. He speaks a dozen languages fluently and can speak 20 others passably, including Basque.

Cyrus has left his body and traveled around the universe, completely against his will. He wants nothing to do with such experiences. Crystal-stroking new-agers pick him out of a crowd and want to associate with him. He has an old soul, they tell him. But he wants nothing to do with people who want to associate with his old soul. He prefers to associate with people who tell dirty jokes and worry about money. Cyrus is a firm believer in law and order.

After studying my palms, he told me that my drive to travel was consistent with my nature and was probably a reasonable way to whatever I was looking for. But, he said, "your desire to document everything and to write has nothing to do with what you're looking for. It's completely irrelevant to your goals. Your public aspect is superfluous to what you really know is a spiritual mission."

Cyrus explained it to me from the beginning.

The most basic aspect of our existence is our consciousness as physical beings. Because we are anchored to our experience by physical bodies, with thoughts influenced by scars, with emotions influenced by chemicals, with sights seen from one angle at a time through physical eyes, it takes tremendous effort for us to understand the universe we live in. Yet if we could see the real consequences of our actions, he said, the world as we know it would be an entirely different place. If we could see that physical life is only a fragment of the totality of our lives, we would act differently. But we are physical beings, and it is not surprising that we do as we do, limited by our ignorance. The chasm between us is immense, he told me. You recognize that and seek to do everything in your power to expand your physical boundaries. Writing about your experience, though, is inconsequential.

I asked him what could be done then, trapped in a body like this.

The only way to learn anything lasting in this physical existence is through other people, he said. Your relationships are spiritual because they help you transcend your limited physical being by understanding other physical beings.

Now that Thom's days were numbered, Jane moved beside me and, after examining my hand, declared that my lifeline displayed ominous signs of disease or injury. I was pleased that Jane had read my palm just as the sun was about to go down on the verge of winter, and that her forecast of doom was inspired by an ancient *Vogue* magazine, whose spiritual influence would reappear a few days later when she handed me a measuring tape.

The sun dipped lower each day, and the light would be gone soon. The transportation channel merely said, "No flights until August." There were no more helicopters flying around. No Sprytes back from sea ice camps. No polypacks of shit from field camps. No long food lines. No trash from Pole. No DVs. No journalists. No researchers. Just frozen darkness and a pressurized pot of potential pathos.

One day I saw a UT with his truck hanging around a pile of useful shelves and crates I had stashed for myself outside the Waste Barn. I approached and said (like a security guard at Wal-Mart who suspects someone of shoplifting), "Can I help you with something?"

"I'm just checking your heater and fuel tank," he said. I saw one of my crates in the back of his truck.

"Oh, okay. Did you just take that crate?"

"Yeah," he said. I laughed.

"This is my shit, dude," I said, removing the crate from his truck and putting it back in the pile.

"Oh, I thought it was skua," he said. "At least I'm an honest thief."

We both laughed and introduced ourselves.

The skua shack right outside the Waste Barn gets passers-by into a foraging mindset, so our food and clothing sometimes disappear from the Waste Barn and the break--shack. A week after I foiled the scavenging UT, a box of V-8 went missing from the break shack. V-8 was very important for Sunday's Bloody Marys. And if we ran out, that could mean no Bloody Marys until August. Someone was fucking with our drinks.

Thom had by chance seen one of the UT's by the break shack one afternoon with a box in his hand. Jane called the UT and told him he'd been seen leaving our break shack with a box the same size as one that had gone missing, and asked whether he knew anything about a box of V-8.

He didn't do it, he said, but maybe it was the other UT.

Jane said it was best if they sorted it out "within their department" and got our juice back "promptly" before things went to "the next level." Jane was good at this sort of thing. She knew how to use a "work stoppage" or a "safety concern" to our department's advantage, and could keep a straight face while speaking the code words of the week. The code words are not handed to us, so we have to pick them up along the way from meetings and emails, but many of the potent code words are introduced at Orientation, in the beginning of the summer. That's where we had watched an ethics video from which we learned that Integrity, Respect, and Teamwork, as well as Quality, Innovation, and Citizenship, were accomplished by avoiding Inappropriate Behavior. The video urged us "to continue the tradition of unquestionable ethics" and to "keep the ethical message alive." Afterward, a video about bloodborne pathogens taught us to "assume that all blood from all persons is contaminated."

A week after Jane made the call, the box of juice was returned to our break shack with a note from one of the UTs saying that he had thought the break shack was the Skua Shack. It was also around this time we noticed that the store was now stocking V-8.

Winter work routines fairly settled, people began to look toward their recreational winter projects. In March a woman emailed all the other women on station that she was producing a play called *The Vagina Monologues* and that they should contact her if they wanted to participate. She hung flyers on the bulletin boards around town. A recipient went to HR and said she was offended by the email. The HR guy contacted Denver, and an order came down that the play could not be performed in any public place in McMurdo, which is everywhere, except maybe the dorm rooms. A few days later women were wearing shirts that said "Got Vagina?" and men wore shirts that said "Vagina Friendly," and someone made a logo that looked like a peace symbol but with a suggestive triangle in the middle, and these were hung everywhere in no time.

People wrote emails to managers asking for specifics and "expressing their concerns." A steady stream of people went to HR to see what was going on and why. I talked to the play's director. She had asked HR for something in writing saying she could not perform the play, but the HR guy told her she couldn't have anything in writing. Instead, he told her she should write a letter of apology to all the women she had contacted about the play. She said okay, and wrote an email to all the women to apologize for using the word "vagina." She told me that she sympathized with the HR guy because he was just doing his job and was in a tough position.

I first met the HR Guy at a Glam Rock theme party in BFC. We sat on the couch and drank and talked for about an hour. He was tall and skinny, with glasses and braces. He said he had worked in the HR business for four years and he knew which companies were good and which were bad. I asked what he thought about Marriott. He rattled off some statistics and said they were a great, world-class company. I asked if he had heard about the guy who was fired for hitting on a man. He said he had. He shrugged. I shrugged. Then we talked about something else.

When the Vagina Ban didn't lift, the New Zealanders at Scott Base offered to host the play, at which point Denver decided the play could be held in the McMurdo library, but that the flyers for the play couldn't use the word "vagina," and that the play must have a doorman at the entrance warning the audience, with an average age of 36, that they might be offended if they came in. The director conceded, and rehearsals continued without further incident, but now everyone knew that the community harbored a sensitive mole. The grapevine rumbled. What would become of the winter art show? Would nude drawings be banned? Who would use anti-harassment policies with such sweeping scope? Why is the mole in the driver's seat?

In mid-March we fired up the Grinder.

The Diamond Z Tub Grinder is a machine that eats wood from McMurdo's scrap Woodpile, which grows so colossal as to have hills and valleys. Inside the spinning tub of the Grinder lives a legion of rotating hammers that make quick work of even the largest timbers. The chips thus produced fall onto a conveyor belt that moves them to a second conveyor belt, where they immediately clog in shifting mounds and must be stabbed at with picks and shovels while the conveyors spin and the Grinder spews plumes of dust onto workers like a wooden volcano.

It takes three or more days to grind the Woodpile, during which town trash retrieval halts and dumpsters bulge impatiently. A delay in grinding, from broken equipment or high winds, exacerbates the trash jam. Grinding infests clothes with wood dust, as if they were full of ticks.

Grinding is so violent and impressive that people from town find excuses to drive that way and idle their trucks on the road to watch for a few minutes. Chunks of plate metal the size of forearms and pieces of 4x4 covered with nails shoot from the Grinder, but usually in a great arc that allows for easy escape. When an irritable Waste supervisor grumbles to a work center about trash mixed in a Wood dumpster, at the heart of it lies the memory of fleeing for cover in a rain of shrapnel. Where the work center sees an unfortunate oversight, the Waste supervisor sees attempted murder.

Once fueled and started, the Grinder is in control. It must be closely monitored, and you should not turn your back to it. Friction from the hammers pummeling larger timbers sometimes causes fires, when the spray of wood dust and snow from the tub mixes with smoke. The tub must be kept full of wood; otherwise the Grinder becomes angry and starts throwing debris hundreds of yards—in one case a healthy chunk shattered the window of a loader—or vibrating violently because the hammers have nothing to pulverize. Once the power is cut, the hammers take five minutes to stop whirling. At lunchtime we would grind out the contents of the tub, disengage the hammers, and idle down the engine.

Typical lunch conversation in winter might include prison rape, gruesome tales of parasitic infection or, as when we arrived from the wood grinder one afternoon to sit at our regular table in the dim back room of the Galley, Roger Moore's dubious qualifications as James Bond. This topic led Ben and Thom to a brief argument over the merits of *Mission Impossible 2*, but the Rec guy broke up the argument, as it was a rehash from yesterday's lunch. Sometimes we would carry a theme, such as dead pets, throughout the lunch hour, with everyone at the table throwing personal stories into the kitty. If someone was on a roll, everyone else would just listen to his or her stories. Or we would spend the hour scarfing down stuffed grape leaves or warm hamburgers and unpeeling the strange secret life of someone bundled in the same clothes as 200 other people but identifiable from a distance by his walk, though we didn't know where he was from. Since we hardly ever talked about our lives outside of The Program, we would be fascinated to learn, after knowing him for much of a year, that the MEC mechanic had for several years run a computer store in a shopping mall.

But mostly we talked about work.

One day Jane told us that she had recently found Construction Debris in a Burnables bin by the Heavy Shop Supply building. She was rooting through the bin and noting the variety of junk that was, first of all, not bagged and, second of all, not Burnables anyway. There was cardboard, a broken coffeepot, and wood. One of the Supply guys drove by, so she flagged him down.

"I know, I know!" He threw up his hands. "I know what you're going to say. I didn't do it."

Jane explained to him that this particular dumpster had been graciously allowed slack on two distinct occasions already, and that she was tired of doing their work for them just because they were lazy fuckers. One of the other Supply guys came over. Jane described him as bearded and trollish. He argued that garbage is garbage. Jane cited spreadsheets and categorized milvans to prove otherwise.

"But we don't have any bags!" he screamed.

"Call Central Supply!" she screamed back.

After everyone had simmered down, Jane realized with horror that our new welding console that had arrived on Vessel, been lost in the melee of Offload, recently been found, and been delivered to the Heavy Shop instead of to the Waste Barn, was in the hands of these goons. She asked them about the welder.

At the lunch table we stopped eating and leaned closer to hear.

"Yeah, well, it's not exactly on our priority list," said the troll. "You think maybe you could just pick that dumpster up and—"

"Whuh-ohhh!" from the lunch table.

"I'm not picking the dumpster up," she retorted.

"Ha!" from the lunch table.

As we ate breaded prawns and Jane finished her story, we caught the last part of a conversation at the next table, where Thom was talking about some asshole at the bar who was telling him never to get married. "All you get is screaming kids and a used-up pussy," the guy had told him. We batted around the filthiness of the phrase "used-up pussy" for a while; then Jeannie began exploring the implications of the phrases "Fuck your brains out" and "Fuck the shit out of you."

The soft-spoken and polite Heavy Shop supervisor had come to the back room to sit by himself a few tables away. He was shaking salt onto his food.

Jeannie was chanting now, "Fuck your brains out, fuck your brains out, fuck the shit out of you, fuck the shit out of you..." The Heavy Shop supervisor stood up, took his tray, and returned to the other section of the Galley.

A few days after we finished grinding, I was running *Terminator* around town collecting trash. There were two Construction Debris dumpsters by the JSOC construction project. I'd already dumped one, but when I went to get the other I noticed a lot of wood in it, so I climbed from my loader to examine it. The project foreman saw me rooting through the dumpster and came over.

"This dumpster was over there and before I knew it they put all this wood in there," he said, implying that I should take the dumpster as it is.

"I can bring you another wood dumpster for over there," I said.

"It's just bags at the bottom under the wood," he said.

"This wood needs to go in a wood dumpster," I said, before we went too far. "Wood gets dumped in the Woodpile. We grind it up. We can't grind up whatever's in these other bags, and I can't dump that much wood into Construction Debris."

He nodded with his lips pursed. "But what about all this stuff?" he said. "It's 40 feet long and won't go in a dumpster."

I followed him across the road to see the broken sides of long crates that this winter's construction materials had been packed in. On the way I introduced myself. We all wore the same socks. And, disconcertingly, in a few months our farts would smell exactly the same. I looked at the pile. These enormous crates had been ordered at the last minute, so The Program had to pay top dollar. Now, because the crates had cost so much, there was some elaborate scheme brewing to save them, while up the hill we were grinding half-sheets of ply for hog chow.

"That's good it's stacked," I said.

"It was a pain in the ass to stack."

"Do you have any cargo straps?"

"No."

"I'll bring you some cargo straps. Just cargo strap these up and they'll be good to go. Do you have any pallets?" I asked him.

"No."

"I'll bring you some pallets."

"But look at this shitty wood," he said, snapping off a piece of wood with his foot. "This stuff is going to fall all over the place."

"What do you suggest?" I asked him. I noticed suddenly that his fingers were as thick as oak saplings, his thumbs even thicker.

"Bring us a big container we can throw it in, and then you guys can sort it out from there."

Bighand was brand new from stateside, where construction projects had easy access to landfills. But we were on a remote island where the burnpiles and landfills had been discontinued, and waste is ugly cargo that must be processed and packaged just as precious cargo must, to leave by boat. Waste is Antarctica's main export.

"We have to grind all this wood; we don't send it out as-is," I explained. "And if it spills, it spills. But it's less likely to spill if it's strapped than if it's not strapped."

I didn't want to come across as a mere bureaucrat, so I lightened the subject and told him the cost of these crates that he was destroying and that we would eventually grind into chips that The Program would pay a hog feed factory to use as fuel for its furnaces.

"Are you shittin' me?" he said.

Rumors had been heating up all month about a medevac flight in April. Finally it was officially announced, and our Operations Manager gave us some details at a morning meeting in the Heavy Shop. He didn't know anything about the person or people being medevac'd. He said that no one knew when the plane would come in or which planes would come in; it would either be Air National Guard or Kiwis. If the ANG flew down, they would bring a complete extra crew, extra rotors, and extra parts, leaving little room for freshies or mail, he said. If a Kiwi plane flew down, he said, there would be plenty of room for freshies and mail, because the only things the Kiwis would need for themselves are the Sports section and a pint of milk.

Like other McMurdoites, he had a low opinion of the Air National Guard, whom people describe as "prima donnas" or "whining clowns." Most ANG come down for only three weeks at a time; they're issued free humidifiers for their rooms, won't eat Grasshopper Pie unless it's labeled "Mint-Chocolate Pie," and erase videos to record football games. They are short-timers who complain that McMurdo is miserable because there is no good TV and there are weird couscous salads and other tragic products of civilian culture. Though individual courtesies are exaggerated between members of the two groups, and outright hostility is rare, there is little recreational mingling between civilians and the military. Whether by choice or because of rudeness from the redcoats, the green jumpsuits gather at their own tables. Whereas almost every facility in town remains unlocked and open for use by all, a sign on the door of a lounge once read that it was off-limits to anyone but ANG "and their guests." Their dorm buildings prohibit entry to anyone but ANG "and their guests."

The Air National Guard replaced the Navy as air logistics provider to The Program. The Navy had founded McMurdo in 1955 and, even with the increasing role of NSF administration and defense contractors since the 1960s, continued to play a big part in running the show. Navy culture still permeates the base with terms such as "Galley," "Ship's Store," "Fleet-Ops," and "Midrats." In 1998, the Navy was phased out of The Program, and the ANG was brought in as a hired gun rather than as a powerful partner. Unlike Navy workers, ANG never stay for the winter. The terrible relationship between the civilians and the ANG has been exacerbated by a few incidents in which winter-overs have stolen things from ANG storage. The predation by winter-overs was summarized by an ANG guy: "As soon as the last aircraft leaves, everything on Ross Island belongs to whomever is left and can get to it first."

With the previously military foundation removed, the ex-military old-boys network is slowly disbanded, and a more corporate order emerges yearly. Official memos now refer to the "Dining Facility," when no one calls it anything but "the Galley." In 1958 the McMurdo beer selection was Budweiser, Pabst, and Schlitz. In 2001 the alcohol selection included Sierra Nevada Pale Ale and more than one Pinot Noir. In 1958, "dirty jokes or smutty sayings" were not allowed. In 2001, "inappropriate behavior" was not tolerated. The extensive collection of military history books in the library has been discarded to make room for self-help and pop-psychology books.

After a long, relaxing weekend in the U.S., NSF suddenly croaked out a date for the medevac flight. Since Monday in Washington D.C. and Denver is Sunday in McMurdo, the Fleet-Ops operators were hustled in on Sunday to groom Pegasus Runway. Time is of the essence! The mission is critical! After a few days, Fleet-Ops had the runway ready, just in time for the flight to be delayed for obscure reasons.

As soon as the plane was official, people started ordering New Zealand groceries over the Internet. Laz ordered 20 pounds of chicken-flavored potato chips and some cigars. We heard that ANG was coming down with over 30 crew members for a "rescue mission." There was still sunlight, and the weather had been good. An ex-military friend told me they had so large a crew because if one goes on a "rescue mission," one receives a medal, which is useful for promotions.

We started a pool betting on how many people would go out. Some said two, some said ten. The high numbers were wiser. Even if the plane was officially coming to get only one person for medical reasons, a plane is a plane. That meant that people who didn't like their winter so far could quit, and managers who didn't like their employees could fire them. Also, anyone who went into Medical for a minor injury would be taking a risk. Despite the emails from the Safety Guy in Denver ordering us to report our injuries, with a plane coming, we knew that a minor injury was as good as schizophrenia on the paperwork, and anyone reporting one risked being sent home. Wherever management saw a problem, the plane could solve it.

Nero, Ivan, and I sat in Gallagher's one night, drawn to Sunday Burger Bar, where volunteers serve greasy planks of meat between stale, frostbitten buns. It wasn't even dark yet, and we all agreed the vibe was strong. Nero had been in

McMurdo the winter of the hammer attack. He had wintered a few times and
said it felt different this year, that something big was going to go down.

I cleared the napkins and other burger paraphernalia from the center of
the table and got out a piece of paper and we came up with a chart we titled the
"Projected Mayhem Index."[7] On the bottom of the graph I listed the months
from March to October. On the side, numbers ran from one to ten. We agreed
that Level One constituted a normal state of affairs, with backbiting and minor
one- or two-week scandals and such. Level Three involved minor skirmishes,
perhaps pushing and shoving. Level Five required violent interaction with
injury, as well as the presence of extreme paranoia in a party to the interaction,
as with the woman who one winter thought her ex-boyfriend was rappelling
into her third-story dorm window and doing such things as moving her
hairbrush, all of which she explained to HR, who brought the accused in for
questioning. Level Seven would be the equivalent of the Hammer Incident
or other violence with hints of psychosis. And Level Ten would be anything
as bad as the full-fledged Soviet chess game axe murder, which, because it
displayed remarkable brutality while hinting at the pettiest of motives, was the
worst we wanted to reach with our chart, shying from the realm of cannibalism
or occult matters.

One year a winter-over had revealed that he was the reincarnation of
Galileo. (This would not appear on the Projected Mayhem Index, as it fell
short of mayhem, because Galileo might be fun to have around.) When Siple
Dome was a year-round base, some of the crew had splashed chicken blood
in the snow, scattered torn clothing around, and reported someone missing.
The prank so frightened one of the winter-overs that he thereafter slept alone
in an abandoned shack.

And just last night there had been some trouble in Southern.

Injun Joe, an ironworker, was kicked out for hooting at the top of his
lungs every few moments. As someone escorted him out the door, I hooted
to him. His lively yelping was the only sound audible over Bad Company and
Lynyrd Skynyrd, to which Tracker at the bar was pounding shots and playing
a sizzling air guitar. Joe broke from his escort and stumbled over to shake my
hand and put his arm around my shoulder.

"That muth-fuckuh is a fuckin' racist!" he said. I caught a shower of
spit. "I'm an ironworker!" I thought both he and Tracker were ironworkers. I
pointed at Tracker, "What's he then?"

"What's he? He's a fuckin' monkey!"

He flipped Tracker off and grabbed himself by the crotch before he walked out the door and went to the other bar. Injun Joe was still drunk at breakfast, hollering in the Galley.

Munching our burgers in Gallagher's, we each drew lines on our chart showing our predictions for the tumult of the winter to come. We noticed patterns of agreement. We all agreed, for example, that the Winfly flight in August would bring a sharp decrease in Projected Mayhem, as there would be new people around and the end of the winter would be near. We also agreed that something like a fight in April would be compensated for by a calm May. We also agreed that June and July would be banner months for deranged mayhem. While Ivan and I both forecast a Projected Mayhem of Level Seven for July, Nero's indicator shot all the way up to Ten that month.

"C'mon dude," I prodded. "You really think something like an axe murder is going to happen this winter?"

"Man," he said, "Something real weird is going to go down this winter. I can feel it."

CHAPTER 6
NOTES

[1] "'Do you see that black thing over there?' Hassel called out urgently as they were making camp on the 13th. Everybody saw it. 'Can it be Scott?' someone called. Bjaaland ran forward to investigate. He did not have to run far. 'Mirage,' he reported laconically, 'dog turds.'" —Roland Huntford, *Scott and Amundsen*

[2] Poopypants would later find herself hitchhiking on a desolate road in New Zealand with little hope of catching a ride, when an eight-seat van carrying three people approached. She recognized the passengers as people who'd shared her special time on the world's seventh continent, where people in a hostile place come together in order to survive. The van sped by her while a woman hung out the window and yelled, "Good luck getting a ride, Poopypants!"

[3] Paul Siple reported that during the first year at Pole they received a phone patch from Art Linkletter, a TV emcee: "The men learned from him which movie actors and actresses were still married and which had divorced... There was also a contact with a somewhat gay Dean Martin,

the singer who was in Las Vegas. The men related that he sang a line from a song, then said he wished he could talk longer but 'I have to go back to the bar.'"

[4] Some scientists at Ellsworth Station in 1957 drew a chart called the "Ronne Rating" to index the relative degrees of contempt they received from the Commanding Officer and base manager Finn Ronne. 1 represented the most hated, where Ronne "completely lost control," and 8 began to taper off as "nonentity." 9 meant "nice fellow."

1 South Pole Station. (Photo: NSF) **2** Robert Scott's hut at Cape Evans.

3

4

5

3 McMurdo Station. **4** McMurdo's Uppercase dorms overlook Discovery Hut. **5** When a storm ripped the ship *Aurora* from its anchor, ten men were marooned in Antarctica for two years. The anchor remains at Cape Evans. **6** The Ironless Hut on the sea ice.

6

7, 8, 9 The strange world of South Pole.   **10** Penguins encounter a McMurdo kitchen crew.

11 Unwanted treasures collect in the "skua piles" in the dorm entryways. **12** Cupcake on a string found in one of the tunnels. **13** A fraction of the dozens of pallets of McMurdo's historic hot dog stockpile. **14, 15** South Pole's puzzles and board games.

16 The Playhouse about to collapse in the wind. **17** Inside the Dome at Pole. (Photo: Melanie Conner, NSF) **18** Fuel tanker offload at McMurdo. **19** A pickle roams one of McMurdo's many cargo yards. **20, 21** Deltas on the sea ice.

27

22 The Terra Bus. **23** McMurdo's fleet of orange trucks waits to be retro'd back to CONUS.
24 A portion of McMurdo's fleet of heavy equipment. **25** A Case M4K, better known as a "pickle."
26 USAP parkas at the Clothing Distribution Center in Christchurch, New Zealand. **27** Standard issue
"bunny boots," with air-valve. **28** Training for Antarctic Hazmat Decon in Texas.

29 Admiral Richard Byrd. **30** A Soviet winter-over removing his own appendix. **31** Historic explorer Sir Robert Scott. **32, 33** Recovery team inspects and bags the remains of one of the passengers after the crash of Flight 901. (Photos: John Stanton) **34** A tourist enjoying Flight 901 before it crashed against Mount Erebus. (Photo: Unknown passenger) **35** McMurdo Mass Casualty Drill.

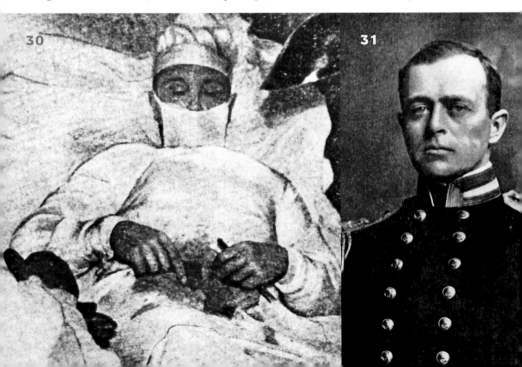

40

36 One of the tunnels leading out of the Dome.   37 Drifts block the Waste Barn door after a winter storm.   38 The Wood Pile.   39 Some still claim to hear the footsteps of restless ghosts in this freezer building.   40 The Chalet: NSF's McMurdo headquarters.   41 McMurdo's faithful worship the Holy Ghost in the Chapel of the Snows.

42 Orthodox priest ponders polar pagan prank. **43** The Cosmonaut and Polees being run over by a Snowbug. (Photo: Rick Monce) **44** "IMAX" crevasse. **45** Better safe than sorry. **46** The Snowbug expedition. **47** Black-Ops party: bystanders extract Barbie Doll from a winter-over's Saran-Wrap-and-ketchup cocoon. **48** Boozy the Clown in top form. **49, 50** Found photos of "Natasha Petronovich," used to entice a McMurdo ironworker to Moscow. **51** Boozy the Clown and his frozen friend share a moment of slumber. (Photos: Erin McVoy) **52** A technician humps the alien autopsy prop at the Black-Ops party.

53, 54 The angry unicorn and the frontier penguin ride the wind in this winter-over drawing. **55, 56** A crazed pig blooms flowers in the blood-red city in this painting by a winter-over. **57** A company psychologist's appeal to today's polar workforce. **58** Amidst a rash of end-of-winter controversy surrounding room-inspection penalties and bonus cuts, "rose-colored glasses" were dispersed to winter-overs.

Need a place to talk?
Support Groups starting soon...

57

Contact Esther at 653
or
esther@mcmurdo.gov

58

For
Winterovers

CHAPTER SEVEN

The Ice Annex and the Medevac

There I was in a tent on the side of Mount Erebus, with the temperature at 10 degrees below, with snow buffeting the tent, and a planeload of mutilated bodies outside.

– Constable Stuart Leighton, NZ rescue team

You see on everything you see about Antarctica, there is going to be [a] photograph of a penguin, and so that is what people want to see.

– Dr. Donal Manahan, Chairman of the Polar Research Board at the National Research Council

We would not have to deal with the dead bodies, he said–just the wounded.

As we hauled military-green stretchers into the airport shuttle, a gray-bearded, earnest man whom I had somehow never seen before explained that the vans, not the airporter, would pick up the dead bodies. The airport shuttle, with its tall, sloping, gray-tinted windows and high roof for standing passengers, was not designed to hold stretchers for victims of a disaster. So we practiced maneuvering the stretchers in a tight turn just through the narrow door before laying them across the aisle with the handles resting on the seat backs. It wasn't too cold, but our frozen breath filled the cramped shuttle.

In the summer I had not been allowed to volunteer for the Mass Casualty Drill, because I was already on the Spill Response Team. If a river of fuel thick with bodies were roaring down the hill, my duty would be to the river, but in the winter there was extra time to train for multitasking.

The Mass Casualty Drill aims to prepare community volunteers and emergency personnel at the Firehouse and Medical for incidents with high body-counts. Traditionally, the scenarios are cataclysmic. One time a phantom helicopter crashed into the gym. The gym, piled with basketballs, hockey nets, and frisbees, was engulfed in imaginary flames. Invisible fuel leaked from the carcass of the helicopter, threatening to further aggravate the situation with imaginary explosions that might kill the already immobile victims pretending to be wounded. The helicopter was played by a Spryte (manufactured by Thiokol, the same company that made the O-rings for the space shuttle *Challenger*), and the flames and fuel were supplied by stern emails of officially sanctioned delusion. The victims were volunteers, feigning the throes of death and color-coded by emergency response managers. Green tape meant the victim was "walking wounded." A yellow victim was immobile, but not in need of immediate medical attention. Red would probably die without immediate assistance, and black was either dead or about to be dead, and so passed over for care.

Recent drills had added the intrigue of a criminal element. In one, a loader stolen by some ill-intentioned community member crashed into 155, cutting off heat and power to the Galley. In another, an illicit still exploded, killing its shameful owner and starting a fire in one of the dorms.

On November 28, 1979, 237 passengers and 20 crew flew over Antarctica on commercial tourist Flight 901 from New Zealand. The tourists took pictures, drank champagne, and ate a dessert called "Peach Erebus." Then the plane hit Mount Erebus, snapping all of their ankles simultaneously. The wing engines were destroyed immediately by the impact with the mountain, but the tail engine continued to give thrust, and the plane tore into the snow and ice like the blade of an ice pick. As the aircraft disintegrated, passengers on the left side of the plane were thrown out, some tossed into nearby crevasses. Passengers on the right came out as flaming fragments. No matter which side they were on, Air New Zealand's lawyers determined that each passenger was worth NZ$42,000 to next of kin plus NZ$240 for unchecked baggage.

Workers were brought by helicopter from Scott Base and from McMurdo, and a police team was flown from Christchurch. Reporter Michael Guy wrote, "[The first rescue workers] were confronted with a scene which defied description. Bloodied bodies, charred bodies, bones, unrecognisable pieces of flesh, wreckage. Handbags, money, cameras and a myriad of personal belongings—the pathetic impedimenta of violently terminated life—lay silently in the snow..." A psychological report by A.J.W. Taylor and A.G. Frazer on the rescue workers read: "Several mentioned the sight of heads with smashed faces, opened skulls empty of brains, bodies without feet, and corpses that were charred." The Antarctic weather was sometimes a hindrance to the salvage operation, but also "made the task of handling bodies less unpleasant for them than they had expected it to be because there was no putrefaction and stench from decaying flesh."

Recovery teams worked in shifts, camping at the crash site and receiving food and body bags and other supplies by helicopter. Some bottles of champagne, wine, beer, and brandy had somehow survived the crash and were put to service.

Skuas joined the recovery teams in searching the wreckage for human remains. "Bloody Skua birds are ripping the plastic bags open and eating bodies all over the site," wrote one of the crew. In those days McMurdo was better armed, and lent a rocket-launcher to shoot the birds, but it proved too dangerous to use with all the oxygen tanks around.

The psychology report described that some of the salvage workers "became angry as a response to their work, and they were able to displace their feelings onto convenient targets. Some displaced them onto the skua gulls, another onto those of his fellows who were cursing the gulls... Two were bitter about those who had formed premature opinions about the cause of the disaster, and resentful that because of the crash Antarctica might become anthropomorphised as 'hostile and evil'..."[1]

McMurdo old-timers say that the bodies were first stored in what is now the food freezer, then moved to the gymnasium, before it was finally deemed more efficient to store them at Willy Field, where they would eventually be flown. To sanitize radio communications, the body staging area at the runway was codenamed "Ice Annex" and the bodies themselves "Delta Cargo." When Delta Cargo arrived by helicopter, workers at Willy unloaded the bodies, which "had begun to thaw and slither from the effect of the sun's heat on the plastic bags. The juices frequently squirted out as the bags burst, and on one occasion a handler who caught the body liquids full in the face earned the admiration of the others as he wiped his face with fresh snow before continuing his job." When they had stacked over 25,000 pounds of remains, they loaded them on a plane bound for New Zealand.

The morticians and investigators in Auckland were met with 347 plastic bags punctured by bones and full of human flesh smelling of jet fuel and hydraulic fluid. As soon as bodies were identified, relatives of the Japanese passengers appeared in New Zealand with a Shinto priest and wanted to be flown to visit the crash site on the side of the smoldering volcano in Antarctica. In the following days some of the mortuary staff became vegetarian. One had a recurring dream "of being locked in an iron mask in a house with locked doors and windows from which there was no escape…"

When the siren sounded for the Mass Casualty Drill, I went to the Firehouse and helped the other stretcher-bearers carry emergency equipment from the Mass Casualty Equipment Shack through the snow to the Firehouse. We wore yellow reflective vests. We rode in the airporters to the scene on the Scott Base road, where a head-on collision had been arranged. Three victims lay on the ground feigning concussions and compound fractures and waiting for us to move them. Airporters idled. Fire engines and ambulances (one is named "Graverobber") with proud flashing lights crowded the roadsides at the top of a slope that fed down onto the white rippled sea, stuck to the bottom of the twilit sky.

Some of the firefighters were a quarter mile down the road looking for victims who may have crawled off to die. In past seasons victims have been overlooked, the most serious mistake emergency workers can make. In one drill, a vehicle driven by a pretend drunk rolled off the embankment and down the hill. The simulated drunk was an authorized handful, hooting and shouting and trying to bewilder her rescuers. Chernobyl, who had worked in McMurdo that year, was overlooked as he sat quietly in a gully with a serious imaginary head injury.

The firefighters called for stretcher-bearers, and we hurried out of the airporter to the wounded, who were getting chilly from lying prone so long on the cold ground. We collected two victims and joked with them about their mutilations as we drove back to the Firehouse and carried them inside.

The Firehouse garage served as the emergency room. Casualties with imitation hypothermia and lacerations were stood over by calm rescuers scanning folders of paper. Bright yellow "Do Not Cross" tape separated the treatment area from the wounded queue, and from the waiting area for the stretcher-bearers. The yellow tape crisscrossed the garage at chest level, obstructing transport of victims.

After the drill, once the Firehouse garage had been cleaned up and the oxygen tanks put away, the doctor invited us to the classroom in the back of the Firehouse for a debriefing. Here I once took a fire extinguisher class and saw a movie in which fire researchers set up a room with tasteful upholstery and chairs and lamps and curtains, then torched it all and filmed it. Pictures of summer and winter fire crews from seasons past hung on the walls, and in the back of the room were beautiful pictures of burning houses, elegantly arranged.

The doctor told us he thought the drill went well. Someone asked how many victims a Mass Casualty Incident requires. He said that three simultaneous victims would tax the resources available in McMurdo. My interest waned during a dispute about how best to get people to muster for the drill, so I was looking around. The guy standing behind me was already watching me. I didn't know him, but had probably greeted him a few times in the halls. Our eyes met, but mine suddenly felt like the glazed marbles of stuffed game.

His name was Perry. One of his co-workers, a law student named Wilson, told me stories about him. One time Wilson was bent over scraping something off the floor in the 203 remodel when he looked up to see Perry standing over him with a length of two-by-four in his hands, poised as if to bash Wilson over the head.

"Hey Perry," Wilson laughed.

Perry was giggling.

"You got me good there," Wilson said.

Perry lowered the two-by-four, still laughing.

Perry told Wilson a story of his childhood on the farm. The family dog had a litter of pups, and Perry's father told him that if Perry didn't find a home for the pups he would kill them. A few days later Perry was sitting on the porch idly popping shots at birds when one of the pups crossed the yard in front of him. He shot it; the bullet ripped through its skin above its shoulder blades, and most of the skin on the puppy's back flew off, the remainder hanging off in tatters. The pup ran into the barn where the rest of the litter was. When Perry went into the barn, the other pups had surrounded the injured one, and when Perry approached, the biggest pup started growling at him. He put the gun to its head and shot it.

"Then I shot the other one," Perry giggled.

One of his favorite jokes was to approach Wilson with a tape measure and take his measurements to see how big to make his coffin.

"I think our crew is all right because we're his buds," Wilson said, "But I think everyone else on station is in the red."

Wilson explained that Perry didn't like it here at all. He wanted to winter at Pole. Wilson had told Perry that if he didn't like it here he probably wouldn't like it at Pole either. Perry had told him he wants to be out away from everything.

Though at first I suspected Perry was a psychopath, my later conversations with him convinced me that he wasn't so bad. Sure, he had a brooding and distant temperament, and he would probably snap someday, but in these remote places you have to learn to get along with people. As for my hasty judgment based only on a few stories, there are countless tales of explorers devouring dog brains and pony meat. Though most are tales of survival, some aren't. On the *Discovery* expedition, Robert Scott, disgusted by their eating each other's shit, ordered a litter of pups killed. Once Richard Byrd and some other men, standing on the ice edge, stabbed whales with shovels until they bled, which got the men so worked up that one suggested exploding one of the whales with dynamite. John Behrendt, a seismologist at Ellsworth Station under Commanding Officer Finn Ronne, described how Ronne and an assistant once caught and killed two penguins to take back to the Smithsonian Institute:

> First the Great Antarctic Explorers jabbed the birds in the eye with an ice pick hoping they would die when the brain was pierced—they didn't. Then they kicked them down and stood on their heads. Next they tied ropes around their necks and dragged them back and forth across the snow in an effort to strangle them and clean the blood off their breasts.
>
> After they dragged them around camp from the airdale building to the garage, the one with the injured wing died. The other got up, and with blood streaming from its eyes tried to walk away. Finally Ronne kicked it down and stood on its neck until it died. The whole operation took over an hour.[2]

Ronne's books include *Antarctic Command*, *Antarctic Conquest*, and *Antarctica, My Destiny*.

So when Perry, who lived two doors down from me, put up his first door decoration—a grainy black and white photocopied picture of a deer being hit by a car, its body contorted in the split second just after impact—it was as if a famous explorer had moved in next door.

Laz had had a sore neck for a few weeks, and it didn't seem likely to go away. He could endure the soreness, but it also interfered with the movement of his head. So, when all else failed, then and only then, he went to Medical. The doctor looked at Laz's neck and told him it would be fine and to treat it at work by applying a hot moist rag four times a day. Laz, who spent most of his time working outside, remarked later, "Yeah, I'll just stop by the hot moist rag bin every now and then."

Medical is to be avoided at all costs. If you go in with a health problem, you come out with a political problem. Sometimes we are told there are no punishments for going to Medical, but there are plenty of indicators to the contrary. One woman told me she went in for an icepack and was denied it, but was then stuck with the full consequences of the paperwork for a recordable injury.

The minute you enter, you begin the paperwork, and the paperwork follows you back to work, where you've just made more work for your supervisor. Someone up the chain checks in with a friendly personal email to "see how you're doing," while sending out mass emails complaining that "things" flow downhill and they're feeling a lot of pressure about Injury Rates. While Denver ostensibly encourages the reporting of injuries, Denver has also awarded cash to departments with the best safety statistics, in practice encouraging concealment of injuries. That the right hand and the left hand don't communicate is illustrated by the following excerpts from separate memos:

"It has been brought to my attention that some employees are of the belief that if you are injured and go to medical for treatment it can or will somehow he held against you and your bonus. I want to tell you all right now that there is absolutely no truth to that."

— Safety Guy, October 26, 2000

"Our safety and health performance will play a role in determining not only our contract award fee, but also each of our individual deployment bonuses."

— RPSC President, July 26, 2000

Whether one is following orders or merely requires routine medical advice, even the least serious trip to Medical has a way of snowballing into a "situation." If a medevac flight is imminent, the repercussions of reporting an injury are even dicier, because it matters little if the doctor thought you were fine. A corporate executive with no medical credentials in an office far away could ultimately pull you out against the McMurdo doctor's recommendation and terminate your contract under "medical" auspices, as is illustrated in these email excerpts from the RPSC Program Director to a McMurdo physician (April 2001):

". . . you may make a call for an evacuation, but the final approval is neither yours or Charlie's— it's the National Science Foundation's, based on my recommendation."

"Based on the information I've received on the case of the patient with [diagnosis deleted], I believe it prudent that we evacuate him along with the others."

"We're fighting a losing battle with Corporate. The Legal department doesn't want a repeat of the [patient name deleted] injury situation. I'm afraid [other patient name deleted] will have to depart."

Each day more people got scheduled for the medevac plane. Besides the legitimate medical evacuees and the cost-effective manager-selected evacuees, it began to look as though there would be some shitkicker evacuees. An ironworker threw a drink in the face of a bartender, who then threw the ironworker on the floor. The ironworker, who had recently attacked someone with a pool cue, was certain to go out on the plane. A painter who was wrestling with the Kiwis over at Scott Base crashed his face into the corner of a table and would be flown out for reconstructive surgery. Two guys at the bar had a heated argument over who had been to Black Island more times. One threw a bottle at the other, cutting his hand. The incident might be overlooked, or not. We would find out when the plane arrived.

One night I stopped by Laz's room to talk about résumés. His room was decorated with camouflage netting, metal shooting targets, an artillery shell full of Christmas lights, and a mock rifle for which he was once summoned to answer after a "fire" inspection. The funiture was arranged around a flat-screen TV and a DVD player he had ordered over the Internet. Laz and I were going to apply for jobs at a camp in Kuwait. Laz pulled up their website, which showed the view from camp. In one direction a series of smokestacks blasted out gray plumes. All other directions showed a flat brown horizon with a gray haze floating above it.

Laz's eyes glistened as he regarded the desolate shithole.

"Hey look here," he said, pointing out that the camp boasted a burger stand called Uncle Frosty's Oasis. "You should begin praying now that you don't become my underling," Laz taunted in an aristocratic slur, "for I will most certainly be without mercy. As I relax in my government-issue tent and receive correspondence on the fax machine, I will occasionally peek out from my doughy quarters and—should I find your pace unsatisfactory—bark out a piercing 'Chop chop!' only to see you tremble out there with the hired Bangladeshis. Perhaps if your pace has not diminished, I will do the same, regardless."

"Fuck that, Captain. I shall work at Uncle Frosty's. And when your neck is on a chopping block for some monstrous act you've committed and your bewildered pleading rings through the dusty plaza, it will be I, in cap and uniform, name badge gleaming like the blade above you, who dispenses frosty shakes of rich vanilla by which the mob forgets its heated vengeance. Custom will demand that you be indebted to me for life, and you will live out your days in freedom but for a variety of interesting skin grafts rotated weekly."

"Hi-ho, sir, you weave a fantasy which neglects the improbability of even the filthiest bistro considering you as staff, unless perhaps it is to persuade the vermin in their walls to seek more reputable lodging."

Like most station residents who migrate around the world chasing cashflow, Laz has varied work experience, but he has stuck with marine and air cargo for over a decade. One time he worked in the woods in Alaska, hired by biologists to camp by a river and guard a fish tally device threatened by bears that Laz would shoot in the ass with rubber bullets. For a while he worked in a prison dispensing medication. He wore a white smock and scuttled between cells with a tray of paper cups holding an array of pills. He went into the cells and yelled out names for people to get their medication. At first, people just lay in their bunks and didn't respond, or they would say, "Over here!" and try to get Laz to bring the paper cups to them. Laz sympathized with the prisoners' goal to regain some of the power they had lost over their lives, but he was not going to play that game. He bellowed out their names until they fetched their pills. It went on for a week like that until Laz noticed one day that as soon as he began yelling names people lined up to get their meds as quickly as possible. He discovered that one big bruiser who was always trying to sleep had promised a beating to anyone whose name was called more than once.

In the women's prison they would tease and taunt him, asking him how he liked it and how big his cock was. They always wanted him to call the guard; when he did, the prisoner would bother the guard about this or that, and then the guard would be mad at Laz. One time a woman called out to him that she was sick and asked him to fetch the nurse. Having learned his lesson, he first asked what was wrong.

"I barfed up a turd," she moaned.

"Miss, if you could barf up a turd, then you wouldn't be alive right now," he said.

"I did!" she cried. "I barfed up a turd. I saved it in a cup."

Though we were still on the front end of winter, we had already seen most of the safety videos, because safety meetings were mandatory each week. For the meetings, Cuff and Cory would come down from the Haz Yard; sometimes Red and Jeannie would come up from Fuels. Sometimes Ben would stop by if Fleet-Ops was having a slow day. We squished together on the couches in the little Waste break shack and drank coffee or cocoa as the frozen creases in our clothes thawed and the wind screamed outside.

Most of us had seen most of the videos at least once. Videos were preferable to verbal meetings, where we would agree that no fewer than two people should hold a ladder being climbed and that no one should ever walk on ice while working outside. These notes would be recorded and turned in to satisfy the Safety Representative, who was just as easily appeased by our watching a video, which was more fun and far less trouble. We had several times watched *Shake Hands with Danger*, in which a variety of errors made by careless workers leads to dismemberment. We were tired of *The Roll of the Drum*, a classic cataclysmic compendium of workplace injury, in which an incongruous snare drum announces severe injuries involving heavy equipment. Later in the film, when you hear a drumroll, you know a fantastic collision will occur and the operator will become deformed or disabled. We had seen *Remember Charlie* twice. Charlie's main qualification to instruct was having had most of his skin burned off in a chemical explosion. Charlie said he was just like us, hating the safety equipment, trying to take shortcuts so he could get off work early, and then one day he was floating in a burn unit acid tank surrounded by the screams of the dying. Charlie had worked for an oil company in the southern states, and was now paid by the oil company to give safety lectures. To put it another way, once he had a terrible accident, Charlie was given a full-time contract that involved travel. We'd watched even the video about restaurant safety, the main point of which was not to leave boxes lying around on the kitchen floor. I liked to remember this video when I saw the ironworkers standing on the slippery beams of a two-story unfinished building in the howling wind, faces masked and goggles fogging.

The main theme in the safety videos is that horrible results occur when one ignores Safety. The videos promote self-preservation as crucifixions promote brotherly love. The result of watching them was that over time we became jaded about safety warnings and numb to the carnage that results from ignoring them. Since we had depleted the supply of safety videos from the Safety Representative, Jane had begun hitting up the Fire Chief for videos. So we went from watching videos about slippery floors and proper lifting techniques to watching bodies being pulled from the wreckage left by the Oklahoma City bombing.

One day we watched a video called *Alert 3: The Crash of United 232*. The back of the video case called the story "a tragedy turned to triumph," which meant, in Emergency Response lingo, that the flaming carcass of the airliner was subdued with extinguishing agents, an impromptu morgue was established (chosen for the presence of floor drains), and the bodies were successfully tracked through the forensics process without losing any of them. We listened to witnesses describe how the plane ripped open on impact and some of the passengers, still buckled into their seats, tumbled down the runway end over end, eyes wide open and alive, until they weren't anymore. Between horrifying shots of the plane smacking against the earth were inspirational keyboard music and flyover shots of sunsets and monuments in Sioux City, Iowa, where the crash occurred. When the video ended, I knew I never wanted to fly again, unless it was to vacation in beautiful Sioux City.

The highlight of our Safety Program was a video released to Jane with a whisper from the Fire Chief that this one was not for everyone.

At a restaurant in Texas a gunman drove his truck through the front door and shot people as they devoured chicken and spuds from the all-you-can-eat buffet. The police officer in the video remarked that the gunman's tactic of blocking the exit by driving through the door was effective, in that buffet-goers who fled to the rear of the restaurant were consolidated for easier murder. The gunman had placed one of his empty guns on a plate with mashed potatoes at the buffet line. We were shown repeatedly the restroom antechamber where the gunman finally shot himself in the head. Many lingering close-ups showed

slain diners with food on their clothes and napkins over their faces—in respect
for the dead, said the police officer. Repeatedly we saw images of pudgy dead
people slumped over on the floor after their last meal. Finally, the officer
explained to the camera that although this was a terrible tragedy, the situation
was dealt with professionally.

The morning of the medevac flight, 30 people in parkas lined up with
their orange bags outside the HR Office, to fool the HR Guy into thinking
they'd all decided to quit. The atmosphere was jovial, and someone from FEMC
brought the Tin Man, a man-sized mascot of theirs with a phallus through
which margaritas and sangria are dispensed at parties. He was reported by
someone as indecent to the HR Guy, who told FEMC to get rid of Tin Man.
He was sealed in a coffin, to be stored on a cargo line until a safer era.

Eleven people were flown from McMurdo, and the station doctor was
evacuated from Pole. NSF was quiet about the McMurdo evacuation but
enthusiastic about the second annual doctor evacuation. This time the flight
actually was in the middle of winter. Though more slobbery papers such as
the *Los Angeles Times* and the *Washington Post* tried to recapture the magic
of the previous year with headlines of the "mercy mission" and the perilous
journey, the American press was only mildly interested this year. The doctor
had gall stones.

A story from Agence France-Presse was unique in reporting on the dual
evacuations. The reporter did not understand why one of the evacuees had a black
eye and broken facial bones that required reconstructive surgery. The reporter
was also curious about why the plane went to pick up four people, and returned
with 11. "Eleven men [sic] came back, and reporters were blocked from access
to the aircraft as its passengers departed Tuesday night. In contrast to the lack of
information on the McMurdo rescue, reporters have been swamped with details
about the condition of a sick U.S. doctor who was rescued Wednesday from the
Amundsen-Scott-South Pole station." A New Zealand military administrator said
the lack of information on the McMurdo evacuation was for "political reasons."
An NSF spokesman said it was an HR issue.

CHAPTER 7
NOTES

[1] The anthropomorphization of Antarctica precedes aviation disasters, however. As if the wind and cold each bore intent, these elements have often been described as hostile or merciless or malevolent, precisely by those walking pouches of warm blood who saw fit to tramp into the heart of Antarctica swaddled in canvas jackets. Even better-equipped military expeditioners have described their achievements as those of overcoming malevolent forces, or of conquering an enemy, as Richard Byrd wrote: "From the war there was a heritage of powerful new weapons which could be adapted for exploration and turned from fighting men to overcoming the even more malevolent elements which guard the secrets of Antarctica." Ernest Shackleton once described his Antarctic experience as the "white warfare of the south." An advertisement by Bell Helicopter boasting of the twin Hueys once used in McMurdo said, "All Antarctica seemed to conspire with the elements to keep them down."

The stock footage of Us versus Them sounds good, and it is still repeated, but with diminishing spunk. If Antarctica is still an enemy, it is a mild one whose secrets are "unlocked", like an unfriendly foreign intelligence agency. If Antarctica is still an enemy, then it is one who welcomes platinum-credit tourists. The cry of 'Charge!' fizzles at the thought of vacationers wandering around the South Pole like campers at a roadside plaque.

The conventional theme of struggle against a ruthless and malignant foe is worn out and in need of replacement. Almost any mythology will do. The robust market of civilization has yet to vend on the continent all but the most popular brands of legend. Despite that Shackleton was a Freemason, for example, and that Antarctic history is teeming with Freemasons, the occult fellowship, including Scott and Byrd, has been uncharacteristically lazy in raking its exciting and colorful Masonic legends over the barren continent. Obediently aping the simplest sentiments of conquest, young or aspiring Masons have not yet planted the Eye of Horus at the world's southernmost Entrance to the Temple of Solomon. Had a true Freemason been consulted during the 1979 Erebus crash, surely Antarctica would not be suspected of hostility or of "evil" but of murder, to which the passengers of Flight 901 were accomplices. An astute Freemason would understand that this was an act of vengeance, by brooding forces, for events ancient but not forgotten.

The central figure in Freemasonry is Hiram the Builder who in the Bible was a worker from the industrial-sounding city of Tyre. King Solomon contracted Hiram to build pillars and to do some heavy construction on the House of the Lord. In the Phoenician city of Tyre, a hub of paganism, your average pillar represented Melkart, the god of the City, the first Builder, and the inventor of "all the things useful to man." Hiram the Builder, a born-and-bred Phoenician, not only built Solomon's pillars, but he named them, thus professionally infusing the monotheistic House of the Lord with the pagan pillars of the Phoenician Cult of Melkart. According to ancient mythology, Melkart's association with pillars symbolizes his union with the earth and the trees. Water was his enemy. He slew Prince Sea and King River, and he was the first to navigate open seas, riding upon a tree trunk. Melkart (as god of Hiram the Builder, the central figure of Freemasonry) was born and thrived in an ancient world without Poles, where civilization grew from great rivers mastered so as to irrigate fertile soils, and in a time when a vast realm of frozen untamable water could only be fiction.

Antarctica, with its colossal useless beauty, is no place for Melkart, the inventor of "all things useful to man". Stolid before a lake or the largest river, which can be put to industrious tasks, Melkart is but a puny micro-god before the lording power of Captain Icecap. Even should he import the sturdiest oak as his vessel, he would be unable to break far through the ice shelf before its wintry power matured, engulfing the frustrated lackey and sending him back to the coast to scratch out a place for himself on Ross Island. Intent on proving his mettle, planning to build a Hall of Pillars, or perhaps a more unassuming House of the Forest like the one his devoted vessel Hiram built for Solomon in his prime, there is not a single tree to be found, and even if there were, only the smallest fraction of the continent consists of exposed earth or rock suitable for building. Even were he to find a few good acres and import enough supplies to build a great Hall of Judgment, his existence would be contingent on a camping permit, his domain that of a few vacant lots in a sprawling hostile empire.

Melkart, siphoning strength from earth and trees and fire, has been murdered by Antarctica, which each year draws more tourists admiring the beauty of absence, of uselessness, of what defies life to exist. Melkart, a god of utility, is an obsolete deity ambushed by an opponent he could not have foreseen. (Similarly, Hiram the Master-Mason was killed by three builders—perhaps McMurdo, Pole, and Palmer?—who "planted themselves at the Three Entrances of the Temple.") According to Phoenician legend, upon Melkart's death his wife "wreaks a bloody vengeance upon one of his many murderers. She cuts him with a sickle, winnows him with a shovel, scorches him with fire, grinds him in a mill, and then scatters his flesh over the field as food for the birds..." Then, after death, Melkart becomes God of the underworld: in Greek myth, a region named Erebus.

[2] One day after the birds were killed, while Ronne was away on a helo trip, someone stole the two penguins. Later the headless penguins were found lying in the main tunnel, and one of the heads had been put in the seat of Ronne's personal tractor.

CHAPTER EIGHT

DISASTER CITY

do you eat. what kind of animals. do you see.

— curious 7-year-old correspondent to McMurdo worker

Nothing is changing on them except the wording.

— HR responding to concerns about
mid-season changes to bonus criteria

T O THE GREAT DELIGHT of the McMurdo community, the medevac of 11 people and one from Pole led to conspiracy stories by some of the shadier news outlets on the Web.[1] Some said a virulent disease had been unleashed from the ancient lake under Vostok, where a clandestine agency was drilling to uncover a lost city, and Antarctic personnel were stricken with plague. That table salt was flown to Pole during the medevac was regarded as an ominous indication of the secret drilling because, as we learned from a website by Michael Bara and Richard C. Hoagland, "Salt is crucial to survival in outdoor conditions in Antarctica. The air is so dry, that unless someone exposed to the outdoors there has a good supply of salt, they are likely to face the possibility of death by mineral depletion and dehydration." Frantic engineers were draining the crucial salt supply! Pouring salt on their faces and in their clothes to endure the winter cold as they burrowed to Atlantis! The conspiracy theorists had done too much bad research, and it was the simpler points that led them astray: "Obviously the Base, after years of operation, would have a pretty good handle on just how much salt is needed until the next re-supply plane arrives. So how is it that they suddenly find themselves desperately without *any* of it left?!" The dedicated conspiracist assumes that The Program is a sleek sorcerer, a master at layered deception and covert treachery, rather than the bloated carnival barker it more closely resembles, willing to use any trick up its sleeve to keep the show going. Pole ran out of salt because someone didn't order enough salt, just as the next winter Pole would run out of beer.

Upon the approval of the local Operations Manager, we began planning a Black-Ops Party to be held in June in the Waste Barn. We researched the Chupacabras (the Goatsucker) that plagues South American villages, appears on the Web in grainy photographs always as a smudge in the distance, and sounds suspiciously like bored teens making slurping noises. We had decided that Antarctica's goat deficiency proved the Chupacabras' decimating presence.

We asked the Fire Chief for one of the old CPR training dolls. We didn't know what it had to do with Black-Ops, but it seemed like a good prop. He brought it to the Barn one day with an extra suitcase full of fake blood, wounds, and make-up used for victims at Mass Casualty Drills. Astonishingly, rubber lacerations and burns had been requisitioned, flown to Antarctica, and entered into inventory. The frontier required this equipment. One of the wounds had a tube poking through it that ran to a bulb at the other end for squirting fake blood.

The Fire Chief stayed for a few minutes. He told me about a disaster training class he had taken in Montana. The instructor took them out to lunch, and when they returned to the classroom several of the students found fake bombs planted in their belongings. This was a lesson to them, the instructor said, in how easy it is to plant bombs. The Fire Chief spoke of the meth labs of Missoula. He said many of them were boobytrapped to injure intruders or destroy evidence. The Fire Chief was excited about these meth labs. So was I.

I had acquired a taste for Disaster Culture in Texas, training to be on McMurdo's Spill Response Team. Solid Waste, Haz, and Remediation workers were flown to Galveston to attend a week-long course in Spill Management at the Texas A&M extension college. We slept in the Hilton, swam in the pool, and woke up early to gather in the lobby and drive out to our classroom, a small building tucked between the freeway and some filthy body of water. In the mornings our instructor showed us videos of successfully managed oil spills and taught us how to reclaim "product" in various environments through the use of containment boom, sorbent, and little oleophilic balls that soak up oil but not water. Everyone loved the word "oleophilic," and we used it whenever possible.

Our instructor was an expert on managing spilled contaminants. He wore cowboy boots, had a white ring on his back pocket from a tobacco can, and always tucked his t-shirt in. He continually smiled shyly, as if permanently embarrassed, and a Texas accent bobbed on his patient voice. He looked like a boy but occasionally mentioned his wife. He taught us about the properties of benzene and diesel and other common solvents. His repetitive lecture style dulled the subject somewhat, but there was usually enough enticing jargon to make up for it. We learned about the Incident Command System, the pros and cons of each oleophilic system, how to set up decon stations, and how to keep journalists satisfied with minimal information.

An array of brochures filled the cabinets at the rear of the classroom. A trade magazine called *Fire Talk* had a picture of a state-of-the-art emergency response dummy of a person with a severed leg, and articles mentioned "local, state, and federal players." The magazine showcased the Communimeter, designed to measure "communication effectiveness," and had an article on an emergency response cartoonist who does a comic called *Manimals* "about animals doing or saying things common to humans." The cover story was about "Disaster City," built solely to train for disaster. "Disaster City will provide a realistic city infrastructure," it read, including a strip mall, an apartment building, and an office complex "all in various stages of collapse." A map of Disaster City marked "Freight Train Derailment," "Single Family Building Collapse," and the "Weapons of Mass Destruction Office." When I asked our instructor if he had been to Disaster City, he said, "Oh yeah. And I tell you, that place is somethin' else."

In the afternoons we cleaned up ruptured barrels of pretend benzene or scrubbed orange soap contaminant from each other's chemical suits at a rehearsal decon station. Our instructor had us walk around the building in the heat to illustrate how uncomfortable and cumbersome the suits were. As I walked around the building, looking something like a tottering white robot, a man watering his garden watched me from across the murky slough. I waved to him, but he just glared, so I wondered if these strange processions had crushed his property value.

Other times our instructor took us to a beach on an even filthier body of water crowded with shipbuilding yards, repair docks, and disused oil rig platforms. We trained for Antarctic spills on this beach in Texas, where it was always at least 100°F and black flies ate us alive. A man in a motorboat spilled cotton seed in the water to simulate fuel, and we contained it using boats and boom and assorted oleophilic devices, while our manager pretended to be a journalist who interfered with our operation.

In the middle of an uneventful day, Jane and I were cleaning out a skua bin in the barn. Some evil fucker the previous summer had brought down hundreds of little plastic E.T. figurines, which had infected the station like a virus. No one could resist putting one on top of the computer monitor, or by the phone, or on the counter next to the pencil holder. Whether you went to get a part at the Heavy Shop or to put in a work order at FEMC, or to ask a question at Finance, one of these things would be there, somewhere on the desk, looking cute. They infested the skua bins: I found them fallen in Tupperware containers and coffee mugs, in boxes of food, trapped in folds of clothing, or scattered at the bottom of the bin. We surmised that it would be years, maybe even a decade, before the alien-figurine population normalized.[2] I didn't know if these things had made it to Pole yet, but I was determined to stop their advance, so I threw them away whenever I came across them.

In one of the bins Jane found an old boot with pills in it. Later we got on the Internet and in a few minutes determined by their identification code that they were meclizine, a boring old antihistamine. It would have been much more difficult to identify the bootful of pills were it not for the Internet, which has of course changed the stations deeply. Since the Internet arrived, Antarctica is just down the street from Denver and Washington. Directives from off-ice managers are disseminated to all relevant persons and have immediate influence. Bulk threats against the employees' bonuses can be administered daily rather than at occasional meetings. Even the lowliest supervisors sometimes report to off-ice managers, and easy communication exacerbates Denver's tendency to think of the Antarctic stations as mere annexes to its office park, where Midwinter's Day is no longer an observed holiday.

When the Internet first arrived, people took handwritten messages to the Chalet, where the National Science Foundation censored them, then typed and sent them to the specified email address, which was, for many people, that of a man in Pennsylvania who for years printed or retyped emails from the stations and mailed them to the specified physical address.[3] Internet access has long been commonplace, and these days workers can easily write stories for their hometown papers, even in the winter.

With communal computers, problems inevitably arise when people forget to log out of their accounts. Some of the stunts are mild, as when the Safety Guy didn't log out and someone sent an all-station email from his account saying that ice had been renamed "Safetywater." Some of the pranks have been far more abrasive, however. When a winter-over survey was taken and a happy-go-lucky woman won a "Good Citizen Award," she received an American flag that had been flying on one of the buildings for many years and had recently been replaced. One of the town Stamp Collectors, whom I will call "Scott," protested that he deserved the flag, presumably because of his dedication to preserving local historic relics. An unwitting bystander, whom I will call "Shackleton," forgot to log out of his terminal one day, and someone wrote this message to "Scott" from "Shackleton's" account:

> From: [Shackleton]
> Subject: American Flag
>
> Dear Miss [Scott]. I say "MISS [Scott]" because you are obviously a very little girl hiding inside an amazingly ugly man's body. I'll keep this brief…
> Fuck you and your American flag bullshit!!!!!! You claim to be a veteran? Maybe a veteran of cocksucking and having a dick shoved up your ass but other than that you are less than human you piece of worthless white trash motherfucking shit!!!!!!!
> How fucking dar [sic] you claim to be more deserving of anything at all including an American flag?
> If it will make you happy, I will gladly buy you a flag of your own and then shove it up your fucking ass!!!!!!!!!!!!!
> You suck! Your whole existance [sic] is an offence [sic] to all that is good and pure in this world! If you love this place so much then why don't you throw yourself into a crevasse and become a part of it!!!!
> I shit on you! I jerk off and shoot sperm on you! You probably like that though don't you because you are obviously a sick and perverted individual!!!!!!!
> Cry Baby [Scott]! That is how you will be remembered down here! Do you like that?
> WHAAAAAA!!!! WHAAAAAA!!!! WHAAAAAAA! I want a flag too!!!!!!!!
> There is nothing in this world that can be done to you that is horrible enough to compensate for the sick, useless life that you

have lead [sic] so I pray to God that he will see fit to punish you in a very deserving fashion.

[Scott], you are the woest [sic] excuse of humanity that has ever walked the earth!!!!!!!!!!

The only good thing is that you are obviously impotent and cannot get an erection with a woman therefore you can not [sic] breed more fucking dick-drip assholes like yourself!!!!!!!!!!

You just keep fucking other wasted old men like yourself. Up the ass is what you like and deserve. You are the sickest thing ever!

If you fuck with [the good citizen] and her flag again then be prepared to die you shit eating enema loving dick licking fuckwad !!!!!!!!!!!!!!!!!!!!!!!

Hey! I heard that you love to eat forskins [sic] for breakfast. That does not surprise me because you are the most fucked up person to step on this rock.

PLEASE DIE [SCOTT]! PLEASE DIE [SCOTT]! PLEASE DIE [SCOTT]!!!!!!

Receiving an email like this in the middle of winter in an isolated community of 200 people is troubling. "Scott" immediately reported this correspondence to HR, who hauled in "Shackleton" for questioning. "Shackleton" had obviously not written the email, but regretted not logging off; he apologized to "Scott", and all was forgiven. News of the event trickled through the grapevine. In an uncanny turn of events, "Scott" one day forgot to log out of his account, from which someone sent this message to "Shackleton."

Subject: A Lifetime of Mistakes

[Shackleton],
I must admit I have made a mistake. When I first received your message I was taken aback.

I was taken aback for two reasons. First by the fact that someone would hate me as much as you obviously do. Secondly I was disturbed by the fact that someone I barely even know has seen beneath the facade I have carefully constructed over an entire lifetime.

You are absolutely dead on in your characterization of me. I do love to eat foreskins. I do love to fuck and be fucked by old men. My dick does drip relentlessly from years of self abuse. I realize now that if someone I hardly know has seen beneath my facade I should do away with it completely. It takes a tremendous effort to maintain and, as you have pointed out, I am an old man.

Thank you for showing me the error of my ways. It's bold

people such as yourself that can truly help people and allow them to take a real look at the way they are.

> Thank you again so much [Shackleton].
> Love,
> [Scott]

PS If you are ever lonely and need to talk please feel free to approach me.

Right after work one night at 5:30, Jane and I went to Southern. It was a special occasion; usually the bar didn't open until 7:30. This rare Happy Hour at the bar was renamed "Social Hour" so as not to suggest drinking. We all showed up in our work clothes to eat tacos and jalapeño poppers and drink beer. Even though all the food came from the same frozen inventory, it was a welcome change from the routine of eating in the Galley.

At Southern, Jeannie reminded me that I was subbing for her on the bowling team that night. Their bowling team, consisting of Ivan, Nero, Jeannie, and Kevin, was called *The All-Hand Jobs* until someone complained and the HR Guy told them to change their name.

Both of the McMurdo lanes are warped. The pin-setting machines are operated by attendants, who get paid about five bucks an hour after work to sit on an elevated shelf behind the lanes until the ball smashes through the pins and thuds into a carpeted barrier, whereupon the pin-setter hops from the shelf, rolls the ball to the bowlers on a track between the lanes, gathers the pins into the pin-setting machine, then manually lowers them onto the lane in the usual formation. Rumor has it that these are the only two manual pin-setting machines in the world, and that Brunswick has tried to get their hands on them by offering to replace them with fully automated lanes. In the bowling alley are about a hundred balls, an old ballwashing machine, a stereo so bowlers can argue over what to play next, and a fridge full of beer that works on the honor system, with each bowler paying one of the pin-setters, who emerges rattled from his post at the end of the match.

After bowling that night, we went to Southern for a drink. The team trademark was to wear afro wigs procured from the Rec department's costume closet, and we wore these at the bar also. While Ivan and I waited at the bar for drinks, Nero and Kevin went into the bathroom. While they were taking a piss, Ted the Racist came in.

Antarctica is difficult for white racists, because there are almost no minorities to hate. So, in the quirky spirit of ingenuity at the last place on earth, the devout racist must improvise.

"What is this," said Ted, "some kind of nigger-pissin' convention?"

Though no urinal was free, Ted already had his dick in his hand.

"Hey man, what are you flapping about?" Nero asked.

"Nigger, nigger, nigger," Ted spewed.

"Whatever, man..."

Kevin made robot noises. They finished pissing and left.

At the bar Nero told me what had happened. Later he described how HR had recently ordered him to remove from his door a photo of two bunnies humping in the wild.

One Saturday in mid-May we had an All-Hands Meeting, our first since the medevac plane had left in late April. We crowded into the Galley in our work clothes. The first speaker was the technician who maintains lab equipment. There was not a single scientist in McMurdo this winter, but if anyone could be labeled a "researcher" to make it easy on the newspapers in the U.S., it would be he. He showed us some video footage of the volcanic activity in Mt. Erebus accompanied by the Pink Floyd song "One of These Days (I'm Going to Cut You Into Little Pieces)." Afterwards he told us that the green laser in the Crary Lab had been fixed, and that if we wanted to see it we could call him and he would turn it on for us. He reminded us not to climb on the roof to look at it from above, because it would permanently blind us.

In the winter the green laser shoots from the top of Crary into the sky while everyone goes about their business. To see this green laser while I hauled garbage was the central reason I had decided to winter. In a strange world hardened by routine, the rub between the fantastic and the mundane creates a spellbinding itch.

The next speaker was the winter Galley Manager, with whom I had worked my first year down here, when he was the baker. I would take breaks from washing pots to hear his stories about being a chef in the Playboy Mansion, where he spent much of the time making hot dogs and PBJs. Now he told us that his new oven had been stolen. Parts of it had been sent to him with ransom notes, threatening its destruction unless he sang "I'm a Little Teapot" at the All-Hands Meeting. He sang one verse and sat down, but everyone cheered for more, so he did it again, and we cheered even louder.[4]

Then the Operations Manager took the floor and reminded us to check the hours on our machines, and to remember to bring in our machines for PMs, or Preventive Maintenance. "Also," he said, "if you have an accident, you need to report it."

Then Franz, the new Station Manager, stood up to talk. He had replaced the previous station manager, who went out on the medevac flight. Before his new appointment he had been working as a supervisor in Materials. Though he was a fingee, Denver liked him for his management experience in a hotel in suburban Denver.

I had first met Franz in the summer, when he was Butch's roommate. One day after work Butch and I were hanging out in his room shooting the shit. When Franz came in from work, he busied himself on his side of the room for a while before saying to Butch:

"So, I'm going to take a shower now. I'll be five or ten minutes. Then the place is yours."

Butch looked at him without understanding.

"I'll just be five or ten minutes," Franz repeated, suggesting that we leave the room so he could take a shower, in the bathroom, behind a closed door that had a lock.

Franz read some statistics from a study he had scavenged on the Internet concerning the psychological effects of wintering in Antarctica. "Many of you at this time of year will have sleeping problems," he said, "and may become depressed, irritable, or bored. Five percent of you," he said, "will suffer effects that will clinically categorize you as in need of psychological treatment."

I was excited to see what personal dementias I would face, and realized that if my disrupted circadian rhythms or thyroid activity were to show any symptoms, since it was May now, they should be kicking in any day. I wondered if I would collect pictures of animals, or draw eyes on all my belongings, or come to despise asymmetrical shadows.

In the dark ages a withered priest might have warned us that the Devil was on the loose and that we had to purge ourselves of sin. Now we had scientific evidence to remind us, via a former hotel manager, that the individual's predetermined behavior and aberrations are the product of devilishly powerful external forces, such as the planet's tilt. There was little practical reason for any manager to warn us of winter psychological effects, since they are disregarded in daily affairs. You would still be written up for tardiness, regardless of "sleeping problems." A "support program" for the "depressed" would not be authorized until the end of winter. And "irritability" would still be met with dorm room inspections in your absence. Whatever the initial intent of these academic psychological studies, their field application is as an orientation to employee culpability.

After the meeting I stopped at the store to see if *Rosemary's Baby* was in the video collection and to buy some Skoal. The McMurdo store is miraculously well-stocked. Though someone is always likely to complain that this or that item has run out, the store has Pringles and Rolos and jars of hot salsa. There are a half dozen kinds of beer, most common types of liquor, and a considerable selection of red and white wine. (Every fourth bottle will be rancid by the end of the winter, because the wine is stored upright and the arid air will have ruined the corks.) There are hundreds of videos for free checkout just by giving the liquor clerk the last four digits of your Social Security number. There are windscreen facemasks for sale. There are aerial posters of Ross Island, a few kinds of soap and shampoo, nail clippers, and anti-fart medication. For years there have been hundreds of unsold postcards of a velvet Elvis painting that someone photographed at the Pole. When the Navy first opened the store, they stocked mosquito repellent that no one bought because there are no mosquitoes in Antarctica.

Much of the souvenir merchandise in the store is contracted for manufacture to a company in Denver. The souvenir t-shirt selection is large, but with two basic varieties. The first and most common variety centers around the penguin. These shirts may also include icicles or the sun, and their style staggers toward stark romance. They might say "Wild Antarctica" or "The Last Frontier" on them. The second variety may also include the penguin, but the styles imitate tired surf or snowboard designs. These designs include men in parkas with surfboards, or "Antarctica" written in the style of the Ford logo. They refer to Antarctic "powder" and say things like "eternal sun" and "chill out."

Some of the goods at the store are depressing, like the bumper sticker that says, "Antarctica: Been There, Done That," and some are confusing, like a cap embroidered with a colorful bass biting a fishhook and the text "Bite Me—Antarctica."

At the counter I browsed the Antarctica pins that I never buy, and scrutinized one that depicted the Antarctic continent flanked by American flags. The clerk told me that last summer NSF, which usually has little to do with the running of the store, instructed her to remove the "Made in Taiwan" sticker from the backs of the pins before displaying them.

The next day, in the middle of a Sunday afternoon, on a dark road coming down from T-site, Bighand flipped a truck. He came down too fast and went over the embankment by the Cosmic Ray Lab, launching the acetylene and oxygen tanks into the air from the back of the pickup. The truck rolled but landed on its wheels, and Bighand drove it back to town after gathering the pressurized canisters of volatile gases. He hid the truck behind one of the orange fish huts where scientists in summer stay warm while fishing for specimens (there are no Antarctic bass) through the sea ice. Then he found his boss at the bar and reported the incident.

The Heavy Shop assessed the truck's extensive damage. HR summoned Bighand for questions as to why the cab of the truck smelled like beer, and he said that the mechanics must have poured beer in the truck to frame him.

The grapevine lurched into action. At dinner the next day someone said, "Shit, I didn't even hear about it until after lunch." Bighand was in and out of the HR Office all day, and at break we speculated on the company's strategy. We determined that since Bighand was a foreman he wouldn't be fired straight away. He would stay on to work and would probably be sent out at Winfly in August. Had he been in some menial position, he might have been made an example of and put on minimum wage until he could be flown out, but since he was a foreman and necessary for construction of JSOC, he would be kept on until someone new could be brought in. HR would give him the impression that he had been forgiven, but he would be fired just before the first flight out.

The next few days were marked with investigations by HR and Safety. Both of those departments this winter totaled two people. They brought in everyone who was at T-site on Sunday and pumped them for information with which to convict Bighand.

T-site is the hub of all radio transmission in The Program. The road up to it is long and windy, with signs along the way warning of exposure to hazardous doses of radiation should you stray into the garden of transmitters. Because of the importance of uninterrupted communication around the continent, a couple of people, one of whom must always remain on-site, live at T-site in swank and roomy quarters. They have a pool table, a band room stocked with instruments, supplies for brewing beer, a well-stocked pantry and kitchen, and comfortable couches. Just off the ordinary living room lie corridors lined with banks of transmitter components: some of it state-of-the-art, some of it antiquated but reliable gear from the early Cold War era.[5] One can get up from the couch in the warm and carpeted living room, pad in one's socks down the corridor full of vigilant technology sprouting bundles of wires and silently ricocheting voices or strands of data around the continent, and seat oneself on another couch by the pool table in the equally comfortable rec room. Looking out the window in the summer, one's view weaves through the dozen or so enormous spidery transmitters nearby for an otherwise clean view of the Transantarctics and of White Island and Black Island, where another transmission outpost stretches the range of communication from T-site. Going to visit the comm techs at T-site brings a change of scenery, where the relentless sound of loader back-up beepers in town is faint.

Bighand had been driving down from a band rehearsal held that afternoon in the T-site rec room. Franz, the new Station Manager, and the HR Guy called everyone who had been at T-site that day into the HR Office one by one to sign a "warning" acknowledging that the signer had violated an NSF policy by using government vehicles to enter a restricted area; presumably this aimed to fill a hole somewhere in the documentation of T-site's restricted status. Franz told Nero that HR was "just going to shred them up at Winfly anyway," but Nero didn't see why he should sign a "warning." Many people did sign it, but many refused.

By the time he flipped the truck, Bighand was already notorious around town. His drink of choice was a tall glass of Jim Beam topped with Wild Turkey and a splash of Sprite. Then several more. When I wore a skua'd priest shirt to the bar one night, he got down on one knee before me with his eyes rolling back in his head and began babbling incoherently, so I blessed him and howled "Demons be gone!" When he tried to leave, he walked into the door and almost fell over before going outside. I didn't think he would make it home, so I followed him outside, where he was just getting up from a fall on the ice, and walked him to his dorm. One time Bighand filled a truck with diesel instead of mogas. That's a pain in the ass for the Heavy Shop, who must then drain the lines. Now that he'd also flipped one of the new red trucks, he was a bona fide public buffoon. Trying to blame the Heavy Shop for the beer in the cab had also created enemies, as well as a potential rift between Ironworkers and Mechanics. Perhaps this was why someone crept into the JSOC job shack one night and took a shit in Bighand's hardhat, wiping their ass with a piece of the project's blueprint.

Aside from "Been there, done that" and "We need to touch base," managers are particularly fond of the phrase "It's a harsh continent," which has two uses. The first meaning is that of the manager speaking of some hassle or burden on himself. In this case, the manager says, "But hey, it's a harsh continent," expressing a noble resignation. In the other case, the manager, awed by the big decisions coming down from someone more powerful than herself and fantasizing about making such decisions herself, says, "Well, it's a harsh continent," which translates as "Tough shit for all of you." Though these uses may seem opposed, they really express different shades of the same sentiment: submission is survival. To work hard and increase one's competence is nearly irrelevant. The most important things are to occasionally seek decisive assistance, to mimic the mannerisms of the immediate superior, and to occasionally let out a squeak or yelp of fear or pain.

Managers also like to joke about "putting out fires." Fire is the direst threat at an Antarctic station, where the dry air makes the buildings tinderboxes that can crumple minutes after the first flame. In manager parlance, though, "fires" are problems of any kind, and the manager knows there is no end to the fires, so he usually follows the reference to extinguishing them with a fatigued sigh. Once a fire is put out, he moves onto the next fire. Each new flame is addressed as a unique problem, unrelated to anything that came before it. He rushes around the room extinguishing isolated flames, emphatically smothering anything in the vicinity of the smallest wisp of smoke, lest the snoozing overhead detector be aroused and its shrill scream betray his failure to control his sector.

A band called Monkeybox had an upcoming weekend show at Gallagher's, for which they hung flyers on the recreation board during the week. The town mole reported to HR that she was offended by the word "Monkeybox." Franz determined that the band could no longer be called "Monkeybox" or put the word "Monkeybox" on their flyers. ("Monkeybox" was an anatomical epithet from the controversial *Vagina Monologues* performed at the beginning of the winter.) He told someone that if people could name their bands whatever they wanted, the next thing you knew they would be nailing babies to the wall. A righteous fury swept the community. Now people were putting up flyers of the First Amendment around town, and pictures of monkeys with boxes were everywhere. People were angry enough to discuss a work stoppage.

Monkeybox was an isolated flame that needed to be extinguished, and Franz was surprised when the standard tried-and-true and universally practical method of restriction made the flame even bigger. Creating a bigger flame threatens to trigger some shrieking overhead authority, so he thoughtfully assessed this unsettling public grease-fire. Alert and intelligent, he decided that continuing to douse the flames with more restriction might create an inferno, so he tried a different approach: the Monkeybox censorship was revoked, and the public outcry died down.

Thus did Monkeybox become authorized.

The Chapel of the Snows at McMurdo has burned down twice: in 1978, and on the evening of May 18, 1991, the same day that Denver released a memo—in mid-winter—saying that wages and bonuses would decrease and that the retirement fund for contract employees was being cancelled.

God has a tough gig in Antarctica. The few Catholics, Protestants, and Mormons are surrounded by drunks, scientists, drunk scientists, and other assorted heathens who hold yoga classes in the Chapel, sweating and groaning in skin-tight clothing and assuming positions, such as "Downward-Facing Dog," that sound as if lifted from some ritual of fire and semen in praise of Baphomet. There are no sandy sunset beaches to depict in inspirational calendars, and no majestically soaring gulls; only variations of merciless frozen waste, and dirty brown scavenging skuas that eat their own kind, their bills and feathers crusted in the summer with lard and the juices of spoiling meats.

It is tempting to conclude that McMurdo's secular character stems from Antarctica's image as a place of scientific research. One might imagine that a concentrated contingent of scientists would naturally emphasize reason, logic, and observation over faith, hope, and obedience. But after a while one notices that everything religion was once good for—encouraging sacrifice and devotion to a higher power—has been recalibrated to fit the new science and technology theme. The National Science Foundation acts like fat papal bureaucrats in distant Rome; policies have replaced commandments, "inappropriate behavior" has replaced sin, the leverage of Heaven has been replaced with the withholding of a substantial percentage of wages as a year-end bonus, the threat of Hell has been replaced with the more immediate threats of termination and exile, and blessings take the form of Antarctic service medals, issued by the government, that read "Courage, Sacrifice, Devotion" and fetch about 30 dollars on the Internet. There is already enough hocus-pocus in the mix without all that obsolete hoodoo about angels and bleeding saints and magic underwear.

Though one can still believe in spirits and not be considered as insane as if one believed in aliens, the religious ceremony is sparsely attended, and its consecrated ornaments dusty. The Erebus Chalice, a communion goblet sealed in a case in the Chapel, was first brought down in 1841 by a lieutenant on Sir James Clark Ross' vessel HMS *Erebus*, for which the volcano and chalice are named. In Greek mythology, Erebus is the son of Chaos, the embodiment of primordial darkness; he shares his name with the gloomy part of Hades through which the recent dead must pass on their way to darker counties. That the holy cup is so old, has so much goth snazziness, and sits forbidden behind a barrier, unavailable for slamming tequila shooters, lends it a certain mystical air and makes the Chapel not a bad place to move in on your date.

The Chapel is inviting because in the summer it always has hot water on for tea, and the Chaplain (only present in the summer) doesn't mind if you watch horror movies on the TV/VCR as long as no one is trying to pray in the meditation area. An attractive stained-glass window inside depicts the trinity of a penguin, the Antarctic continent, and the Erebus Chalice. The space is warm and offers a good view of the Transantarctics from the window behind the altar, where there's always a pair of binoculars on the window ledge. One time we asked the Chaplain if we could film a scene for one of our movies in the Chapel, and he said it was all right with him, as long as we didn't mess with the altar. We respected his wishes, of course, but reportedly the altar in this "southern-most house of worship in the world" (as described in a Chapel of the Snows brochure) has at least once been defiled by copulating rascals.

The Chapel's spiritual significance was explained to me during my first summer, when a military chaplain sitting across from me in the Galley said my tortellini soup looked good. It certainly was, and with that we began chatting. He had a sharp nose, a chronic smile, and small hard eyes. His manner was confident, strong, and friendly, but with the practiced air of one who demands firmly that no door be closed on the friendly. He wore full camouflage fatigues marked with his name and a small cross sewn onto the breast.

He had an office in the Pentagon with four or five other chaplains, he told me, all working for the Department of Defense, known as the War Department in the days of Little America. His job was to visit areas of national emergency, natural disaster, or remoteness and "assess community needs." I apparently didn't ask the right questions, because he never explained what "community needs" meant or why a chaplain was the right person for the job, but he did explain the difference between a military and a civilian chaplain.

A military chaplain, while a man of the cloth, holds rank. A lieutenant colonel chaplain holds the same power as any other lieutenant colonel, with the exception that while a lieutenant colonel can be subpoenaed to testify in a military court against a subordinate, a chaplain—of any rank—cannot.

The Pentagon Chaplain gave me an example of religion's place as a political amnesty clause: "A pilot confides in me that he's using marijuana, or has some other substance abuse problem. I have the rank to command his superiors to reassign the pilot without telling them why. They obey me because I have rank, and the pilot is saved from embarrassment and disaster."

Civilian chaplains are not bound by nondisclosure policies, he told me, except under the flaky and tenuous standards of their own whimsical brands of faith, so the soldiers don't trust them. Regardless of their faith or promises, they have no place in the political hierarchy. "The soldiers won't invite a civilian chaplain to their social events," he said. I could understand why. I felt a warm filial feeling for the candid Pentagon Chaplain, and I wanted nothing to do with those other blabbermouth friars.

While I was talking with the priest, Ben walked by and shoved his salivated pinky in my ear, as he liked to do. I flipped him off and called him a motherfucker as he walked away smiling and victorious. This reminded me that I had been swearing as heavily as usual even while talking to the Chaplain. Perhaps the Pentagon Chaplain registered my brief flash of hesitation.

"The main point," he continued, "is that a civilian chaplain is mainly concerned with the chapel." He leaned across the table, glancing around to see who might be nearby before whispering, "We don't give a shit about the chapel."

On Saturday, the night Monkeybox was playing, Jeannie held Ghost Stories night in her room.[6] When I arrived with a gift of a Spring Rain douche priced just that evening at a quarter for clearance, she was lying on the floor with her face painted white and her eyes open as if dead. I put in a Burzum CD, which we played all evening. Each new arrival bore a different variety of douche (none were able to pass up the low, low price) and asked what the music was. Burzum was a Norwegian heavy metal guy with a keyboard recording his neo-pagan pre-Christian tribal fantasies while in prison, apparently for stabbing his friend Euronymous in the head and burning down a 600-year-old church. We crowded on the beds and floor and told ghost stories, of which a few were local.

One time Nero was in the food freezer, where, he says, you can hear the door opening from any location within. You can hear anyone walking or talking from anywhere inside. There was a request for seven cases of cheese danishes, so he climbed to the top of a stack of pallets, opened a new crate of danishes, pulled out seven cases, and tossed them onto the floor below. He descended immediately, and there were only three cases on the floor. He figured maybe he somehow only pulled three cases, so he went up again, opened the crate, and saw that he really had pulled seven cases. He thought he was losing his mind. He went down again and looked around, finding nothing. Then he saw the other four cases. Though he had thrown the cases toward the middle of the warehouse floor, they were now neatly stacked in a pile between two pallets of food off to the side.

"Oooooh…" we moaned in unison.

After the Erebus plane crash of 1979, when corpses were brought to McMurdo, the freezer was used as a morgue until, upon consideration, the gym was preferred. People still hear strange things in the freezer, said Freezer Guy, and see what they think is someone's breath, only to look around a corner and find no one there.

A man who'd worked on the ice and died in the States requested that his ashes be scattered in Antarctica. The urn was put into the care of an absentminded acquaintance, who brought it down and kept it in his room, waiting for the right opportunity. Nero saw the urn sitting in different people's rooms and finally spilling onto the carpet during a party, so that the remains shared a vacuum cleaner bag with coffee grounds and foot powder. Nero suggested that these events might have something to do with the angry ghost in the story that followed.

Nero told us of a DA in the Galley who confided one night that he was afraid to return to his room. He had awakened in the middle of the previous night. He thought he saw someone standing on the other side of the room, but shrugged it off as a hallucination and lay back down to sleep. A feeling of proximity stirred him to open his eyes. A figure was hovering directly above him, face to face, with only inches between the ghostly eyes and his own. He let out a yelp and shut his eyes. When he looked again, nothing was there, but when he tried to sit up, he was unable, as if something were pressing down on him, or pulling the blanket on each side from below. After a brief struggle he sat up, then jumped out of bed and ran from the room.

Nero has heard several versions of this story. People call it the Grab'em Ghost of McMurdo Station.

By June our routine was hopelessly solid. Each of us in Waste could distinguish the sounds of different loaders even from afar. Every Saturday we checked the glass and aluminum bins at the bars to make sure they were empty. Every Monday we checked the same bins to see if they were full. The Galley pumped out a daily stream of Burnables and Cardboard and a medium stream of Plastic and Light Metal. FEMC produced a lot of Wood and Light Metal and Construction Debris. The Firehouse hardly put out anything at all, but when they did, they separated their trash poorly. The Heavy Shop made a lot of Construction Debris, and we had to make sure to pick up their Heavy Metal when it was only half-full; otherwise we might have trouble dumping it, because one of our loaders had some hydraulic problems at max capacity. The Carp Shop could fill a Wood dumpster in a day or two. The dorms were steady with Burnables and sporadic with everything else. The Coffeeshop Glass bin only filled with wine bottles, and we appreciated the bartenders' separating by glass color even though it wasn't their job. The power plant dumpsters had been requiring attention this winter, because the engineers were cleaning house, and they called us to pick up their cardboard frequently, but that's because they didn't break down their boxes. Crary Lab took forever to fill anything but Haz Waste or Plastic.

Passing conversation ever more often involved Christchurch, an Antarctican's Heaven, where the year's grinding work would be rewarded with sushi and botanical gardens, Thai food and titty bars. There would be rain on windows and the sound of wet tires on pavement. Fresh off the plane, we would seep into Christchurch like diesel into snow. We would be full of money. We would scatter about the hostels and hotels, then clump again into smaller groups at restaurants throughout the city. Ice people would be everywhere, stopping on the sidewalks to ask each other what they ate for lunch, because now lunch would not be the same for everyone. To avoid tables for ten with confusing bar tabs, one would avoid the Monkeybar Thai restaurant. Bailey's, a bar at the edge of Cathedral Square, draws so much business from the USAP that they have sent kegs of Guinness down to special parties on the ice. Bailey's would replace Southern Exposure, but without parkas by the door, and the work stories would be full of nostalgia instead of details. The talk would concern beautiful future beaches and bloodless Antarctica.

In Christchurch we look pale, weird, and menacing, but soft as adult-sized newborns. People who were attractive in thick brown Carhartts and all manner of accessories to cover necks, faces, and hands appear in the Christchurch summer as a mass of elbows, kneecaps, and toes. People wear shorts and sandals, exposing pasty flesh and propensities for camping. We are no longer Carps or Fuelies or Plumbers. Our cold-weather clothes are taken away, our intertwining community vines pruned; we suddenly have separate destinations.

By June, work was sometimes a wearisome prospect. I was sleeping longer on weekends and tired on weekday mornings, even when I went to bed early. When I did laundry, the clean clothes got put away just in time to do laundry again. Shaving was a chore. My room was getting messier. My memory seemed weaker.

One day while I was welding a dumpster I had problems explaining something to Jane.

"In this case it'd be better to hold the steel plate than to…" I hawed. Jane waited patiently. I couldn't think of it. I pointed to the clamp lying on the floor. "What's that called?" I asked her.

"Clamp," she said.

"…than to clamp it," I finished. Jane said that pretty soon we would be speaking in grunts, merely pointing at things to name them, and staring into space.

One weeknight there was a "Political Discussion Group" in the library. The topic was the First Amendment. The moderator, a former defense attorney, rambled for over an hour before opening the floor for discussion, and the topic quickly disintegrated from the First Amendment into general law and hypothetical employment practices in people's home states, during which a normally subdued guy who worked in Supply erupted in aggravation.

"So if my right to practice my religion conflicts with a seven-day work week, and I can't find anywhere that doesn't work on Sunday, then it's not fair!"

His voice was tinged with a flash of mania.

Psychologists have been prying into the winter-over mind since the early expeditions. A report by Lawrence A. Palinkas, *On the Ice: Individual and Group Adaptation in Antarctica,* says that Antarctica "has long been viewed as having enormous potential as a 'natural laboratory for the social and behavioral sciences' (Shurley, 1974; Pierce, 1985)."

The study is accurate in many cases. For example, it details the "Winter-Over Syndrome," the name for all staring, grunting, and absentmindedness after April or so, and which the Antarctican simply calls "getting toasty," or less frequently, "T3." The term "T3" comes from the change in T3 thyroid hormone levels triggered by prolonged exposure to cold and darkness, which reduces the body's activity so as to conserve energy. What this means is that in June or July your clothes get heavier and the air around your legs turns to mud.

Palinkas' study found in the winter-over "a complete absence of Stage IV sleep as well as sizable reductions in the amount of Stage III and REM sleep." This means it is not a bad idea to bring a stash of sleeping pills. The "winter-over syndrome" of the "Antarctic microculture" caused by the "perceived absence of social support" within the "social and environmental context" simply means that when people are stuck together like monkeys in a box they start to get on each other's nerves. And the researchers' "analyses of the human experience in Antarctica suggests that there are few, if any, traits that serve as useful predictors of performance during the austral winter." This means that a few psychos will always slip through, and also casts doubt on the value of psych evals.

The study describes "long-eye" or the "Antarctic stare" as "the occurrence of mild hypnotic states," which have been observed in Antarctic expeditions as early as 1900. This is perhaps the spookiest of winter traits, when we leave off in the middle of our sentences to stare at the wall or ceiling. Thousands of half-sentences disappear into the void during winter, and the winter-over seldom tries to retrieve them. By July or August, your story is finished, not when the narrative finds closure, but when you stop talking. Everyone seems to understand, and no one comments on the behavior.[7]

The study also cites another study claiming that "…approximately 5% of winter-over personnel experience symptoms that fulfill DSM criteria (American Psychiatric Association, 1994) for a psychiatric disorder and are severe enough to warrant clinical intervention (Palinkas et al., 1995; Palinkas, Glogower, et al., in press)." This sentiment is illustrated locally by the "Toast List" that Nero revised throughout the winter, and which included those whose behavior sometimes hinted at the subject being "over the edge" (Nero, et al., 2001). Nero would freely divulge the subjects on his list, especially in their presence, and it became something of an honor, creating an unbalanced elite. Thus subjects on the edge of the black crevasse of insanity met approval for their amusing achievements rather than scorn and hostility.

The study falters when it emphasizes the effects of peer interaction and the "extreme physical environment" as the primary hardships of working in Antarctica. This is contrary to actual experience. I have never heard one person say that the most difficult thing about Antarctica is working outside, or being cold. I have never heard one person imply that Antarctica's tough physical environment would be the main reason not to return. I have never heard of one returnee who finally quit because it's the world's highest, driest, coldest, or whatever. People leave because of the bullshit.

Since the culture at the U.S. stations has been imported from the United States, the small polar society is by default structured so that any scheming pecksniff will feel comfortable making a lunge for the reins. And since the average American community regards "freedom" as any state of affairs other than being trapped in a tomb without food, the obedient and the unscrupulous find a welcoming place to play drug dog. Those who prefer a pristine image to the blemishes of authenticity are able to manufacture accomplishments in such surplus that the extent of privilege—dispensed by bureaucracy like food pellets at the end of a maze—becomes merely a matter of appetite. Any departure from the nickel-and-dime bureaucracy is met with howls of official protest. Without these comforts exported to Antarctica from the homeworld, we would no doubt be crippled by the culture shock, but after a season or two, familiarity brings awareness: whether in Antarctica, or on Mars, or on the brightest moon in the belt of Orion, we will set up shop with the same bag of tricks. Why not go back to the homeland, then, where at least there are fresh California oranges and New York steaks?

The Palinkas psychology study claims that "Within each station from one year to the next, a high value is typically placed on certain qualities such as self-sufficiency, decisiveness, intelligence, the ability to work alone, good communication skills, assertiveness, and independence." Palinkas is wise to avoid saying exactly who values these qualities, because, while it's true that many still prize these virtues in work and friendship, actually demonstrating them in an official capacity endangers one's bonus. Self-sufficiency, decisiveness, and independence, in practice, bring only grief, and "assertiveness" is also known as being "unprofessional."

It takes your average wide-eyed fingee approximately 30 business days to realize that the average manager is far less concerned with the business of managing essential tasks than in staving off the onslaught of accusations and sideswipes that might hinder her progress to the next level. If a forthright supervisor or fingee manager gets right to work with his crew, he won't know what hit him. Blacklisted before the summer's half over, he naively does too many favors, leaving his department open to encroachment and implicating him in other departments' fuck-ups. Not knowing what's going on, or rather, not believing his eyes, he fails to release inky clouds of emails that confuse his opponents or to fire off the right dart with the carefully feathered cc: list in time to save his reputation.

Though isolated Antarctic stations are for obvious reasons carefully designed social environments, the psychological study fritters around with "mood disturbance scores" and the "stress-illness paradigm" to explain hardships. Though each new batch of management emails offers an exhausting blend of ominous warnings and perky pep, the Palinkas study is content to let "prolonged isolation and harsh environmental conditions" pull the battered sled of classic Antarctic burnout. Only briefly does the report mention the influence of "external agencies" as a component of the psychological landscape, which is unsurprising, considering its funding source: the National Science Foundation in partnership with NASA.

The two agencies also co-published a report in 1990 that outlined how they might collaborate in applying USAP techniques to the goals of a permanent human presence on the Moon or a manned Mars landing. Antarctica is for NASA a model for the Moon and Mars: a sort of Mock Mars Drill where, because of its remoteness, terrain, logistical constraints, and the tendency of its crews to "experience stresses that are, in many respects, similar to those that will be experienced by crews on long-duration space missions," NASA can perform tests in approximately lunar or Martian conditions at terrestrial prices. NASA not only slavers over Antarctica's potential for a telerobotic construction outpost, but also claims that "Antarctic bases can provide a testbed for studying operational techniques, human factors, and small-group dynamics in harsh conditions... Command and control structure, crew coordination and communication, and questions of leadership, all critical to the success of space operations, can be studied in Antarctic outposts." Though the report didn't specify what varieties of studying would be involved, or when the studying would commence, the report makes clear that Antarctica is "a compelling place" for these studies of "human factors" and that, in exchange for their cooperation, the USAP "could benefit from developed and proposed NASA data, systems, and technologies that might increase the efficiency of operations or enhance the research program." The report describes this win-win situation as "a proven, rational method to reduce the risks associated with human space missions," which are "high-investment missions." An Antarctic mission, on the other hand—in the words of NSF Director Dr. Neal Lane's 1996 press release about the search for Martian meteorites in Antarctica—is like a "bargain-priced space mission."

At lunch one day, Jeannie told this story:

Jeannie was five and playing with her hamster, Scratcher, while her parents loaded the car for a trip to the cabin. Jeannie had put Scratcher in the plastic hamster ball and was rolling the little furpuff around the room as he ran his stubby legs off inside.

When the family came back from their weekend trip they found that poor Scratcher had spent the weekend in the little ball, soaking in his own filth, rolling around the room in futile gyrations like a lost atom. Jeannie took Scratcher out of the ball and lovingly bathed him in a shallow pan full of warm water and Dawn dishwashing liquid.

The hamster did not respond well to the dish soap. Scratcher's hair fell off in clumps while his tender naked body developed unwholesome scabs. He was in a bad way, and Jeannie's dad told her they would need to put Scratcher to sleep. She thought this meant they would drive the hamster to the veterinarian for euthanasia, until she caught her dad in the laundry room with Scratcher inside a garbage bag, beating him against the washing machine.

One Saturday night in June, after a month of detailed planning, we held the Black-Ops party in the Waste Barn. It was costume-optional. Before the party Ben poured a bottle of ketchup on his chest and Nero and Ivan wrapped Saran Wrap around his torso. The flattened and smeared ketchup and chest hair beneath the Saran Wrap looked like some hideous organism on a microscope slide. On top of this he poured more ketchup, then added a Barbie doll that was quickly wrapped up as a new appendage.

I went up to the Waste Barn early because I was the first DJ. The Rec Guy was acting like a secret serviceman, telling people as they came in that they needed to talk to "Agent Tuna the DJ" and ask for the secret codeword or some such. Injun Joe arrived and began yelping at me. "You Agent Tuna? What the hey? Agent Tuna! You Agent Tuna? What the hey? What the hey!" I finally realized through the racket I was playing that he was yelling "Where's the head?" I pointed him out the front door, to where Ben had earlier spent a few hours with a loader and a Herman Nelson heater setting up and melting out a u-barrel shack. Injun Joe left for a while and came back. He told me his IQ was 76. He told me he was a Native American. "Navajo," he yelled. He told me to call him Injun Joe. I excused myself, as there were only 30 seconds left on a song, and he disappeared. Later, just after I had played the song "Tuvan Internationale" by Huun-Huur Tu, Injun Joe reappeared and, with stern insistence, saluted me repeatedly then shook my hand for playing "true music."

After my duty as DJ ended at ten and one of the NASA guys took over, I wandered around the party drinking beer. Despite the recent policy of no hard alcohol at parties, it was in abundance, in unmarked containers. A party in McMurdo not on the verge of a stultifying binge is unthinkable.

I spotted Laz dressed as a deranged lunatic and wearing a weird mask found in skua. I called him a murderous dog and explained that while he was away Ben and I had invaded his room and gone through all his stuff, and that I had jacked off on one of his shirts but couldn't remember which one.

Laz and Jeannie had just made the six-hour return trip from Black Island, where they had gone for almost a week to refuel the tanks that keep the generator building heated. On the way back, they made a bet on their ETA into McMurdo. Laz won the bet, so Jeannie would have to deliver burger bar to Laz in his room. At Black Island they had 100-mph winds. They took 20-foot walks to the Delta from the front door before turning back. Laz said longer walks could have been dangerous.

I was eager to hear about Black Island, but Injun Joe soon pulled me away.

He told me he was a medicine man and had visions. He told me I would be rich. I would be a great leader. I would someday meet him on the floor of the Navajo congress. Our faces had to be close together to hear each other, so I took a lot of spit.

"These people here don't understand anything," he said. "I don't belong here. Not in Antarctica. These people cannot understand the Navajo. The Navajo respect humility."

I told him about the Americans I had met in South Korea who had lived there for three years and couldn't order from a menu. I told him those Americans were filthy people.

He told me that if I wanted to know the Navajo I had to learn the language.

I excused myself and went to find another beer.

Later that night Injun Joe, who had been kicked out of the bar early in the evening, was also kicked out of the party. Later in the season he would be kicked out of Antarctica altogether.

The new fleet of red trucks had been around for about a year, and the fleet of old orange trucks had been sent out on Vessel last summer. Only recently, though, had we learned of the trucks' fate after leaving McMurdo.

The Director of Operations was beside himself because he had thought the trucks would fetch more money than they did. Most of us had gauged the trucks' value as being approximately that of their weight in scrap metal, plus the value of any salvageable parts. And that, Denver was now finding out, was their value.

In desperate yet half-hearted attempts by the Waste managers to get us to feel some sense of responsibility for the heat they were enduring, they sent us stern emails about the poor loading of the trucks during Vessel last summer, even though some of the recipients weren't in McMurdo when the trucks were being loaded. The actual sale price was unknown to us, but we knew it was less than they thought, because shit rolls downhill, and clumps and clods were coming to rest around us. Our minimal involvement with the project, contrasted with the volume of shit rolling to us, was a confusing lesson—seemingly to disregard anything that came from uphill.

The "truck problem" began like this: all summer an entire fleet of orange pickup trucks and vans sat on the pier. Whoever was in charge of such things (no one knew who) had determined that the trucks would be loaded and strapped to the deck of the ship. Suddenly, once the vessel had arrived and we were in the midst of Offload, someone decided that the trucks had to be loaded into milvans. We were told that this was to keep the trucks from being damaged on the deck during the long voyage.

It was amusing at the time to hear of concerns about the trucks being damaged. We knew right away that these decisions were coming from Denver, from someone who had no idea what he or she was talking about, from someone who lived in a world where trucks worked for about a decade on unpaved roads in Antarctica and don't depreciate but are treated as rare gems, perhaps to be sold at auction as historic artifacts.

The trucks were a mess. The tires were flat, the rims falling off, the windows broken, the grills busted, the engines full of ice; few, if any, would start. Putting them in milvans was a rush job, and no one was really quite sure whose job it was. At first it was not Waste's responsibility; then, after a few days in which no trucks were loaded, it was, and then, after a few days of loading trucks, it suddenly wasn't anymore. No one knew what was going on, but everyone was in a hurry.

I spent a day helping to load the 50 or so trucks into milvans. The technique settled upon was this: one person sat in the truck to steer while the other chained the front of the chassis to a loader and dragged the truck back across the pad opposite the milvan, making sure not to block the path of semis driving through every few minutes. When the coast was clear, the loader would push the truck backward into an open milvan. Since most of the trucks had flat tires, the rear suspension would usually take a heavy hit bumping into the milvan. Since there was no side clearance, the mirrors would get ripped off, and the sides would get scratched. Since the trucks didn't start and the loader couldn't push them far enough into the milvan, a pickle was brought down to push the truck to the back. A pickle is designed to lift pallets and ill suited to moving large vehicles. Loud snaps and pops and the uncomfortable screech of warping metal rang through the chilly air like a church bell in a metal baler.

Saul, manager of Waste Operations, and Don, his boss, manager of Waste Programs, had come down to watch all of this. Saul and Don, often referred to as a unit, had a good rapport with us. If they made a mistake, you could accuse them of smoking crack, and they would return the accusation. They usually left us alone to do our jobs, a management style we appreciated. Don knew our department's responsibilities well, and therefore he knew the responsibilities of other departments also; he had a protectiveness toward us that at times seemed strictly territorial, but at other times paternal. He smoked, and he had a belly on him. He was self-effacing about his age and his brains and his weight, but he kept a well-groomed moustache, boasted of his computer prowess, and left no doubt that he was the king of his domain. Don knew The Program's politics as well as almost anyone. I asked him once why the relationship between NSF and the subcontractor doesn't always seem cut and dried. He said, "NSF is a science outfit attempting to oversee what is essentially an industrial operation. The people who have risen into the upper echelons of the NSF come from a background of science, and science administration. They're not used to hardhats, so they make bad decisions that cause hundreds of thousands of lost dollars in the blink of an eye. Eventually the contractor they hire realizes this and begins to exert their expertise, sometimes where it is not, politically, wanted." The Program has an elaborate structure of departments and agencies that no one quite understands. Experienced managers who have spent a lifetime commanding vast budgets and enormous crews at government contract sites around the world have stumbled out of Antarctica in complete bewilderment. From years of experience, Don has lucid insights into a system of almost mystical complexity and opacity. He enjoyed talking office politics, and I probed him about them whenever he was in town. Don would eventually have an Antarctic island named after him.

Saul, second-in-command, also maintained a familiar rapport with us. We could play darts and drink beer with him and never have to watch our mouths. He was self-effacing also, and responded with good humor to being called a bald dwarf. Saul was like a vibrating nerve; even in good spirits he never seemed completely relaxed. We said his knees never stopped jerking, because when a problem arose, his preferred solution was the one quickest to implement.

Saul and Don came down to the ice pier to watch us load the trucks. When not chaining a chassis to the forks of the loader, I stood with them, shooting the shit, exchanging jibes and insults. We laughed at the absurdity of the task that had fallen to us at the last minute from muddy skies—these pathetic trucks stuffed into milvans to protect them as precious cargo when they were not precious, nor was this a solution if they had been. But if that's what needed to happen, that's what needed to happen. We laughed.

But now the trucks had hit the spreadsheet.

CHAPTER 8
NOTES

[1] "Last year, midwinter, that party of ten, eleven researchers and staffers got evacuated out of McMurdo. Biggest incident of its kind ever. USAP was a little vague with its explanations, don't ask me why. Maybe the beakers came down with cabin fever, went a little crazy, got into an old-fashioned punch-out, and were embarrassed to admit it. Or maybe the caginess was just a typical bureaucratic reflex. Next thing you know, though, you got thousands of conspiracy theorists on the Internet posting bulletins that they made first contact with flying saucer people. *There's* Antarctica for you."— from *Cold War*, one of Tom Clancy's "Powerplays" series, 2001

[2] A can of fiddleheads had been floating around the skua piles for several consecutive years. Someone told me that he finally ate them just so they would go away.

[3] "Censorship by the NSF of electronic mail (e-mail) continued to infuriate scientific parties operating out of the U.S. base at McMurdo as recently as 1990. Then the NSF Representative would have the e-mail printed out to check it for possible personal messages before it was released

for transmission. However, by my latest trip in 1995, technology, the vast bulk of e-mail messages, and common sense had solved these problems. I was able to log into my computer in Denver from a terminal at McMurdo and send and receive messages directly." – John C. Behrendt, *Innocents on the Ice: A Memoir of Antarctic Exploration, 1957*. University Press of Colorado, 1998

[4] The earliest known performance of "I'm a Little Teapot" in Antarctica was by a civilian at Ellsworth Station in March of 1957.

[5] One of the comms techs told me that the roof of the T-site building had once blown off in a storm and when the storm ended some of the equipment that is still used today was packed in snow. The tech at the time holed up in a shed and ate cookies until the storm ended and someone could come up and get him.

[6] "While I was sitting reading in my cabin this afternoon at half past one—the men have washday today—I suddenly heard three or four long, terrible screams. I thought the noise came from the afterdeck and hurried there together with the doctor and Koren. There was nothing to be seen. Then we ran to the engine room but there was nothing to be seen there, either. Everyone was inside. The commander was walking on the deck and had heard nothing. Lecointe and Racovitza were on the ice and had not heard anything either while Arctowski was asleep. The doctor, Koren and myself were the only ones who heard the terrible screaming. I do not know what it was but I have recorded this event as accurately as possible for a number of reasons." – Roald Amundsen, Belgica Diary

[7] "Even thinking seemed too great an effort. Men became absentminded, staring vacantly and having difficulty concentrating on anything. Discussions usually did not stay on one topic for long, and talk tended to become assertive and unresponsive. Conversation turned more and more to badinage—the language salty and the banter ribald." – Historian Eugene Rodgers, description of Little America inhabitants by Midwinter's Day in June 1929.

CHAPTER NINE

THE UNITED STATES
EXPLORING EXPEDITION

*The outcome can be a more benevolent future for all citizens in
all nations. . .*

— Dr. Neal Lane, NSF Director, at a meeting of the American
Association for the Advancement of Science

*The Author having laboured so long and done so much to serve
and instruct the Publick, without any advantage to himself, has at
last thought of a project which will tend to the great benefit of all
Mankind, and produce a handsom Revenue to the Author.*

— Jonathan Swift, "A Project for the universal benefit of
mankind," in which Swift satirically announces to publish a
work describing the unexplored territory
Terra Australis incognita

26 June 01

David,

I have received my first classic Antarctic injury. I have
frostnipped the tips of the fingers on my right hand. No, now, don't
worry. It required no medical attention, and already the pain is

going away—though they are still tender—and there is no visible disfigurement. This is the way of classic Antarctic injuries; they are wrought covertly, the weather teaming up with the body to seize control of strategic facilities until their demands are met. In this case, I was walking in a class-action storm trying not to spill the can of beer clutched in my ungloved hand. The back door of the dorm, wherein lay our supplies of liquor and handy ice buckets, had frozen shut and no amount of vigorous kicking and pummeling would jar the latch mechanism loose, so the band of hearty explorers and I, sound and seasoned in all cold-weather survivalism, decided to go around to the front door. In this merciless frontier where one's life is only a temporary concession by the whimsical crushing forces of nature, my beer had grown warm, and I knew the mere hundred-yard walk to the front door would replenish the quality of my supplies. Like a company considering its contract workers, I had given little thought to the biological tools that merely facilitate the logistics of some vague inebriating purpose. The front door was open and we continued our research, me being the only ungloved, running my hands under warm water for a short period emitting nervous laughter.

After concluding some pressing research, we were very drunk and completely ravenous... [So] we bravely ventured out into the fray to get to the variety of meat and rice dishes that awaited us in the institutional cafeteria where a big screen TV continuously airs *Sesame Street*... The next day the entire station would receive an email saying that we could be terminated for disobeying orders to stay inside during a Condition 1. One young woman, N, who read this email and then deleted it received a call within minutes from her supervisor, E. E told N that she had received a call from the Station Manager saying that N did not read the Safety email and that it is mandatory that she read all Safety emails. Apparently there are electronic functions that allow the sender of an email to determine whether a message has been opened before being deleted. N, who like everyone else uses Microsoft Outlook, a program capable of personal settings which can allow the user to view a message in a frame without actually opening it, had been flagged by the Safety Girl, who alerted the Station Manager who alerted N's supervisor who assured N that this was a very serious issue. There are other reasons the Safety Girl is very funny. I'll tell you why.

You see, since the beginning of winter an entire crew of carpenters and painters and various tradesmen has been remodeling dorm 203A. It has recently come to light that the tile flooring and some of the drywall in that dorm has asbestos in it. I don't know how the initial question came up at all, but once the cat was out of the bag, it was discovered that a report in an office of some medium-level building coordinator who isn't even on the ice and who is no doubt involved in important matters in Denver, indeed confirmed that there was asbestos in said flooring. Flooring that was ripped up, cut up, and smashed by hand so as to fit into the dumpsters by workers who, during the demolition, continually came to lunch covered with a fine dust, and who were unaware of the results of the report that no one told them about, perhaps to be saved for a rainy day's reading by some giggling accountant aware of the costs of asbestos abatement. There is much ado about much involving the incident, though I brought it up only to make this point: the Safety Girl has written exactly no emails about asbestos while her regular reports about slippery ice and safety glasses and injury records and safety statistics continue unabated. My supervisor tells me about the Supervisor's Meetings and revealed to me that the Safety Girl's contribution to the matter at last Saturday's meeting was this: a safety video about asbestos is now available for our weekly safety meetings.

When the workers on the 203 remodel discovered they had been exposed to asbestos, they stopped work in the building. The FEMC Supervisor at a meeting accused NSF of "criminal negligence," and wrote in a follow-up report: "An incredible error was made in removing the sheet vinyl with no abatement procedures, and this error was compounded by aggressive sweeping of any possible remaining asbestos-containing dust. There can hardly be a worse procedure for asbestos-containing material."

Though the exposure had already occurred, and though the asbestos flooring in the building had long been removed, the Safety Girl took air quality samples, after which the Safety Board in Highway 1, usually plastered with color charts of injuries broken down by body part and department, displayed only an array of charts showing that the asbestos levels in the buildings were currently within OSHA standards.

Fingers pointed in all directions, and contract supervisors, who had overseen the work but had not orchestrated it, had to defend themselves from Denver's immediate thirst for nonmanagerial blood. Even the unlikely head of the Paint Shop supervisor was prodded to see if it would look good on the stake.

The key element that prevented Denver from pinning the negligence on some expendable and unsuspecting local supervisor was the asbestos report by AECOM, a subcontractor that had performed an asbestos inspection of McMurdo and Pole Stations from October 25, 1991 to December 12, 1991. The asbestos report had been gathering dust, ignored much as was the Royal Navy's cure for scurvy in the heroic era of Antarctic management. The report lay on a bookshelf in the office of a full-time FEMC administrator who had left at the end of the summer to work in Denver for the winter. Local winter supervisors had never heard of the report, which stated that the vinyl flooring in 203 contained 25–30% chrysotile asbestos. The authors noted, "Sheet vinyl flooring was observed in the vestibules, laundry rooms, and janitor's closets. This material has been damaged in several areas and the friable backing has been exposed." The inspectors suggested, "These areas should be repaired with duct tape or otherwise encapsulated to prevent the release of asbestos fibers and should be scheduled for removal."

Wilson came to my room one night to tell me about a conference call he had with Denver. He had led the push to accurately document the incident. Some workers on the 203 project, the foremen, the station manager, and a few others sat around the speakerphone. On the other end of the speakerphone were several people in Denver, including Jim Scott and the Safety Guy. The previous summer the Safety Guy had answered questions from children at a grade school in the U.S. He wrote, "My job is to try to keep people safe from occupational hazards that may come from their particular work place…" Now he discouraged the workers from reporting their exposure to the doctor. He urged them not to overburden McMurdo's overly busy medical staff. This sort of advice is probably what a USAP Safety Review Panel had tried to prevent when it suggested in a 1988 NSF report, "Contractor support for [the tasks of the Safety, Environment, and Health Officer] must be totally separate from the U.S. Antarctic Program prime support contractor in order to avoid real and/or perceived conflict of interest." Jim Scott and the Safety Guy would not answer any questions about whether OSHA policies had been disregarded. Wilson asked what the plans were for disciplinary action against management. Everyone was told to leave, and Wilson sat alone with the speakerphone, alone with Denver. While those excused from the room wondered whether or when the mesothelioma would start, Jim Scott yelled at Wilson for asking about disciplinary action against management in front of the others, in violation of policy.[1]

A year earlier NSF had awarded a $160,000 grant to two scientists at the University of California, Riverside, for "A Philosophic and Scientific

Assessment of the Use of Scientific Evidence in Toxic Tort Law." A UCR press release said that the goal of the study was "to determine whether judges are making good decisions in lawsuits related to human exposure to environmental toxic chemicals." Carl Cranor, one of the grantees, wrote that exposure to toxins "can harm us just as much as the grosser forms of violence, theft and deception that have typically served as grist for philosophers' analytic mills." While workers on the 203 project were sweeping clouds of asbestos into the air and an NSF-funded report pinpointing the chrysotile asbestos was gathering dust in some low cabinet, NSF was funding a research project on the "moral and ethical implications of human exposure to the nearly invisible molecules of toxic chemicals." Despite this research interest, not a peep was heard from NSF throughout the asbestos incident in McMurdo. But its 50th anniversary executive summary contains an explanation, of sorts: "NSF invests in individuals and organizations that conduct the work that ultimately leads to the outcomes of the investment process that NSF manages."

Around the time that I went to the Haz Yard lab to witness a few of the asbestos samples test positive, the Safety Guy wrote an email to the Safety Girl expressing his disappointment in the quality of some recent "accident investigation" reports that she had sent. "We have been at this for some time now," he wrote, "and our results are not very positive and it is partly due to people not taking the time to do what is necessary to produce a useful report that will lead to injury reduction." Safety Guy wanted a number of reports redone because they had not properly assigned "root cause," such as that employees were playing sports without wearing safety goggles, and that employees did not wear gloves when handling harsh soaps. Also in question was whether a wrist injury incurred while flipping hamburgers was a strain or a repetitive-motion injury. "I understand that you are busy with the asbestos issue," he wrote, "but please address this ASAP."

As the Projected Mayhem Index had prophesied, June was Level 10, though the slow poisoning of a whole work crew was a dreary genre of mayhem we had not envisioned. Whereas an axe murder or a hammer attack might be followed by an exciting chase and a dramatic incarceration, with work disrupted for FBI interviews, asbestos exposure was followed only by more paperwork. Raytheon's official response was a memo[2] by Jim Scott in Denver, who was not present for the remodel. Those who had worked on the 203 project responded to the inaccuracies of the memo in a letter.[3]

The company memo read that in question was "100 square feet" of vinyl flooring removed by the work crew. The employee letter read that they had also removed vinyl sheeting from four bathrooms and the laundry room for a total of 964 square feet, or "approximately 10 times the amount of square footage listed in your memo."

The memo read that "asbestos in embedded vinyl materials is usually tightly bound, minimizing airborne exposure during handling" and that "the vinyl was removed as a single sheet." The letter read, "We know as workers who participated in removing the flooring that this is not correct. We cut, ripped, and scraped the floor off causing the flooring to be torn in numerous pieces as well as greatly increasing (not minimizing) the airborne exposure during handling. This will be proven if the asbestos sheet vinyl is removed from the construction debris flat racks."

The memo read, "This building was sampled for airborne fibers and found to have levels less than 1/10 the occupational standard for asbestos." The letter questioned "the validity of air sampling after a vast majority of the renovation has been done" and stated that such samples were "not representative of the poor air quality throughout the remodel process."

The memo read, "While some asbestos containing materials may have been disturbed in the renovation of these buildings, based on the quantities involved, time, and the conservative (over estimating) sampling methods, it appears the exposures were very low. In most cases, levels were well below the permissible limit." The letter read, "We are confused at how you determined that during renovation the exposure levels were low and well below the permissible level. Could you please explain this?"

In 1839–1840, the United States Exploring Expedition, commanded by Lieutenant Charles Wilkes, sailed along 1,500 miles of pack ice in Antarctic waters. Land had earlier been sighted in the Antarctic, but Wilkes is said to have been the first to prove that Antarctica is a continent rather than a collection of islands. Many considered the expedition a milestone in American science. Because of this expedition, a large section of Antarctica is named Wilkes Land.

Samuel Dinsman and three other marines who had signed a four-year contract of service in November 1836 saw it expire in November 1840, while the vessels *Vincennes* and *Peacock* were harbored on the island of Oahu. When Wilkes refused to discharge the men from service, the marines refused to work.

The court statement of Samuel Dinsman says that on November 16, Wilkes put them in double irons and sent them ashore at Honolulu, where they were each put in solitary confinement in "a low, damp, filthy place… abounding in vermin"; they were fed fish that was "in a rotten state." On November 27, Wilkes ordered their rations halved. On December 2, three of the marines were brought back to the *Vincennes*, where "Wilkes asked them if they would go to duty, and upon their respectfully stating that the term of their enlistment had expired," Wilkes kept them in double irons and threw them in the brig. Two days later he brought them out, gave them a dozen lashes each, and threw them back in the brig until December 7, when they each received another dozen lashes. Court documents state, "After this system of lashing and confinement, for the preservation of their lives, the said marines were compelled, against the terms of their enlistment and against their free will, to do duty… under the command of said Wilkes." They were finally discharged in the United States two years later.

Wilkes stated that "the officers knew not whom to trust at the time" and that the marines' imprisonment ashore helped ease officer concerns about mutiny. He said that the prisoners' quarters were "a comfortable place of residence" and that the food supplied them was "wholesome, palatable, and invigorating, consisting of a vegetable called 'taro,' and fish…" He claimed that their care was left to a sergeant whose duty was to report to a lieutenant, who in turn was to report to Wilkes, and that the sergeant "never did report that [Dinsman] was suffering from confinement or otherwise in want of proper food or raiment; that such report, if ever made, must have been made through the first lieutenant of the said ship, and never was made to or through him; they further showed, that… it was the duty of said sergeant of marines to make report to said first lieutenant of every case in which any vermin of any sort or description were found upon any marine, or among his clothing, and no such report was made to the said first lieutenant by the said sergeant of or concerning the said plaintiff…"

In defending his decision not to release the men, Wilkes said he had "explored and surveyed the Antarctic region as far as it was possible, and in that service the said ship *Vincennes* received extensive and serious injury" which required all available hands, not only to overhaul and repair the ship, but because the natives "were exceedingly troublesome" and "the said ships were then to visit the wild shores, and the officers and men to come into contact with the ferocious savages, of the Northwest Coast of America, where the marine force was especially needed; and it was deemed of the utmost importance to keep that force as large as possible, and… that it was with this view deemed essential to the public interest to keep said plaintiff on board said ship..."

Having summoned Dinsman from the brig, Wilkes "pointed out to plaintiff how essential his services were to the public interest, and he still refused; that defendant then ordered him to receive twelve lashes on his bare back, and the punishment was accordingly inflicted in the manner pointed out in the rules and regulations of the navy..."

The marines felt otherwise, and Dinsman suggested that his forced service beyond his contract "was not essential to the public interest, and that defendant had no reasonable or probable cause to believe that such detention was essential to the public interest."

Whether the prison quarters were light and clean, or dank and vermin-infested; whether the fish was "wholesome and invigorating" or rotten; whether the irons were lined with felt or the lashings administered with a licorice strip, Wilkes and those working for him had very different ideas as to what "the public interest" demanded of individuals.

A senior NSF representative once said that McMurdo "looked like a John Wayne movie about a mining camp." In the 2000 edition of NSF's annual Antarctic Press Clips, the introduction explains, "Antarctica is a continent of amazing natural beauty as well as the focus of worldwide scientific curiosity. Most people will never visit 'the ice.' But many will experience it vicariously through stories they read in their newspapers or watch on television."

I had my first Antarctic TV experience at an outdoor survival course commonly known as Happy Camper School. There we learned techniques for anchoring tents in both drift and hard ice, how to use the camp stoves, handheld radios, and HF radios, and useful details about camping in local conditions.

One of the first things we learned was how to build an emergency survival shelter of the "snow mound" variety. A group of us piled our bags of personal equipment, then began burying them in snow. After the pile was covered in enough snow, we would dig an entrance through the side and remove the equipment, leaving a hollow sleeping space.

While a dozen of us were shoveling snow in a pile, the TV engineer and his assistant arrived in a Spryte and brought out their equipment. The TV Guy said, "All right now, when I count to three could everyone give me a real good shot of you shoveling snow?!" We were shoveling snow. Most people stopped and waited for him to count to three before shoveling harder and faster than they were before.

After we had made the snow mound and a few people began digging through the side, he asked us if we wanted to be interviewed. When two scientists said they did, the TV Guy had each of them wear Hawaiian shirts he'd brought along and stand with the expanse of sea ice behind them. He told them to rub snow in their beards. The TV Guy asked questions about the turn of the millennium. The interviewee answered; then the TV Guy helped him hone his answer into a shorter, wackier version of what he'd just said. Sometimes the interviewee's answer was funny on its own, which delighted the TV Guy. The second interviewee was more nervous and had trouble thinking of answers for some of the questions, which prompted the TV Guy to give his own suggestions, which the subject accepted. In order to relieve the interviewee's tension, the TV Guy told him to "Jump around for me," which was promptly executed. Each of the interviewees was filmed counting down from five, then screaming "Happy New Year!" I loitered nearby, fascinated. The TV Guy said he was trying to get this footage out now in the hope it would be picked up by one of the networks for their live New Year's Eve broadcast.[4] The date was November 19.

He wanted a group New Year's countdown shot, and two women began hollering to get everyone together. "I'm just a stick-in-the-mud," I thought. "No one else seems to mind hamming it up for the camera. What's my fucking problem?" I joined the group. The TV Guy filmed us counting down and yelling "Happy New Year!" Then he wanted to film it again with more excitement. Then he wanted us to put on our parkas so it would look colder out. Later I asked the TV Guy if I could take a picture of him. He said okay. I asked him to pose with his camera, and he obliged. I asked him to pretend he was filming people shoveling snow. He put his eye to the viewfinder, and I snapped a picture.

About a week after the asbestos was discovered in mid-June, I went to a "Sockhop" at Gallagher's one Wednesday evening. I had seen the signs for it in the hall and in the dorms, and I asked the Recreation Coordinator if he had organized it. He said he hadn't; it was the idea of one of the community members and he had merely provided the resources.

I was drawn to the Sockhop after finding in skua a stack of mesmerizing old magazines called *Reminisce*. Letters to the editor pined for "the good old days." There were some timeless and useful how-to articles about crafts, farm chores, and cooking, but the rest of the magazine was a collection of readers' flawless childhood memories and accounts of people's unrelenting efforts to bring back that special time. It was part Laura Ingalls Wilder, part Norman Rockwell, and all Rousseau.

At the Sockhop, the stereo played Buddy Holly, and a sign above the burger window read "Arnold's Diner." Color photocopied menus on the tables listed the Fonzie Burger, the Potsie Burger, and Ralph Malph Shakes. The Sockhop's inspiration was not the 1950s, but a sitcom set in the 1950s. I ordered a Fonzie Burger from the organizer of the event, who flitted between tables in a poodle skirt taking orders.

My relationship with Poodleskirt had been cordial but distant since I first worked with her in the Galley. She had been one of the Galley Office people, and occasionally caused grief for menials who met her disfavor. She had insisted that DAs put the salt and pepper shakers on the side of each napkin holder closest to the TV. Poodleskirt had yelled at one DA for improperly performing this pointless task. Only my friendliness with her boss had spared me such troubles.

Poodleskirt brought me my burger and I thanked her. As I ate it I tried to remember plots of *Happy Days* episodes, but I couldn't, though I was sure I would if someone prompted me. I could only remember a collection of reassuring objects—hamburgers, old cars, the leather jacket worn by Fonzie, and the mechanical jukebox that played whenever Fonzie gave it an authoritative thump.

I gnawed on my burger and silently slew *Gilligan's Island* memories that rushed in whenever I tried to access *Happy Days*. This whole Sockhop business reminded me of the nice couple who lived next to Kath in Dorm 211 last summer. They measured the efficiency of their shampoo usage by marking the shampoo level on the bottle with a line and the date. On New Year's Day 2001, after most of the community had drunk themselves into comas and would doubtless greet the new year with suffering, the nice neighbor woman, at exactly 10:01 a.m.—one minute after regulation quiet hours lifted—began vacuuming up the confetti in the hall.

Kath occasionally burned a quarter stick of incense in her room, and the neighbors didn't like that. They would stomp up and down the hall saying to anyone they saw, "Are you burning that smelly stuff? Do you know who is? That stuff's forbidden." The neighbors rightly suspected Kath. The woman said good morning to her in the bathroom, but with averted eyes. The man, departing from the politeness he showed everyone else, responded to Kath's greetings with strain. The nice neighbor woman asked Kath's roommate in the dirty hours of one morning while she was brushing her teeth if she knew who was burning incense in the dorm. Kath's roommate feigned ignorance and reported to Kath that the neighbors were on a manhunt.

Eventually the neighbors posted signs in the dorm:

NOTICE TO ALL RESIDENTS

Burning of incense or candles is not permitted anywhere within the building.

Smoking is not permitted anywhere within the building. This includes the vestibules. Do not light your cigarette in the vestibule before stepping outside because the air handlers draw the smoke into the building.

If you bring dishes home from the Galley, it is your responsibility to return them to the Galley. They are not to be left in the lounge area.

The doors at the end of the hallways are fire exits. They are not meant to be used for normal entry and exit. The slamming of the doors and pounding up and down the stairs is very disruptive. Please use the interior stairwell and the double doors at the center of the building for normal entry and exit.

Kath, having kept me abreast of their antics, took one of the signs and showed it to me. That evening Kath posted signs I had made for her:

ATTENTION ALL RESIDENTS

NSF policy prohibits the unauthorized posting of notices.

Displaying NSF regulations for the purpose of enforcing personal motives constitutes fraud and violates NSF policy and United States civil law.

All notices not directly issued by NSF authorities are in direct violation of this policy and will not be tolerated.

Like their sign, mine bore no signature, but the magic thump of authority cast on the fidgeting snouters was immediate and lasting. Despite Kath's continued burning of incense, she never heard another twitter from the neighbors about it, and thereafter they greeted her enthusiastically in the halls.

A Condition One storm at the end of the month left huge drifts all over town. A dune of snow blocked the Waste Barn doors, so we busied ourselves inside until Fleet-Ops came to clear it. All the milvans were blocked with snow, and I was relieved that I had done a lot of the milvan loading of Glass, Food Waste, and u-barrels the previous Saturday. Fleet-Ops was out all day moving snow for other work centers so they could get their jobs done. Two people had gone out to Silver City (a hut on the ice shelf near Scott Base) on Saturday night and, because of the storm, they were stuck out there until someone could fetch them.

The minutes from Saturday's POC (Point of Contact) meeting were sent out in the morning. At the weekly POC meeting, the head of each department relates current events of their department that bear on the community. A secretary takes notes and disseminates the Town Meeting Minutes to the supervisors, who pass them on to the workers. Jane read through them and told us that an announcement about the bonuses had been omitted from the Meeting Minutes. HR had changed the written criteria for bonuses with this explanation: "Nothing is changing on them except the wording." The HR Guy said that the bonus structure levels were applied too liberally by supervisors and that the company now, instead of looking at Level 3 as baseline performance, would like to see Level 3 as the "top end," and there should be more Level 2s. I remembered when Raytheon first took over the contract and sent a representative to the Waste Barn to talk with us. He told us that Level 2 was essentially a non-rehire. The previously reprehensible Level 2 was now appealing because, if it became the new baseline, the company would save at least 2% of labor costs.

When Jane called the HR Guy that morning to ask why the item wasn't included in the minutes and why the bonus criteria were being changed mid-contract, the HR Guy told her, "You're a supervisor. Just buy into it." When Jane got off the phone, she remarked that sometimes coming to the ice felt like joining a cult.

At the same POC meeting, the Quality Assurance Representative reported that a project in which he was physically involved had been postponed the week before "due to weather." He was cleaning out 157, which is used mainly for storage and thus minimally heated if at all. The temperature inside, he said, was down to zero. He was canceling a project "due to weather" inside a building, out of the wind, with the luxury of zero. We amused ourselves for a few days with that one. We decided that this warranted the addition of Conditions 4, 5, and 6, to denote indoor weather states with safety criteria based on nippy drafts or whether a building had plumbing with hot water.

No one seemed to know what the Quality Guy did or why he did it. People said he showed up at their work centers and wandered around looking at things and watching people work. His Quality Assurance investigation reports turned up problems with the quality of brooms and proposed "Flag detail—acquisition and installation of new flag to fly over McMurdo." I first met Quality Guy when I went to Pegasus with Laz to collect some Herman Nelson heaters after the April medevac flight. Quality Guy was out there for some reason. I asked him if he was at Pegasus when the plane landed.

"Yeah."

"That must have been pretty cool," I said.

"It wasn't much."

"Yeah, but I heard there were burning drums along the runway so the pilots could see and there was black smoke everywhere when the plane landed."

"It was just smoke," he said. I suddenly understood why boredom was a problem in Antarctica.

I met him again while loading half-ton triwalls of food waste into a milvan with the pickle. Two triwalls barely fit side-by-side in a milvan, so a maladjusted pallet can require fancy work to avoid splitting one of them open. I had been loading waste for a few hours and thus was in the Zone, where speed and quality of physical labor unite in job satisfaction. Inside the pickle, and in the winter dark, you are essentially blind and deaf to the rear. Because the pickles are old, everything in the cab rattles, adding to the loud engine noise.

I rolled backwards from the milvan, barely seeing a red-coated figure in the dark walking around. Workers know not to fuck around near machines without making eye contact with the operator. I was annoyed. I put the parking brake on and opened the door, and looked out at the figure. It was Quality Guy, with his digital camera. He came over to the machine.

"I'm just taking some pictures," he yelled over the noise.

I looked at him quizzically. "I told Jane about it," he yelled, waving his hand toward the break shack where Jane was working in the office. He felt no need to explain it to me because he had already explained it to my supervisor. "Let me just get a picture of you," he yelled. I declined with a wave of my hand and shut the door of the pickle.

Once I had finished loading food waste, I went into the barn where Quality Guy was standing with his camera, watching Thom and Jane work. I walked over and introduced myself. He said he was there to do a QA report on Waste Management for Denver, so I explained our most recent project to him as we watched Thom use Terminator to flip a metal dumpster over on the floor of the barn.

"We're fixing broken dumpsters," I explained. "Some of them have bent latches, missing braces, and severed tongues. If a rocking dumpster has a bent latch, it can sometimes roll during transport and dump trash on the road. If a dumpster has a missing brace it can be troublesome when trying to fork it, and when tongues are missing it takes more time to dump them because you have to chain the dumpster to your forks. So we'll use a grinder, an acetylene torch, and a welder to reshape the latches, attach new braces, and mend tongues. They're basically minor repairs, but when we move thousands of dumpsters a year the repairs can save a lot of time and annoyance."

Quality Guy nodded his head. He later explained to Jane that he was just there to do a "warm and fuzzy piece for Denver."

Later in the week at the end of the day, Laz stopped by the barn to tell me there were auroras in the sky. I crunched beside him in the cab of his loader, and we drove out to the Pass, away from the town lights. A half-mile from town we stopped, switched off the lights, and stood outside next to the idling machine and stared at the fading and intensifying green lights in the black sky. Streaks of green rose vertically, as if the earth were inside a cone of charcoal smoldering with green fire. When the aurora changed, we were in a vast box with green light leaching through a black lid barely cracked. A science writer for the *San Francisco Examiner* (funded by NSF for a one-week visit) once wrote that "scientists risk their necks" to "analyze the shimmering aurora that flickers across the night sky like a great curtain." The radio in the cab of the loader crackled with voices. "Auroras at the Pass," someone reported. Every minute or so another vehicle would speed up, park, and turn off its lights, and doors would slam in the darkness before another truck did the same, some speeding by to go further toward Scott Base and some driving up the Ob Hill road that leads to where the old nuke plant used to be, looking for the optimal view.

After about ten minutes we got back in the loader and headed back to town.

Later we received this email:

Please read the attached message. Aurora chasing is not considered work related travel. Please adhere to the policy regarding no personal use of Government vehicles.

Thank you!

-----Original Message-----
From: Scott, Jim
Sent: Thursday, June 28, 2001 6:28 AM
To: [Franz]
Subject: Vehicle Use

It has come to the attention of DHQ that government vehicles in McMurdo continue to be used for personal reasons. Please discuss with the community ASAP that this use of government property is unacceptable. Every person on station was briefed of this when they arrived. If they respond differently they are not being honest. But to provide them with one final warning, please counsel all personnel that government vehicles are "not to be used for personal travel or convenience."

Any person who further abuses this policy will be given a written notice. This will be entered into their file in HR and it will impact their bonus.

Regards,
Jim Scott
McMurdo Station Area Mgr.

I had spent the morning repairing dumpsters. I stopped grinding at 11:30 and took a loader to lunch. Down the hill, three pedestrians were almost to the awkward island of the three-road main intersection in town. I pulled a quick right through the stop sign, rolled down to the Galley, parked the loader, set the forks on the ground, placed the accelerator stick so the machine wouldn't wet stack, and walked the hundred yards or so to 155.

One of the pedestrians was coming down the road. I couldn't see who it was but I waved routinely. As I was going in the door, the pedestrian, station manager Franz, pulled down his hood and scowled. "You should stop at that stop sign," he said.

"Okay," I said mechanically.

"Especially with the NSF Rep there," he added. "It looks bad."

"I used to work with a guy who was deaf in one ear," Sasha told us at lunch as we fed on squares of greasy pizza and oily pasta salad. "When we became friends I asked him how he lost his hearing."

"You won't believe me," he had told her.

"Yes I will. Otherwise I wouldn't have asked."

"Do you promise not to laugh? I never tell anyone because they laugh."

"I won't laugh. That would be terrible," she had said.

When he was a kid his friend had a monkey. One day he went to his friend's house and they were playing with the monkey when suddenly the monkey latched onto his head and started fucking him in the ear.

"It was so hard not to laugh," Sasha said as we choked on our food.

"Did the monkey come in his ear, or did it break the eardrum?" Jane snorted.

"I think monkeys are just dirty, so it infected the guy's ear."

"Well, yeah," said Thom, "it sure was a dirty monkey."

CHAPTER 9
NOTES

[1] "Mesothelioma is a cancer of either the pleural lining or the lining of the abdomen. It is a fatal cancer believed to have little or no threshold limit; theoretically, exposure to asbestos through inhalation for as little as one day could spur the cancer, which may not be detected for fifteen to twenty years." – AECOM report

[2] Appendix 2

[3] Appendix 3

[4] "Quality video production services go a long way to effectively support and expose science projects that outline the purpose for USAP. With a video production department working side by side with public affairs, we could make a useful department more effective, thus increasing exposure and possibly future funding for the NSF. The possibilities are endless. Lets [sic] put our resources together to come up with a Video Production Plan to take us into the new millenium [sic]." – McMurdo Radio and Television Broadcasting and Video Production, AFAN Affiliate Station Manager/Executive Video Producer

THE ANTARCTIC
SERVICE AWARDS

*We live in a golden age of science, which we hope will continue
to unlock the secrets of the unknown for the benefit of all
humankind.*

— Dr. Neal Lane, NSF Director

*Great holes secretly are digged where earth's pores ought to suffice,
and things have learnt to walk that ought to crawl.*

— H. P. Lovecraft

THE WHITE HOUSE
WASHINGTON
June 19, 2001

I am pleased to send warm greetings for Midwinter's Day 2001
to the scientists, researchers, and other professionals from around
the world who are stationed in Antarctica. This June 21 observance
is a special time to recognize your contributions to learning and
knowledge.

More than 40 years ago, 12 nations pledged their commitment
to a unique experiment based on international cooperation, scientific

understanding, and peaceful co-existence. The Antarctic Treaty brought together an international community of scientists to collaborate on new discoveries and shared global problems.

Today, the international science community working in Antarctica is carrying on this proud legacy, helping us to learn more about global processes affecting Earth's environment. Consequently, we will have the solid scientific information we need to develop sound environmental policies. Exciting discoveries, like the recent astrophysical breakthroughs in understanding the nature of the Universe at its infancy, also inspire young people to sharpen their math and science skills and to prepare for the opportunities of tomorrow.

The United States is proud to support your important work in Antarctica. Your spirit of cooperation, demonstrated recently by an international effort to rescue a sick colleague at the South Pole, inspires people everywhere. I applaud you for your courage and professional dedication as you work in a tough and unforgiving environment.

As you observe Midwinter's Day 2001, I send best wishes for a productive and rewarding experience in Antarctica. May God bless you and bring you safely home to your families.

George W. Bush

McMURDO STATION
ANTARCTICA
July 4, 2001

Dear Mr. Bush,

Thank you very much for your warm Midwinter's Day greeting. Midwinter's Day is an important holiday for us in Antarctica as it marks the halfway point of our service to international scientific cooperation this winter. I wish to return your acknowledgment of our holiday here with the warmest greetings for you on Independence Day.

Though I am a garbageman and I spent Independence Day sorting through vomit-covered aluminum cans, the warm glow of your Midwinter's Day greeting reminded me of my contribution to learning and knowledge. In your letter you addressed "scientists, researchers, and other professionals" so I have humbly included myself in the greeting. Actually, at McMurdo, the largest U.S. station in Antarctica, there are exactly zero scientists serving here this winter. There is a science tech who fixes some of the automatic data collecting machines. He must be the researcher you mentioned. The other two hundred of us contract-workers such as janitors, plumbers, and construction workers must be the other professionals you mentioned. I'm glad we are helping students become better at math and science. In all honesty, I was never very good at math or science, which might be why my clothes caught on fire today while I was grinding down the surface of a dumpster for repairs. I am very good at reading and writing though. Perhaps you could send a greeting to U.S. students to tell them that math and science will help them be a fraction of the Antarctic population while reading and literature will help them be garbagepersons with burning clothes.

Of course, one of the greatest benefits of serving international scientific cooperation in Antarctica is the natural beauty that we encounter as we do our daily work. The storms are fantastic to see, and bright green auroras sometimes appear in the sky. Actually, because of the streetlights at McMurdo, we can't see the auroras unless we travel about a mile out of town. Recently we have been forbidden to do so by the National Science Foundation, the government agency who runs the station, because all the vehicles, here in this cold desolate place where we eke out our existence in unspeakable polar climes in service of science, are government property and we are told that if we drive away to look at auroras for ten minutes we will be terminated. Since you are in charge of the government, I was wondering if you could give us permission to use the government property vehicles to drive one mile out of town for ten minutes when we see an aurora in the sky, not more than once per week, say, just to be fair. We could walk out to see the auroras, I suppose. Today the temperature here was −32F and windchills were below −80F. How cold is it in Washington D.C.?

With all respect, I hope you had a glorious and heartwarming Independence Day full of amazing friendship.

Darin Nicholas Johnson

I realized one week in early July that it had become difficult to imagine being elsewhere. At the end of each day I stood at the fuel pumps looking down at the ice pier while my loader filled with diesel, then drove away with no one to pay. We filled five-gallon juice coolers in the office of the Heavy

Shop when we needed water for the break shack. We lived within a two-minute walk of a meal prepared by someone else. We knew each other too well. We received mail according to weather and season. We saw everywhere at all times ice-covered roads, tendrils of snow, growing drifts, diesel smoke, and lines of dumpsters. I practically lived in a Caterpillar—what would I do elsewhere when I needed to move a five-ton steel box? I could barely remember how things were anywhere else.

I mumbled this to Jane ("Caterpillar allatime. No grocery shopping"). She agreed that our routines were overwhelming. She pointed out that to walk into the Galley and sit down with a table of people one didn't normally sit with would be a very strange thing. Though we still had a few months left, the social code discouraged new relationships. If you didn't know someone already, there was little chance left in the season of getting to know him or her, although when the Winfly crowd arrived the winter-overs would all nod at each other in the halls. Our cliques had solidified, comfortable and courteous, with a tinge of uneasiness marring any extraordinary encounter.

Ivan and I began to play *Tomb Raider* on weekday evenings, whereas previously we had only played on the weekends. After playing the game for a few hours here and there all winter, we were on the last level. Once a level is completed (weapons found, foes killed, treasures collected), a short animation rewards the video-narcotized gamer with the next installment in the game's story. The ravenous treasure-seeking and slaughter of wild dogs overshadow the finer points, but in *Tomb Raider 3* the story goes something like this: You are out to collect ancient artifacts also sought by other forces, both evil and good. One of the evil forces is a company that uses the ancient magic of the artifacts to mutate humans into murderous monstrosities. After three or four levels, after you have collected all the artifacts you thought necessary to complete the game, a purportedly good force shows itself to be an agent of the evil company and steals all your artifacts. Now, in order to complete the game, you must battle the company at its research headquarters to regain the artifacts that you worked so hard for. On the next level you are surrounded by ice and snow in Antarctica.

We battled half-seal, half-human mutants and researchers with red parkas and automatic weapons. We stepped over their corpses and rummaged through their offices looking for clues to the whereabouts of our artifacts. On the office walls were maps of Antarctica just like ours.

"Dude, do you think we're the first in Antarctica to get to Antarctica?" I asked Ivan. "Mutant."

"I see it." Ivan dispatched the mutant with a shot to the head. "Good question." He shrugged with his eyebrows. "Even if we're not, we're probably the first in Dorm 207 to get to Antarctica. And if that's not somethin' to be proud of, then I'll let that mutant eat my head." Ivan shot the mutant.

We also began to watch more TV. Ivan and I held weekly gatherings to watch old *Star Trek*. We watched *Star Trek* because outer space is where it's at. It's the final frontier, not some half-assed backwater frontier. On *Star Trek* there was no chance that once they entered the darkest reaches of space the criteria for their ten-year mission bonuses would be rewritten. When a succubus on an alien planet sucked the salt from a red shirt's husked corpse, the Enterprise Safety Department didn't remind the crew that alien succubi "are your responsibility." Mr. Spock didn't perform mind melds on the crew, send the results off to Starfleet Command, and then tell the crew that the results of the mind melds were none of their business. Unless they had been infected by a malicious energy vortex, the crew was not tense and angry, and we could presume that those who liked to direct plays or play music or write newsletters were free to do so without interference from Captain Kirk, who couldn't hide his annoyance whenever he encountered totalitarian alien cultures. The Enterprise, whatever its faults, did not need a Quality Assurance Representative.

One day, as I was wearily loading pasta onto my lunch plate, Gail, the salad-maker who had taken me with her on the seal odyssey, came out of the kitchen to talk to me.

"You are going to love this," she said. Gail was a fellow connoisseur of The Program's small golden moments. I stepped away from the food line.

"The Galley's about to run out of certain foods," she said. "And underordering food is in the Galley metrics."

"Metrics" is a potent word around town. The "metrics system" is one reason NSF slipped Raytheon the support contract. Each department has a "metric" that, if bungled, will reduce NSF cash to Raytheon at the end of the contract year. A command accompanied by "metrics" implies that all other concerns are overridden, as there will be a follow-up report during or after the task's completion. "Metrics" means it's time to bust ass. The power plant has a metric for minutes of power outage, Fuels has a metric for spills, and the

Galley has a metric for food supplies, so that Raytheon could take a pay cut if some staple were underordered. Gail said that after the recent food inventory had been completed, Denver instructed that nearly depleted items be kept in inventory so as to comply with the metric. This meant that if, for instance, the Galley had only one more case of powdered milk, it was to remain in the warehouse so that, on the books, milk had not been underordered. No milk would be served, but milk would officially be in adequate supply.

In mid-July, just before one of our monthly two-day weekends, we received an email saying that a problem with the water intake pipe had left the town officially on water shortage. We were supposed to cut back on showers, do no laundry, and eat from paper plates in the Galley.

The email had little effect. It was hard to imagine dying from thirst. While we could imagine getting permanent nerve damage from exposure to fuel, or falling in a crevasse, or dying from exposure in a snowbank, it was impossible to imagine being in a nice hot shower that suddenly ran dry, or trying to suck dribbles from the drip tube beneath the ice machine. It was hard to imagine this when we could melt snow in the microwaves in our rooms.

One morning someone posted this flyer in several places along Highway 1:

DUE TO WATER SHORTAGE, RESTRICTIONS WILL BE
IMPLEMENTED AS FOLLOWS:

Job Points + (.125 x Months on Ice)
$= $ Gallons H_2O/Day
All Allocations Non-Transferable
STRICTLY ENFORCED
Have a nice day...

At this time the baker had been on an unofficial strike for a few days.[1] Her desserts were exceptionally good and often elaborate, but the community that gobbled them in great quantities had shown no gratitude for her efforts. Her means of protest was to put out pre-packaged frozen baked goods: small crumbly apple and cherry pies still in the tins, "confetti cake" with multicolored sprinkles still on the cardboard circle, and factory-made cookies. Many thought nothing of it, and some were happy for more familiar fare, but a few pastry-snobs could be seen at the dessert counter grumbling, "confetti cake."[2]

The baker's protest—that people in a community should be grateful for each other—rested on misconceptions about the town. When one thinks of a town of a few hundred, one imagines the local shopkeeper sweeping his sidewalk and sneaking free candy to the children. Old men in rocking chairs pet dogs at sunset and wave to passing visitors. One might even expect such things of a small town in Antarctica, without the dogs and children of course, and expect firm handshakes to be delivered after the local barnraising for the newest office module.

In reality, the little polar town has a strict division of labor, and neighboring departments try to foist responsibility on each other for even the most inexpensive cargo damage. Overt interdepartmental favors, such as loaning tools or materials, chap the hide of anyone invested in the chain of command. There is the occasional exhortation to departments to work together better, but efforts to that end generally implode on conception, because scapegoating is the primary form of interdepartmental communication. New bureaucracy-busting plans are forever being formulated and implemented. Progress is achieved by addition, never by subtraction. In every department, people are busy at their jobs. The repaired truck goes out and a broken one comes in. A mopped floor is dirty again within minutes. Dumpsters never stop filling up. FEMC has two years worth of backlogged work orders. The desserts get eaten as fast as they're made. Everyone works in the same ceaseless tide. Pats on the back seem as pointless as heating a shack that has no door. Supervisors have been criticized for writing positive evaluations.

Though the advantages of a rigid division of labor are obvious in the weekly reports and spreadsheets, the disadvantages appear as mysterious aberrations, as problems to be solved individually. A sensitive baker realizes the icy divisions and brings attention to them, if only for a pat on the back. The Operations Manager calls on our sense of community so a water shortage doesn't affect operations.

But that's not our department.

On the Sunday of our two-day weekend, we voted to decide the Winter-Over 2001 t-shirt design. The winning design would be emailed to New Zealand and the shirts sent down at Winfly. There were about ten designs hung in Highway 1 for consideration. Laz submitted a design with a generic male figure fucking a screaming penguin. Above it was the ordinance from the Antarctic Treaty that disallows "molestation" of animal life without a permit from NSF. The pocket design said, "Sure, I fuck penguins, so what?" This sketch was covered with a piece of paper warning that the design might offend. Some of the others were polished four-color Photoshop efforts featuring unmolested penguins. One had penguins holding hands (wings, actually), with Antarctica at the top of the globe.

One design was from someone who apparently learned to draw by studying fusion-rock album covers from the 1970s. It showed a penguin waving a cowboy hat and riding an angry unicorn with flames pouring from its nostrils. The crazed unicorn was charging through wispy blue strands of wind erupting from the mouth of a blue cloud with crazed eyes. The cloud's breath coagulated to read, "Ridin' out the storm." The design with the penguins holding hands won with about 30 votes.

The next day we got an email saying that the problem with the intake valve had been fixed and the water shortage was over. "It's amazing how a community can come together during a crisis like that," Ivan said.

The hint of dark blue in the sky and the imminent arrival by plane of the t-shirts reminded us that Winfly was just around the corner. Winfly, the season from mid-August to early October, brings two opposing emotions: relief that soon you will be in Christchurch lavishly spending instead of working, and disgust that from the first Winfly flight until then you will once again cram together with a roommate, find the Galley crowded, and encounter daisy-fresh assholes running around asking where you're from. Yet, a lot of friends would fly in, there would be new women around (or "Winfly Pussy" as Jane liked to say), and there would be furious storms, so Winfly was not without welcome diversions.

But even though we spotted Winfly on the horizon, it was still very much winter. Ted the Racist was fired from the Heavy Shop. He had already been banned from buying alcohol and from going in the bars, and now he had pulled a knife on someone, which was important news for the Projected Mayhem Index, though the asbestos incident had confounded our notion of what constituted mayhem, resulting in a kind of Mayhem Inflation that calloused our senses. Ted the Racist was still receiving paychecks, but no bonus, and was technically still hired as a "consultant." Whatever the official reason for this, we knew the paychecks were a payoff so he didn't go apeshit and hurt someone.

The Heavy Shop was bubbling with unrest. The mechanics were

grumbling. The Heavy Shop foreman had been promoted this year from his previous position as a welder, despite having one season attacked the stereo with a hammer. Now that he was foreman, he simply turned up the shop radio if the mechanics were playing country, and turned it off when they were playing classic rock, even though he spent most of his time in the office.

He decreed that bumper stickers were to be removed from every machine in the fleet when they came in for maintenance. None of the stickers were remarkable, usually asking "Where the heck is Wall Drug?" or advertising some podunk bar in the remote Midwest. The Heavy Shop GA, charged with scraping the stickers from the machines, was soon told to make exceptions for certain stickers: one for "This is a non-smoking vehicle," and one for "Idaho" (the foreman's home state). Jeannie asked the GA about the "Visualize Whirled Peas" sticker on the fuel truck. The GA said that the foreman hated it most of all, and that the policy was probably an effort to get rid of that one sticker.

The Firehouse was also having troubles. Because of air quality problems caused by the Firehouse ventilation system, the firefighters had been moved to 155 to sleep during their shifts. One of the firefighters had reported to Medical with complaints of nausea, dizziness, and chest pain. When other firefighters reported similar symptoms, the doctor researched the effects of long-term exposure to fumes of the jet fuel that heats the building and found it could lead to convulsions and death, so he brought the problem to the attention of Safety.

Safety was too busy formulating emails about the importance of reducing the overall injury rate to futz with nonscientific, subjective symptoms.[3] One of the firefighters wrote an email to her mother about the bad air, and her mother became concerned. She contacted OSHA, who suddenly had no weight in Antarctica, before calling NSF, who didn't respond. Finally the angry mother contacted a North Dakota senator who faxed a letter to NSF, at which point the firefighters were immediately moved out of the firehouse to sleep in 155 until the ventilation problem was fixed. The whole mess was covered in the *Bismarck Tribune.*

By the end of July, Bighand was officially cut off from the bar. The Station Manager began looking out his office window a lot, reporting people who didn't stop completely at one of the few stop signs in town. Some days were so cold that the hydraulics on the machines barely moved. During these spells, the metal baler could barely even crush a barrel. Tires would freeze with flat spots overnight, and our machines sprang glycol leaks every couple of days and had to be taken to the Heavy Shop.

At the end of July there was an All-Hands Meeting at which the Housing Coordinator, a cheerful woman named Ellie who was universally described as nice, explained the Winfly Housing rules and expectations for room inspections. She said that we had three chances to pass inspection, with penalties from $350 to $500 if we didn't pass the third. Her PowerPoint presentation explained room assignment, with a humorous theme of "It's Not Me," pointing out that all Housing allocations were made in Denver. Friends chose friends to move in with, and others opted for random roommates who would come in at Winfly.

Ivan and I decided to share a room in 155. For a few hours here and there after work throughout the end of July, we cleaned our trusty winter rooms and prepared to move. Once Ivan began choking up:

"Remember that time I was cleaning the shower and you were cleaning the toilet? Ah, those were good times, weren't they?"

"Yes, they certainly were, my friend, they certainly were. Remember that time I needed the Comet when you were finished with it?"

"I do remember that, as if it were yesterday. Those were golden days, my friend. Remember that time I was cleaning the shower and you had to hold your horses for the Comet? Remember that?"

"Like a withered blossom clutching but the memory of fragrance I do. Flawless times, flawless. Hand it over."

"Great god, what an awful stain! I am scrubbing the shower, and I may be some time."

On August 1, Winfly room assignments were posted on the Housing bulletin board. There were problems, and the grapevine throbbed with controversy. Half the window rooms in 155 had been reserved for Winfly people, so a steamed winter-over wrote to Denver Housing: "You are telling me I am unable to get a room with a window because somebody who has been in Denver or any other place with 'sunlight' for the past seven months needs one more?"

Some people who'd selected Winfly roommates were instead given random winter-over roommates or told to move to different dorms. Jane, who had agreed to prepare for a Winfly roommate by the end of August, was told that another winter-over was moving into her room and that she had to be ready for room inspection immediately. She thought it was just a paperwork error.

Jane went to the Housing Office. There, Franz told her to contact Debbie in Denver. Jane called Debbie one morning, while Thom and I were there drinking coffee. Debbie told Jane to talk to Franz. Jane told Debbie that Franz had told Jane to talk to her. There was talk of "miscommunication" concerning the Housing policy, and Jane asked what, exactly, the Housing policy was currently. We couldn't hear what Debbie said, but Jane responded, "I'm not being unreasonable."

Following the phone conversation, Jane wrote an email to Franz telling him that she had consulted Debbie in Denver, as he had suggested, without satisfactory conclusion, and that Debbie wouldn't tell her what the new Housing policy was.

Franz immediately sent for Jane to come to the Chalet for a meeting with him and Ike, the Operations Manager, for whom we all had great respect. Jane asked Ike if this was a disciplinary meeting, and he told her it was not—otherwise HR would be involved. Franz eventually told her that if she didn't comply with her Housing assignment by August 8, her bonus would be affected.

The hardships of moving one's clothes and books and wall hangings and junk to a different dorm in Antarctica in one's spare time are unlikely to stir the sympathies of even the busiest packrat, and are ultimately of minor importance, just as the South Pole itself is little more than an unremarkable point in a landscape of unrelenting monotony. But Jane's Housing struggle is illustrative. There were a few different forces at work. An order to move immediately, retracting the options given at the All-Hands Meeting, was in practice an order to work longer days. NSF policy is that no one will get time off work to move, and to vacate and clean quarters inhabited for a year takes more time each night if done within one week rather than five. Most important in this story of a doomed struggle against power, August 8, the date by which Jane was supposed to have vacated and cleaned her room, was an arbitrary date set roughly two weeks before the first Winfly flight, a line drawn in the sand.

Jane had always put in longer workdays if it was necessary, but to do so because of a management "miscommunication," and with no benefit to anyone, seemed unnecessary to Jane. Until the first flight arrived three weeks from now, her existence in one room or another made only the difference between two cells in a spreadsheet.

For working outside in the wind and cold, shoveling, sawing, welding, whatever it is that you do, The Program, in periodic memos and emails, will tell you that you've made a "sacrifice" for "science." But the cold doesn't consider your sacrifice. The cold doesn't care about you one way or another. The cold is not trying to use you in a media spin. Nor is it trying to make an example of you. You do not blame it, begrudge it, or believe you can profit from an insincere alliance with it. Your experience with the cold is so personal that you hardly ever mention it.

To work a long day in the cold was one thing, but to give up even ten hours of spare time for a low-ball glitch in paperwork, visible to everyone involved, was not the kind of sacrifice Jane wanted to make.

> Franz: What you're trying to get at—you're trying and trying and trying and trying to do everything you can to stay in your room—
>
> Jane: To make something fair—
>
> Franz: Right. And I'm saying you've got two choices, because that's what policy decision—
>
> Jane: Okay, if I don't move out of my room, I want to know what the consequences are going to be—
>
> Franz: I'll write you up. It'll be documented and it will affect your bonus.
>
> Jane: It'll affect my bonus how?
>
> Franz: Because it's a written warning—
>
> Jane: How does one write-up regarding not moving out of your room affect your bonus? Obviously I'll be recommended for Level A, B, or C. Does it move it down one level? Two levels?
>
> Franz: I'll have to check with [the HR Guy], I'm not sure, but it's insubordination.
>
> Jane: Can you get back to me with that in writing?
>
> Franz: No.
>
> Jane: Why?
>
> Franz: Why, why, why is—
>
> Jane: I want to know how my decisions are going to affect me. Why is that so surprising to you?
>
> Franz: It's not surprising to me.
>
> Jane: I want to make informed decisions.
>
> Franz: Right. So one of your decisions is—okay, I've got these two Housing moves, or I could choose to stay where I am and accept the consequences of it—
>
> Jane: Right.
>
> Franz: —regardless of what those are.

Jane: No. I like to make informed decisions. That's why I want to know what the consequence will be if I get written up for not moving.

Franz: Then we'll just have to wait and see. I don't know—

Jane: . . . And I'm asking you to talk to [the HR Guy], find out, and to let me know before the 8th.

Franz: I don't think we can find out "hypothetically"—

Jane: You're asking me to move by the 8th but you can't find out the answer to a question by the 8th?

Franz: I probably could. —I don't understand why "why why why," Jane.

Jane: Why I'm upset?

Franz: No. I don't understand why you don't want to move. Why is this all so emotional and such a big deal for you? Why are you putting this much energy into this? I'm not sure what's behind it, to be honest with you. I mean, it's a very important deal with everybody in the community. I'm giving up a two-room suite with my own bathroom by myself for a roommate.

[Long discussion about the particulars of Jane's Housing status, housing points, job points, etc.]

Jane: Why can't I take until Winfly? Why is that a problem?

Franz: I don't know. I don't know who's coming in at Winfly. I don't know what their Housing points are—

Jane: If I agree to the move, or to have [Sasha] move in with me, why can't we take until two days before Winfly, which is the original time I was planning on—it's still a huge change to move instead of having someone move in with you. Why can't you make that concession? Why can't you say "All right"? Do you know how much respect you'd get out of the community if you said, "Y'know what? This wasn't clear. It wasn't clear because it was our job to make it clear, and we didn't make it clear. Therefore, the few people it affects, we're going to make it right."

Franz: I think it's just unclear to you. I haven't had to have this conversation with anybody else.

Jane: Did you read [So-and-so's] email?

Franz: I did. And it's been resolved.

Jane: You just said it's only unclear to me. It wasn't clear to him either.

Franz: But now it is.

Jane: Because his request was met.

Franz: Right. And unfortunately we cannot meet your request.

[long silence]

Ike: From my perspective, I won't even speak on the Housing

policy because too many curse words will fly out of my mouth. Let's just say I have an issue with them as well. But let's talk about Jane. If you choose to stay in your room, against the policy and against the move, you're going to get written up. You've already got clarification on that. And if you are written up for insubordination from the station manager, I'm not going to be able to assign you anything more than a 2, if I'm very lucky. And I had planned on assigning you a Level 5 if at all possible. And that's why I wanted to sit down with you and talk about that. Now, whether or not this is fair, whether or not this even makes any sense, I don't want to see you lose anything you're due, even though it might be unfair to you, and it may be unfair all around—we'll have to figure that one out later—what I'm concerned about is you getting through the season and getting the fair bonus you deserve for the work you've done, and I don't want to see you lose that because of an incident that may or may not have been your fault, that may be in question. In the end, you're not going to win unless you follow what the rules are supposed to be. Whether or not they're fair.

After weighing principles versus hard economics, Jane decided to comply because, as she told me, it was a lot of money to lose just to prove you can't trust the company. That was the end of it, or so she thought, until the end of the season, when her bonus was cut anyway. The meeting was documented as justification for the cut, despite her compliance, which was soon forgotten.

Though Jane's eventual defeat would by any measure be a small and insignificant provincial affair, the story must continue, because there are details that will change the story from an isolated petty occurrence into a timeless story of the circular seasons of human vengeance. To get there, however, we must understand why, at the end of winter, Jane and the Denver Housing lady huddled together in a janitor's closet.

All year long Jane had received high marks for her periodic work evaluations. But when she received her year-end bonus evaluation, she found that her bonus had been slashed. Jane's evaluation reported that she had been "abusive" to Debbie, the Housing Coordinator in Denver. The evaluation referred to an "attached email" from Debbie that supposedly validated the accusation, but it was not attached, and no one knew where it was, or what it said. Regardless, Jane's evaluation documented that at the Chalet Meeting, "Jane was warned that her near abusive behavior was not going to be tolerated at all."

This was a false statement. I had insisted that Jane take my MiniDisc recorder to the meeting, so we knew that "abusive behavior" had not once been mentioned or otherwise brought into question. And because Thom and I were present for the phone conversation Jane had had with Debbie, we knew the basis of the claim was false as well, so we wrote witness statements attesting that Jane had said nothing that could have been considered "abusive." "Abusive" denoted a spooky subset of "inappropriate" that, if unchallenged, could be met with financial retaliation, a red flag in the HR file, and possibly exile.

"If the call wasn't abusive," HR countered Jane, "then why did your employees write witness statements?"

Debbie, the alleged victim of Jane's abuse, came down at Winfly. She spruced up the Housing bulletin board outside her office, adding to the printouts of room assignments and lists of "job points" that ranked employees by position a glossy poster of a multi-ethnic band of smiling youngsters beneath the phrase "Smiles are Contagious."

Six weeks after she arrived, Debbie and Jane stepped into the supply closet to get away from the crowded and noisy Housing Office. Amid the ammonia smell and brown bundles of paper towels, they discussed the sudden year-end allegations against Jane. Debbie clarified that she had never said or written that Jane was abusive, and was in fact thankful for their positive interactions since Debbie had arrived at Winfly.

But in the course of this irregular meeting in the supply closet, Debbie talked frankly about how the atmosphere in Denver may have influenced Jane's downfall. Over the tops of partitions decorated with photos of families and pets, Denver was still talking about the death threat from last winter.

"People were so worried that things were going to be horrible," Debbie explained to Jane. "I think that they were being very protective of the Housing Office, and that's why they made me do everything from Denver, which was kind of weird, to protect [Ellie]. And then somebody—it was a weird setup in Denver, you know how they have those office dividers—somebody came over and said, 'Whoa, you were handling that person really well,' and the scuttlebutt got around. Someone asked, 'Are people beating up on you?' And I said, 'No, I'm fine.' And they said, 'Nononono, you need to let us know.'"

Management's black eye at the hand of an anonymous winter-over was still remembered in the hive of Denver. Between cubicles, suburban office folk said that something should be done about it. Someone should pay for the death threat. Though Jane had complied, she had first resisted, so she was as good as anyone to atone for events of the previous year, when the Housing Coordinator had told people that policy was none of their business, and in return had been offered a knuckle sandwich. Debbie told Jane, "They wanted to really nail people this year."

Using recording devices to document the behavior of the professional manager is an Antarctic tradition that dates back to at least the IGY in 1957, when scientists tape-recorded the conversations of Commanding Officer Finn Ronne, whose duplicitous documentation to his superiors was inconsistent with events as recorded by seismologist John C. Behrendt in his book *Innocents on the Ice.*

Behrendt records that Ronne censored the messages they sent out by radio, refused to let someone who'd crossed him send messages to his family, confiscated a book called *My Antarctic Honeymoon* that was critical of him, forbade the scientists from fraternizing with the enlisted men, objected to people shooting movies, threatened to lock one of the men in irons, shoved an ice pick in a penguin's eye, and even cheated at ping-pong. Ronne once referred to the field of exploration as "the last of an exclusive fraternity." Behrendt wrote of his time at Ellsworth Station: "[Trust among the crew] is the only thing that separates the atmosphere here from that of a totalitarian police state."

Meanwhile, Commander Ronne sent to the U.S. press releases full of glorious embellishments, which Behrendt recorded in his journals:

> [6 May] Ronne sent another press release which is full of the distortions which I am now convinced that everyone who writes for the public about Antarctica is guilty of, e.g. "Suns rays dipped below the surface 24 April [not] to return until latter part of August. Those who braved elements topside -37°F, 18-mile wind witnessed beautiful sight whole northern heaven aflame." It was actually about 0°F to -5°F with little wind, and we just saw a little color where the sun was. "Temperature hovers between -26°F and -40°F." Actually the range has been around 10°F to -10°F the last couple weeks...

> [25 May] Ronne sent out another press release. It was nauseating, filled with distortions..."Killer whale packs several dozen still poke pointed heads up through ordinary ice floes... Their mouthful of teeth and snorting sound makes one tremble because they will attack human beings every opportunity. They

are the man eaters of Antarctica, wild beasts of the sea. I thought
they had withdrawn long ago." No one has seen a killer whale
since we quit our seismic work at the tidal crack. "Your breath
gives hissing reverberation. Moisture you exhale immediately
freeze[s]. Ice crystals grind together as they leave nostrils or
mouth. One of the strangest things about cold temperatures." I
have yet to observe any phenomenon like this.

[23 June] Just before the movie, while I was taking a
gravity reading, Ronne came in and went over a news release
with Kim, on the aurora program. He borrowed our thesaurus
a few days ago. Kim told him he thought it was too flowery.
Ronne agreed but said that's the way the public wants it... Kim
tried to tame him down but to no avail. Ronne described red
rings around the moon, which nobody has seen, and depicted
the aurora as being all colors of the spectrum. Kim did manage to
stop this last statement; the only colors he (or anyone) has seen
are green and very occasionally red. The Captain changed his
statement to "a symphony of color passing in review." Kim told
him that "symphonies don't pass in review." So he changed it to
"a symphony of color parading in review."

During that time, the civilian scientists and some of the crew expressed
themselves through numerous media: publishing an underground paper
called *The Daily Sandcrab*⁴; keeping journals; drawing cartoons of the
time Ronne slipped and fell on the ice and blamed someone else for
his fall; sending coded radio messages (when one of them wrote to a
friend "Fervently hope you can visit with resupply to observe firsthand
activity here—including Caligulas Rain," Ronne asked what the latter term
meant, and the scientist told him it was a geophysical term); and recording
disciplinary meetings Ronne held in his room as well as radio conversations
to his superiors in which he accused the scientists of "causing hatred and
discord among the men."

Sasha's fall from the good graces of The Program began late one evening
in July. She and a couple of friends had been chatting over a bottle of wine in
the deserted Galley when Franz passed through, perhaps to fetch toast or bug
juice, and approached their table.

"I don't want to be a dick about it," he said, "but you can't drink wine in
the Galley."

"I thought that was just in the summer," Sasha said.

Franz said that wine wasn't allowed in the Galley, even in the winter.

Later Sasha apologized to Franz: "I'm sorry we put you in a tough position."

Franz, who didn't drink at all, nodded and said, "I'm disappointed in you."

Irritated by his moral bent, Sasha wrote to NSF asking about the policy, which had been initiated nine months earlier in the summer with this email:

> To: McMurdo -- All
> Subject: Alcohol in Dining Facility
>
> McMurdo Community,
>   The consumption of alcoholic beverages in the Dining Facility is not allowed, unless prior approval has been granted by the NSF Station Manager.

Generally, only the bars and the dorm lounges were good for drinking, because the Galley, with its fluorescent lighting and food court ambience, was an ugly place for a bender. Prohibited from something they seldom did anyway, much as if they had been forbidden to wear their shirts inside out, enough people nevertheless complained about the directive that an addendum came, explaining that the policy was "established over the concern that there may not be adequate seating in the dining area if people lingered at tables after their meals." Now that the policy had been justified as for the good of the community, the barks of protest subsided.

Then in July, in the dead heart of winter, with the station population just over 200, in response to her question about why a policy to prevent overcrowding was enforced in the winter, Sasha received from NSF an email stating that the alcohol policy in the Galley "...was developed by the USAP Executive Management Board, which is made up of the Senior Representatives from each of the primary agencies (NSF, SPAWAR, 109th, CODF, RPSC)." The alcohol policy would have to be introduced "for reconsideration at the EMB meeting coming up in September. Any change to the current policy would have to be sanctioned by the EMB." The policy initially willed by one local NSF manager and later rationalized as ensuring seating in the crowded summer had calcified over the course of the year into barnacled heritage through the inactivity of a hibernating executive committee including government agencies, two offices of the military, and a corporation, all suddenly helpless to exercise power but for a small annual window period.[5]

On August 1 Sasha was also told to move from her room immediately, without the prior warning promised by the Housing Coordinator in June. Sasha had done six seasons, including winters, and she was fed up. She wrote a sarcastic email to Franz and Ellie asking if there were any other upcoming Sundays that she should plan on working. The next day Sasha was summoned into HR and written up for misconduct. The Counseling Notice said that Sasha's email had been "offensive and inappropriate."

Sasha wrote to Debbie in Denver asking for one extra week to move. Debbie replied that she wished she could grant additional time, but could not. Sasha wrote back, "I'm sorry you're not able or willing to compromise. I guess we're back to our starting point."

Sasha was brought into HR and written up again. The Counseling Notice said, "Sasha was asked to refrain from making any more communication of an unprofessional nature."

During this time, Sasha's supervisor, who had signed her disciplinary notices, called the doctor to find out why Sasha had recently visited Medical. The doctor warned Sasha's supervisor that her request could not be fulfilled lawfully.

On the day of room inspections, Sasha's room was the first to be inspected, at 8 a.m., by Ellie, the Housing Coordinator, who was known as one of the nicest people you'd ever want to meet. Sasha had cleaned her room well, and she passed inspection promptly. However, she had forgotten her wallet in one of the drawers, and Ellie put it in the skua pile in the hall. Ellie called Sasha at work, urging her to retrieve the wallet before someone took it.[6]

During room inspections that day, three people were issued fines of $350 each on first inspection, despite the "three chances" that had been discussed at the All-Hands Meeting. A woman who had been in The Program for ten years was threatened with a bonus cut for leaving some shirts hanging in a wardrobe.

Ellie called the Paint Shop supervisor at 4 p.m. and told him that one of his staff, Ed, did not pass first room inspection and must go to his room immediately to finish cleaning it. Thus far we had been adamantly instructed that all room preparation was to be done outside of work time. The supervisor agreed to send Ed home to clean his room better. Ellie said to hold the line, then passed the phone to the HR Guy. The HR Guy told him to write up Ed for missing work.[7]

About this time, three TV stations and the radio feed went dead because of a problem out at Black Island. Apparently one of the vents was blocked with snow and some of the equipment was freezing. A party departed a few days later to fix it, and one of their vehicles caught fire a few miles out.

By mid-August we had light for about two hours a day, though the sun hadn't come over the horizon. Jane and I drove up to T-site with the loaders to change the cardboard and wood dumpsters. To the south, the sky was dark gray, and so was the ice shelf. The moon was huge, low, gold and streaked with black. To the north the sky was light with colors that predicted nacreous clouds. It takes about 20 minutes to drive from town to T-site in a loader, and at the top of the hill I noticed the view for the first time. All winter there had been no point in looking away from the station, because there was only darkness. The station had become everything. Even with the new light, the colorful moon and the mountains had almost not registered.

With Winfly imminent, one evening we had an Award Ceremony in the Galley. We received medals that read "Courage, Sacrifice, Devotion" and certificates that read, "In recognition of valuable contributions to exploration and scientific achievement under the U.S. Antarctica Research Program." At the bottom of the certificate was an official seal with a mighty eagle standing on a crest that depicted a test tube and a microscope before an ancient flaming lamp on an Egyptian pyramid. This was the old logo for the National Science Foundation, a relic of enticing Freemasonry, before democracy and public funding corrupted the elite society of science and the logo became a globe ensnared by a mob of generic human figures.

Franz brought out awards of recognition for some of the Galley staff for their hard work. A few weeks earlier the Galley staff had been unable to attend the traditional All-Station winter photo because it had been scheduled during lunchtime, so that other departments wouldn't miss a minute of work. Now, as Franz dispensed their awards, made from a template and printed in bright primary colors on the office printer, we applauded.

Just before the first Winfly flight, we had a final All-Hands Meeting. The NSF Rep read us a handful of dates and temperatures associated with Winfly, then reminded us not to get too territorial toward the Winfly people, as everyone had by now become protective of their favorite lunch tables and coat hooks. The doctor stood up and reminded us that Winfly marks the beginning of "the crud," a stew of freshly imported germs that would easily plow through our lazy immune systems.

Franz stood up and said niceties and then opened the floor for questions. I raised my hand and Franz called on me.

"Will our bonuses be affected if we ask questions at these meetings?" I asked. The Galley burst into laughter.

"Not if that's your only question," Franz said through the laughter.

"What other questions would affect my bonus?"

"I think it's on the I-Drive," he joked, and addressed the HR Guy at a table in front. "HR Guy—Disciplinary questions?" Now there was no laughter. "Did you have anything in particular?" he asked.

"I don't want to get in trouble for asking questions."

"Throw it out there," he said.

"At one All-Hands Meeting we were told that we had three chances to clean our rooms..."

"Yep."

"I heard a rumor that there's up to three people who've been charged money and they haven't had those three chances. I want to know if that rumor's true."

"If that's the case," Franz said, "it's an HR issue which is confidential and none of any of our business."

Franz covered the frosty ripple of murmurs by restating himself and someone mumbled "When are you gonna run for office?"

A woman got angry and stood up and asked Franz why we should be held accountable for violating publicly stated policies that were inaccurate and unreliable.

Franz listened to her politely, then said that whether it was one or two or a hundred people, it didn't matter, and that it was a confidential HR issue.[8] Any more questions?

Silence.

I began clapping and a weak applause started and died quickly.

"Thank you," said Franz, "that's very sincere."

Franz drew names out of a hat and gave us prizes of t-shirts and hats and other old stock that wouldn't sell at the store.

CHAPTER 10
NOTES

[1] During Byrd's first expedition, the baker quit baking bread for a week to protest some of the crew's loud parties.

[2] "Talkers" are most obvious at the computers or in the Galley. "Potatoes," they say, as they scoop up potatoes. "One new message," they say as they check their email. "Glass," they say as they put a glass bottle in the glass bin at the recycling area.

[3] The Safety Department had once sent an email to all supervisors with the subject heading "Important Directive from Raytheon." The "important directive" was that future safety reports should be submitted in "10 pt Times New Roman Font."

[4] "Sandcrab," says Behrendt, is slang for "civilian."

[5] On October 26, 2000, in the afternoon, the Foreign Names Committee, with full endorsement of the Advisory Committee on Antarctic Names, officially declared, with electrifying decisiveness, that the ocean surrounding Antarctica might be addressed, for U.S. Government purposes, as the "Southern Ocean," as it has been illegitimately named for decades. The gravity of the landmark resolution was not lost on the reeling Committee, who wrote in their masterfully titled "Foreign Names Committee Report" that "The Committee's most significant decision during the reporting period [April–October 1999] was the adoption of the term Southern Ocean as a standard name for the body of water surrounding the continent of Antarctica." It took this network of responsive agencies just under one year to embrace the dream and, with it, to forge a new reality.

[6] In 1971 social psychologists at Stanford University put an ad in the paper for volunteers to join in a study of prison life for a wage of $15 per diem. Of those who responded, two dozen participants were selected on the basis of their "normal, average, and healthy" responses during the psychological screenings. The participants were randomly divided into "guards" and "prisoners." The psychologists told the guards only to "maintain law and order," not to hit the prisoners with their billy clubs, and that if any prisoner escaped from the "prison" (the basement of the Stanford University psychology department—with offices converted into prison cells) then the experiment would be terminated. Other than that they were left to their own devices. The guards decided that the prisoners should refer to the guards as "Mr.

Correctional Officer," while the prisoners were referred to by their numbers. On the second day, some of the prisoners ripped the numbers off their smocks and made fun of the guards. "The prisoners were punished in a variety of ways. They were stripped naked, put in solitary confinement for hours on end, deprived of meals and blankets or pillows, and forced to do push-ups, jumping jacks, and meaningless activities." The guards also created a "privilege cell" where obedient prisoners were rewarded with better food and a good bed, which created "suspicion and distrust among the prisoners." One of the experimenters wrote that "the group pressures from other guards had a significant impact on being a 'team player,' on conforming to or at least not challenging what seemed to be the emergent norm of dehumanizing the prisoners in various ways." Before two full days had passed one of the prisoners was released by the psychologists for pathological reactions to stress. "[W]e worried that there had been a flaw in our screening process that had allowed a 'damaged' person somehow to slip through undetected," wrote another of the experimenters in "The SPE and the Analysis of Institutions." "If we can attribute deviance, failure, and breakdowns to the individual flaws of others, then we are absolved." The guards woke the prisoners in the middle of the night, and tried to abuse the prisoners when they thought the psychologists weren't watching, though the psychologists had secretly set up cameras. Another prisoner broke out in a full body rash and was released from the experiment. Though the study was meant to last two weeks, it ended after six days because the participants "were behaving pathologically as powerless prisoners or as sadistic, all-powerful guards." The experiment was approved by the university's Human Subjects Review Board on the condition that fire extinguishers be available, since access to the basement was limited. "Ironically, the guards later used these extinguishers as weapons to subdue the prisoners with their forceful blasts."

[7] "At first, any suggestion of a comparison between people in the Antarctic who were in the mould of heroes with prisoners might seem to be either objectionable or fanciful. But both groups were in such geographical isolation and insulation from the outside world as to suggest that in some ways their behaviour might be similar... The prison analogy was to recur at different points in my research, and for me it now no longer remains an enigma. Essentially, adversity can be made tolerable when the boundaries of oppression are identified." – A.J.W. Taylor, "Antarctic Psychology." In a 1981 New Zealand study of the effects of Antarctic isolation on hypnotizability and pain tolerance, Paparua prison was used to simulate cramped Antarctic conditions for preliminary experiments with equipment before going into the field. (The results of this study showed that the sensory deprivation of Antarctic isolation increases hypnotizability. The Antarctic environment enhances the power of suggestion.)

[8] When I asked their manager about the "secret" fines, he wrote: "I knew exactly what the fines were for (as did the [fingee employees]), but I just disagreed with them. Essentially they couldn't be Housing fines because all the people passed their room inspections within 24 hours of the first inspection. So, [Franz and the HR Guy] said they were for non-compliance—not following instructions, namely not having their room "ready for inspection." [The HR Guy] insisted that they should get a written reprimand for failure to follow instructions and that one reprimand meant that they lost all their bonus. Management was being kind by only

fining them $350 rather than taking all their bonuses. I disagreed with the written reprimand and also asked where it said that one meant a lost bonus. I never saw that in my Terms of Agreement, did you? At that point it just became a pissing contest to see who had the power, and they had the power."

CHAPTER ELEVEN

FAITH IN SCIENCE

We must balance respect for life with the promise of science.

— George W. Bush

Ah! hurry, do hurry; out there, beyond the night, those future, those eternal rewards … shall we escape them?

— Arthur Rimbaud, *A Season in Hell*

T HE FIRST WINFLY PLANE arrived at the end of August, signaling the final stretch of winter, with six weeks to go before Mainbody. Winter-overs received brown lunch sacks full of fresh fruit and vegetables. The Galley was loud with new people. Those who came in on the plane were clean-cut, tanned, and wearing fresh Carhartts. Fingees with tucked-in shirts all huddled together, looking around in bewilderment. They had just recently been through Orientation, where they had heard about sexual harassment and diversity. Winter-overs got testy when the Winfly people helped themselves to the fresh fruit in the food line.

The day before the plane came in, I was busy banding a Food Waste triwall in the Waste Barn when Bighand came in.

"Hey Bighand."

"I need a bag," he said.

I showed him the roll of plastic triwall bags. "Like this?" I asked.

"No! Not that kind of bag! A bag! A bag I can put all my shit in! My boots and all my shit!"

Bighand had a temper because he was being sent out on the plane. I took him outside to the skua boxes we'd recently collected from the dorms, and we looked through them for luggage. While I continued searching, he walked to his idling truck and spoke to someone in the passenger seat.

"Tracker! Shut the fuck up!" Bighand listened for a moment. "Tracker! Close your fucking mouth!"

Bighand came back over. I showed him a battered cloth suitcase. "How about this?"

"Fuck. Well, I guess it'll have to do." Those were his last words to me. He threw the suitcase in the back of the truck and drove away.

The first plane took Bighand away and brought mail. Ivan had ordered French sailor shirts. I ignored six months of receipts and bank statements; they reminded me that soon I would be keeping money in my pockets, and using telephone books, and standing in lines and seeing ads for credit cards.

While I had been here all year, Raytheon had sent to my P.O. box monthly issues of the company magazine, *Taking Care: Health Information You Can Count On*. One article, "Kindness Is Its Own Reward," said that "being kind is contagious." It suggested, "Tape coins to a pay phone with a note saying that anyone who needs it can use the money," and said that "These random acts may lead to a new way of living—one that is positive and full of compassion."[1] An article called "How Do You Deal With Anger?" said, "You may feel trapped with people and things that make you feel angry," and suggested, "Try slow, yoga-like exercises to relax muscles and ease tension."

There were articles about how to detect and treat poison ivy and how to avoid getting Lyme Disease from ticks in the woods, recipes for cooking with fresh tomatoes, and an article called "Garden Therapy: Cultivate Your Mind" about the healing power of plants: "When you see a seed turn into a plant or flower, it's nature's magic."

The garden therapy article had been included in the magazine's April issue, which had been published about the same time the Greenhouse Attendant had left on the medevac flight and Cuff from Haz Waste had volunteered to keep the Greenhouse up and running. He worked three or four extra hours a day, before and after his other job, and his long hours had assured the community a small but welcome supply of fresh vegetables through winter.

Greenhouse Attendant is a full-time position, and Cuff's supervisor put in the paperwork for Cuff to receive the wages of the Greenhouse attendant for those hours he spent in the Greenhouse. His bosses approved this, but the HR rep, who worked near brewpubs with salad bars in Denver, did not approve, and said that Cuff should be paid seven dollars an hour. She told Cuff it would not be fair to pay him more than those who worked part-time to help Housing, which was short-staffed because some janitors had quit just before winter started, finding it not worth the pay to stick around. Cuff kept the Greenhouse running, because if he had decided not to do it, there would have been no salads for the latter part of the winter. Some in town might have blamed him, as if he had just walked in and turned off the garden.

Sasha believed that the documentation of her meetings with the HR Guy and Franz omitted some of their discussions, so she tried to bring a coworker to one of the meetings. "This is not a courtroom," the HR Guy said, and told him to leave. She asked to have all their meetings put in writing and entered into her file. The HR Guy said that doing so would only be worse for her. She insisted. She printed out the complete digest of emails that had so far been exchanged and asked the HR Guy to include them in her file. He did so, but Sasha was called to HR every couple of days to discuss the consequences of her latest email outside the chain-of-command, or her latest email to Housing to ask again what—because no one on the ice seemed to know—the new policy was, and he didn't always document these meetings. Sasha said that if these meetings were official proceedings, then she had a right to have them documented.

"You have no rights down here," he told her.

Over 80 years before a DA erected barriers against the eating of toast, before a supervisor cleared a room to shower behind a closed door, before a manager confiscated a shower curtain, Mackintosh, the leader of the *Aurora* expedition, realized one day with horror that one of his party, Dick Richards, had so far been plodding alongside him through blinding blizzards without signing the customary agreement with Shackleton that limited the publication of their personal experiences. In *Shackleton's Forgotten Argonauts*, Lennard Bickel wrote that, as they camped at a grim and vacant latitude, their flesh made brittle by cruel squalls on their trackless slog through a frigid desert, "There and then Mackintosh pored over a sheet of paper, writing in pencil the form of contract as he recalled it. When it was done he called Richards to his tent to sign the document."

"You might need this," the HR Guy told Sasha as he handed her a brochure on travel insurance. He had called her in from work. She had cut short a briefing for new employees, donned her parka and hat, and walked down the road to 155 and into the warm HR Office to be given a brochure she would throw away.

"Is that it?" she asked, confused.

He laughed.

On Monday the grapevine confirmed that Sasha was going to be fired. It was solid, because someone saw her name on the flight manifest. She just hadn't been told officially, and no one knew yet what the cause of the termination would be. Her sarcastic emails, her persistent questions, and her impertinence had stirred hostile sentiments, and it had been inevitable that she would breach some arcane protocol that could rationalize her dismissal. Eventually she would make a mistake.

On the common drive on the network, Sasha had found a publicly available "Supervisor Progress Form," which she printed and retitled "Station Manager Progress Form." She left the rest of the form the same, including the official company logo at the top. She made copies and passed them out in the Galley on Sunday.

"Is this one of those funny papers I heard about?" asked one of the managers who had just flown in.

"No, it's a Station Manager Progress Form," she said, and handed one to him, while Franz stood fuming nearby.

Sasha was really asking for it.

She was called into the HR Office on Monday to sit before Franz, the HR Guy, and her supervisor.

That morning Franz was overheard in the HR Office saying, "I'm going to try not to enjoy this too much."

> Franz: We're here to talk about the Station Manager Progress Form. The final resolution of it is in this letter—let me read it: "[Sasha], effective immediately your employment with RPSC has been terminated. On Sunday the 26th of August you were observed distributing a Station Manager Progress Form. When you were questioned about where you found the document you admitted to creating the document using company letterhead. The creation and distribution of unofficial company documents is strictly forbidden. Termination of employment per the RPSC Terms of Agreement, Section 18, include loss of your bonus and no travel fund. You will

be given a ticket to return to your airport of departure on the first available flight. Due to your actions as stated above you are also no longer eligible for rehire."

HR Guy: Here is your redeployment information. Your room inspection checklist needs to be done. [Ellie] will probably take a look at inspecting your room tomorrow morning after Bag Drag. [The HR Guy handed Sasha some paperwork stating that if an employee is fired, they are not eligible to continue paying company insurance rates.]

Sasha: Okay.

HR Guy: Tonight you need to start packing and get ready for Bag Drag. Housing will do your inspection after you Bag Drag at 8:30. You need to work on getting the rest of your checkout list signed off on.

Sasha: And this is because I used the letterhead?

HR Guy: You cannot create official documents. It is a big no-no.

Sasha: [HR Guy], you've done it. You've asked supervisors to switch from the [pre-season] eval to the post-season eval with the click and paste thing. I couldn't get the logo off. And the logo was created by employees through a contest.

HR Guy: No. You cannot do stuff like that. It's pretty cut and dry. I'm allowed to do stuff like that. I have to get it approved. I don't just get to start creating documents and sending them out. I have to run everything by my bosses, they have to approve it with their bosses, and so on and so on.

Sasha: [Morale is really low and it] was something done to keep people from talking about Franz. So they could vent, and slide it under your door.

HR Guy: [That's my job, not yours.]

Sasha: But nothing was happening. Nothing was being done.

HR Guy: I'm sorry you feel that way. It's unfortunate the course of action you decided to take was one that was pretty unexcusable.

Sasha: A lot of people said that they felt [the form] would be all positive... Everyone was searching on the common drive. There is nothing to give feedback.

HR Guy: There's a Supervisor Progress Report Form out there. If someone truly felt they needed to express a concern—I mean, you guys shoot emails all the time to each other.

Sasha: But that's all I found—"Supervisor"—there was nothing for the station manager. That's all I did was change one word.

Franz: Well, technically, I'm not the station manager. [The NSF Rep is the] station manager. My title is "area manager," so the people we're hired by had a problem with... a form [criticizing] the client.

... Regardless of what it was, you can't forge forms. It's just not your place.

Sasha: Can I see that in writing? A law, or something in the employee handbook?

Franz: [laughs] It's pretty cut and dry.

Sasha: Can I see it though? I've never seen that.

HR Guy: There's nothing down here on the ice. You just don't forge documents.

Franz: It's on the list of 50 [fireable offenses]. It's in my office. I'm sure I can—

Sasha: Can I see that?

Franz: I can go off and get it if you want me to—

HR Guy: It's done. You're going home.

Sasha: And this all started because I asked questions about Housing and because I was sarcastic—

HR Guy: It has nothing to do with Housing.

Sasha: It does. This is it. This is all vengeance.

HR Guy: I'm sorry you feel that way. Y'know, there's, y'know, definitely, what you did was wrong.

Sasha: And who can I tell [all this to]?

HR Guy: You're going home tomorrow, so: nobody. You can talk with people once you get back to Denver if you feel you need to. And that would be Jim Scott. He's the station manager, and he's already approved it.

Franz: He's aware of what we're doing right now.

Sasha: And he's gotten the full story of how this all started?

HR Guy: Oh yeah.

Sasha: He's seen everything?

HR Guy: [Sasha's department boss, who was angry that Sasha was being fired] came in and talked to us this morning.

Sasha: But he hasn't talked to Jim Scott yet.

HR Guy: Yes he has. [We all] had a conversation this morning.

Sasha: And there's nothing I can do. This is it. I'm gone.

HR Guy: Mm-hmm.

Franz: [inaudible]

Sasha: It started out with you going off that you had a personal issue with me. You had me written up for asking questions, for trying to hold Housing accountable, and I still haven't gotten an answer to that. There was a mistake made. And instead, I'm paying for it. I was compliant with all the rules that you guys set. I was out by the time when you said. I've got stuff, [HR Guy], that says that you didn't clean up your room right. Did you get fined?

HR Guy: Franz's the one who inspected my room.

Franz: No, there was no issues at all with [HR Guy's room].

HR Guy: Y'know, and we're not here—it's already done—

Sasha: I know.

HR Guy: So let's focus on getting your stuff packed and getting ready for tomorrow—

Franz: —the checklist.

Sasha: It's not right. I'm trying to hold Housing accountable and this is what it's come to. And that is what started it. It actually started with you [Franz] getting mad at me for [not standing behind you at that meeting.]

Franz: I can't think of what that would be—

Sasha: The one where you said, "Why don't you ream me a bigger asshole." That one.

Franz: Nothing ever came of that.

Sasha: I guess. Then you started after me with a vengeance.

Franz: I don't think that's correct. But regardless, we're here because you were documenting things that have happened up until now, and this is the end of the road.

Sasha: So this is supposed to be my third warning, is that—

Franz: You are fired, Sasha. You can't forge a company document.

Sasha: So it has nothing to do with the other warnings?

Franz: No.

Sasha: I thought you had to give three warnings.

Franz: [inaudible] I thought we were friends. At the beginning of the season I felt that.

Sasha: I did too until you started—yeah—

[Long silence]

HR Guy: I guess that's it.

Franz: Okay!

HR Guy: Thank you.

Sasha, leaving on the next day's flight, had one evening to pack up her stuff. Her friends visited her while she packed, and took pictures of her flaunting her termination letter. Jane put one of these photos on the common drive, but someone across the network deleted it. People promised to mail packages for Sasha and take care of anything she couldn't finish in time.

At the Movement Control Center the next day, Injun Joe and the Fire Chief were ready to board the plane too. I went to Injun Joe and we shook hands. He had hooted and hollered and made noise one too many times. His department manager knew that Joe was noisy when he got drunk, but said that he "worked outdoors every day through the Antarctic winter erecting steel, never a complaint. I watched him many a time sitting up high in the air on a beam in below zero (F) weather bolting joints together." Joe had cussed out the HR Guy at a party in 155. The HR Guy wrote it up as "verbal abuse" and fired him. Joe had managed to get booted from every binge in town, and now he was being kicked out for real. I became embarrassed after a few awkward pleasantries and left him to sit alone.

I shook the Fire Chief's hand, and he said "It's all for the good," but I didn't know what he was talking about and said so. He repeated, and seemed desperate to hear, that it was all for the good. "Maybe it is," I said. I would have preferred to talk again about boobytrapped meth labs, but those days were over; he was out on the plane.

Sasha flew out on the same plane, with the rolled truck on one side of her and two guys from an "Asbestos Abatement Team" on the other. They had come down on the first Winfly flight to assess the asbestos situation. They said they were a little confused about their mission, because there currently was no asbestos situation. The exposure had already occurred, so there wasn't much for the experts to do. They made a brief official appearance, took some samples, and flew back.

Along with the police escort, a sympathetic friend in Christchurch greeted Sasha at the airport. She had worked in The Program even longer than Sasha. She had once been told to furnish a pap smear in order to PQ (Physically Qualify) for her job and explained that she had had a hysterectomy. But a pap smear was a requirement on the PQ checklist, and Denver Medical returned her paperwork as incomplete. She explained that her uterus had been removed from her body, so that it was not possible to take a sample of it. But a pap smear was a requirement on the PQ checklist, and Denver Medical said she needed to meet the physical requirements, just like everyone else. Finally, her doctor became fed up and called Denver. "You tell me what to scrape and I'll scrape it," he said, as if she were waiting in the stirrups. A heavy silence came over Denver Medical, and the checklist finally became complete. She hadn't heard the details of Sasha's situation, but she met her bearing flowers.

Over a year earlier, in a "Welcome to Raytheon Memo," Tom Yelvington had introduced an RPSC "logo award contest" as "an effort to give everyone the opportunity to feel a sense of ownership in the company..." Now, for using the logo, The Program had arranged for Sasha a police escort.

In mid-August, while working in the Greenhouse, Cuff found a bag of vermiculite distributed by W.R. Grace. Vermiculite is a grainy, absorbent mineral that, in McMurdo, is used primarily for packing lab chemicals. W.R. Grace ran a mine in Montana that produced vermiculite contaminated with tremolite asbestos that had killed hundreds of workers. Solid Waste handled vermiculite as one of our waste categories, so Thom did some research and learned from the EPA website that "the bulk of the vermiculite with the highest percentages of asbestos contamination came from vermiculite used for packaging chemicals for shipment," which was the source of much of the vermiculite at McMurdo. So the vermiculite was likely contaminated, but we were uncertain to what extent. Both Thom and I had shoveled the stuff from the floor before in a cloud of dust, but we weren't really too worried, as our exposure was infrequent and brief. However, we agreed that it would be better for Solid Waste workers in the future to know that vermiculite may contain asbestos, rather than think it a benign substance, as we had.

Thom researched and wrote a report on the asbestos contamination of McMurdo's vermiculite, then sent it to Denver and to the Safety Girl. Soon the Safety Girl called him at work to say that she was checking his sources.

"But here you listed one of your sources as 'ibid.,'" she said. "Is that a website?"

He explained that it was referencing the previous source.

"So it is a website?" she verified.

"In this case, yes," he said, "but it means 'same as the last source.'"

"So you're being tricky," she asked.

"Yeah, I'm being tricky," he said.

The Safety Guy, from the Driver's Safety Course last summer, came in on one of the Winfly flights. He came up to the Barn one day to speak with Thom about his report. Safety Guy said he strongly believed in science, and that even though vermiculite contains asbestos, there was not enough scientific evidence that the vermiculite posed a hazard. Besides, employees were always allowed to request PPE, or Personal Protective Equipment, if they felt at risk.

Thom agreed that there were not enough studies to determine exactly how hazardous the vermiculite was, but that yesterday we did not even know the vermiculite contained asbestos, while today we did. Therefore, Solid Waste workers in the future should know it too. If workers don't know there's asbestos in the vermiculite, then they won't even know to ask for PPE.

Safety Guy agreed that low levels of asbestos could be potentially dangerous, but he also said that there was nothing in the EPA investigation to indicate that worker exposure to vermiculite in current circumstances was above the OSHA Personal Exposure Limits. He said that if you tell people that something has asbestos in it, you also have to tell them to wear complete respiratory protection, and that complete respiratory protection poses a danger to the worker because it has, in some cases, caused heart attacks. The final outcome of the meeting was that, in order to prevent heart attacks, future workers would not be told that vermiculite contains asbestos.

Thom had "voiced his concern," as it is said, along the proper chain of command, and had reached the end of the road. Any further scrutiny of the matter would endanger his bonus or his ability to return to the ice. He shrugged. The meeting ended amiably; the Safety Guy departed.

At one pre-season Denver Orientation, a Senior Safety Guy told everyone it was our responsibility to make sure that workplaces were kept safe.

"We need to instigate action to make things happen," he said.

An employee raised his hand and said that the little bit of water remaining in the old pipes of some buildings all winter is not flushed out well at the beginning of summer, meaning that the danger of lead poisoning from the pipes may be greater at the beginning of the summer than later in the summer, when the water sampling team tests the water.

The Senior Safety Guy became angry. "That's why you need to tell someone about it," he said to the employee who had told him about it. "You need to take charge, people!"

The employee shrugged.

While the Safety Girl was struggling to interpret the footnotes in the vermiculite report, Saul and Don in Denver had been writing us emails about our Safety record. Our numbers were too high. Jane had slipped on the ice while we were working outside at the beginning of the winter and had reported a slight sprain. To combat Antarctic hazards, Saul implemented a new Safety Observation Form and suggested that we meet in the mornings for a "Tool Box" talk to discuss "incident" prevention. Don wrote that he had slid into third base and scraped up his knee during the company softball game last Sunday, and that his injury could have been avoided with ten seconds of forethought. He suggested that we take at least 30 seconds, ten times a day, to think about our safety, because "each of you are the first line of defense in your own safety." An incoming Winfly employee told me that this season's

Orientation in Denver had a new segment, which warned that inquiring whether your worksite contains asbestos is "your responsibility."

One day, picking up a box of vermiculite from the Science Cargo building, I noticed, stenciled at the main entrance, the slogan "Faith in Science."

[an email received by the Rec Department, printed as-is]

BINGOTRAVEL PRIZES***WED AUG 15TH***
LAST GAME OF THE WINTER!!

When I saw the sign in the Galley, I said to myself..I have got to go because recreation had saved the BEST for last...The travel prizes!!!

Does this background and lettering tell you how I feel when I went and spent 7 dollars and my free time that night? I am still livid and angry at the prizes that were selected for the last bingo game of the winter. The prizes were CHEAP and PATHETIC that I was just exasperated the whole evening. I played along but I didn't want to win any of the games because of those stupid prizes!

Let me remind you of the prizes that were represented as travel prizes. First game the prize was a black plastic water bottle! Cripes, what the hell would I want one of those when I get a water bottle from CDC. I don't think I need a water bottle on my travels when I am going to be spoiling myself to restuarants/cafes!! Second, is shot glasses...how does that apply to travel...geez, I swear, there was no hope for the best that recreation would outdo themselves by now. Third, a frickin trekkie book. I do not and will not be treking anywhere. Why didn't you just post "Bingo for Trekkies" and then I would have stayed in my room. Fourth was a gift certificate to "Bailies". Why couldn't there be an effort made at Annies Wine and Cafe but no, somebody was too damn lazy. Fifth was a stupid fanny pack that I would flatly not own and Last was a jackpot of 150 dollars... wow! There was no grand prize for a trip for 2 to Hanmer Springs or a Winery tour. Urrgghh!! Cheap, Cheap, Cheap!! I mean it and say it again, I did not want to win and I did tell myself and to the person I was with is that if I did win I will not holler out bingo!!

What happened to the money? In the past, lots of money has been brought into recreation and we had some really nice bingo prizes..

I hope that next winter, somebody better pay attention to the community because not only your department but also the TV/Radio are high profile on how the mood of the winter goes!

Just another upset OAE winter-over who keeps telling herself that this is a FINGI winter![2]

The Winfly flights socially invigorated the winter-overs. One night Ivan donned a baggy rainbow clown shirt and a wig, slapped on some makeup, and walked into Gallagher's to co-host Wednesday night bingo at the invitation of Bingo the Clown, who had amateur clown credentials stateside.

Unlike cheery Bingo with her fastidious clown markings, Boozy was a terrible sight. His makeup looked stale, and his eyes glinted with malice. Before the games began, while people were settling in with drinks, buying game cards, and selecting their favorite colors of bingo daubers, Boozy made the rounds from table to table, ripping up people's raffle tickets, taking gulps of their drinks, and throwing their daubers on the floor. This was a new and exciting feistiness for the crowd at bingo night, who took it in with good-natured laughter. The aptly named Boozy had downed about a liter of vodka and tonic before arriving at the bar.

Boozy's job was to pull the little numbered balls out of the agitator and read them to the enthusiastic gamblers. People bought shots of tequila for Boozy as he slurred out the numbers. Someone yelled out, "Did you say O53 or O63?" Boozy replied, "Both!"—which was simply not the case, and one could on these occasions sense the crowd's good humor becoming brittle.

For some, bingo is as serious as a heart attack. You can shovel asbestos into them, change their contracts midstream, wheedle them with technicalities, and prohibit their commentary, but if you fuck with their chances of winning a penguin sweatshirt or a bottle of root-beer schnapps, then you have made a lifelong enemy. Boozy didn't care. He taunted the crowd and venomously attacked hecklers. He embarrassed the meek ones who barely squeaked out their bingos, and he ridiculed those who bellowed their bingos in excitement. When a winner brought his booklet of bingo cards to Boozy for verification, Boozy said that the gentleman was indeed a winner, but reminded all winners in the audience just to bring up their winning card and not their whole goddamn booklet, as he crumpled the aghast winner's booklet and tossed it on the floor before reaching for the bottle of vodka hidden inside a cloth penguin puppet.

Eventually all the prizes were awarded, and bingo night came to a close. When I went to bed at midnight, Boozy was still absent. At 3:30 I awoke to find Ben sitting at the foot of my bed hissing: "Nick! Nick! We're going to bring a frozen pig in here and put it in Boozy's bed! I just wanted to let you know." That was agreeable to me. I drifted in and out of sleep to the sounds of frequent but careful door openings, conspiratorial whispering, the click of a camera, muffled giggles and, finally, a loud outbreak of laughter that fled through a slammed door, followed by the clown's vengeful grunts.

The next day I saw the photos and learned what had happened.

There had been a plot against Boozy since the early evening. The drinks at the bar were followed by a bottle of rum in the upstairs lounge of 155. To get Boozy in his best mood and lower his defenses, a female operative made out with Boozy in the corner while her boyfriend looked on, understanding the sacrifices one must make for glory. Later, Boozy spent some time bent out the window, suspiciously trying to rid his mouth of spit, and some feared Boozy would spend the night on tile instead of sheets. The entire caper hinged on Boozy returning to bed, but they had underestimated his endurance. Deducing that boisterous company infused Boozy with life, as lightning did Frankenstein's monster, they told him they were going to go sit in the Galley— a wretched place to drink—and it appeared their trick worked. Boozy went off to his room, and the cabalists spent 45 minutes or so in the Galley waiting for him to go to sleep.

When they returned upstairs, they saw Boozy on his hands and knees crawling backwards from Jeannie's room, pulling a frozen pizza on a plate across the floor. Jeannie had a toaster oven, and had invited us to use it any time of the day or night to cook the little frozen pizzas purchased from the bar. As he stood in the darkness of her room watching the glowing elements of the toaster oven thaw the frost and curl the cheese on the miniature pizza, he suddenly worried that he was being inconsiderate of Jeannie. When Ben came across Boozy inching his way quietly from her room, he noticed the still-frozen pizza had a bite missing from it.

Tough measures were called for, and the female operative accompanied Boozy to his bed. I slept, unaware of the brave clown-macking nearby. She left Boozy horizontal and happy, and he plunged into sleep.

You have come to the pristine and stark seventh continent with images of adventure involving physical endurance and rugged beauty. It is the middle of the night on a Wednesday, and you wake up to pee. You emerge from the women's room. A man in the hall runs past you with a frozen pig under his arm, pursued by a lurching, drunk clown.

The pranksters were startled by Boozy's persistence in seeking revenge. He lumbered up and down the halls for ten minutes in a poorly planned circular hunt, but Nero had escaped his perspiring clutches by stashing the pig in the sauna and hiding in the women's bathroom. Standing on a chair, Boozy was about to climb through the ceiling tiles into a room he thought harbored a suspect when he realized he was on a cold trail and returned to his warm bed. The pig was later removed from the sauna and returned to the food freezer.

In the weeks after the last Winfly flight, winter-overs began shaving their heads or their beards, or dyeing their hair, getting ready to return to the larger society as if preparing for a date. The anticipation of summer brought a new vigor to the station. The Safety Guy declared scores of tools unsafe, so people had to sneak the tools from boxes on the cargo line to do their jobs. The skua piles grew in the dorm foyers as 200 winter-overs scrubbed rooms and prepared to leave, while Debbie sent troops of frantic janitors to remove the piles in order to keep the halls orderly. While the company president encouraged us to participate in the All-Employee Opinion Survey, HR hounded us for "a good response rate" to the survey.

Riding this new burst of energy, the Safety Girl audited work centers. At the BFC, she told one of the workers that their work center looked pretty good but for one small problem. The Flamms cabinet held materials that were still packed in their cardboard packaging, which, she said, added an unnecessary fuel source for potential fires. She asked the BFC supervisor to go through the Flamms cabinet and remove things from their cardboard packaging. The BFC supervisor reminded her that there were thousands of cartons of matches in the Flamms cabinet for use at field camps, and asked if she had to remove all the individual matches from their cartons.

"No, that's okay," said the Safety Girl, "matches aren't flammable."

The absurd circus seemed to be approaching some climax. On Labor Day, when Denver took a holiday, we howled with laughter. We were in the final weeks of winter. Soon we'd be in Christchurch—fantastic Christchurch!—eating green curries, drinking black lagers, and bitching if it rained. Nothing could faze us. Then Denver cut our bonuses across the board, and the laughter died.

Once we were busy losing money, we could hardly raise a chuckle, even at the season's last All-Hands Meeting, when a carpenter whose bonus had been cut behind the scenes received a $100 award for Outstanding Achievement in public. Some who asked why their bonuses had been cut were told that if they didn't accept the changes to the supporting documents, their bonuses would be cut further.

On the last day of winter, most of the winter-overs skipped work and went to Daybar to get loaded. Tradition and the principle of safety in numbers protected all but one janitor who, like a weak gazelle at the watering hole, was fired. At the bar himself, the HR Guy had seen the janitor there and signed the paperwork for his termination.

Just a few days before he flew out, one of the FEMC supervisors was written up for an email in which he had referred to Franz and the HR Guy as "fingees," a term so established that it has been used in official government publications. He resigned on the spot.

It was announced around this time that "Rose-Colored Glasses" were available for the winter-overs. They were hung in an envelope on the Housing bulletin board.

While Jane was embroiled in a futile struggle with HR, I was waiting upstairs to complete my room inspection.

When the room inspector (a janitor temporarily outfitted with a clipboard) arrived, I was on the couch playing *Tomb Raider 3*, searching for my artifacts. We greeted each other politely, and I resumed my position on the couch while she began looking around the room. She opened the fridge.

"Are these your Cokes?"

"No, they're my roommate's," I said. "He's not leaving yet for another week."

"Well, when he leaves he'll have to clean them out of the fridge," she told me with a small laugh.

"He's leaving in a week. I'm sure they'll be gone before then."

"Well, as long as he takes them out when he leaves. Are these your decorations?" she asked, pointing to the plastic grapevines that circled the room near the ceiling.

"No, they're my roommate's. He's leaving in a week."

"Oh well, ha ha, I'm afraid I can't sign off on the sheet until they're taken down."

"Do you mind if I take them down now, so I can sign off instead of you coming back?"

"Well, okay." She smiled.

I set about removing the plastic grapevines from the wall on my side of the room, to avoid a $500 fine. As I did this she moved to the windowsill.

"This windowsill is dirty," she said.

"I specifically paid careful attention to scrubbing the windowsill," I said calmly. "I know you always check the windowsill."

"Well, okay," she said. "It must have gotten dirty again in a day!"

During a recent room inspection, the inspector had examined the windowsill and told the room's occupant that it was dirty. The occupant, thanks to the efficient McMurdo grapevine, knew of this season's windowsill fetish amongst the Housing inspectors, and came over in surprise to examine the filth in question.

It was frost.

CHAPTER 11
NOTES

[1] Along with the health magazines, I received from Raytheon brochures advertising Metlife, Raytheon's preferred insurance provider. One of the brochures featured Snoopy, Charlie Brown, and the rest of the Peanuts gang. On the front of the brochure, Woodstock was talking into a tin can, and Snoopy was listening through another tin can at the end of a string. Above this scene was the slogan, "The Word Is Out About Metpay." My first thought on examining the brochure was that it must be expensive to pay for the rights to use Peanuts characters to advertise a commercial product. Later, on January 2, 2002, a friend sent me an article from the *San Francisco Examiner* with the headline, "Insurance firm can't wait for client to die." A Raytheon engineer, exposed to toxic chemicals and radiation in the course of his job, had to have a physical examination done every six months by a medical firm specified by Raytheon. He always passed his physical exams, but when eventually he went to a different doctor, he was told that his medical records showed that his kidneys were malfunctioning and that he needed a transplant immediately. He had two separate kidney transplants, and his worker's compensation claim resulted in Metlife agreeing to pay him disability benefits until the age of 65, or until he died. Nearly ten years later, Metlife terminated his benefits without explanation. The claimant reported that the Metlife representative in charge of his case said, "We weren't expecting you to live this long." The claimant sued Metlife, living long enough to collect back payments and to be reinstated. Less than a year after the case had left the courts, Metlife again terminated his insurance, and the case again went to court, to be processed and digested by the sluggardly cilia of justice as the claimant began to run out of money for medicine. After reading the article, I dug out my Metlife brochure and examined it further. Inside, the Peanuts gang is gathered together, all of them smiling, all of them giving an encouraging thumbs-up.

[2] Old Antarctic Explorer—a self-congratulatory term for someone with a lot of Ice Time. At one point the store offered certificates that certified one as a member of the McMurdo Society of Old Antarctic Explorers. The certificates read, "The society's purpose is to work in partnership with each other to support scientific efforts on the highest, driest, coldest, windiest, and southernmost continent. Continuing the venture of the pioneer Antarctic expedition leaders who launched this endeavor and to pay honor to all those who have followed them to the bottom of the world."

APPENDICES

APPENDIX I

THE IRONWORKER AND THE RUSSIAN BRIDE

IT WAS ABOUT HALFWAY THROUGH the winter when Tracker the Ironworker first learned from a co-worker that the Internet could be useful for finding and corresponding with potential Russian brides. His co-worker had shown Tracker how to open a free email account and how to navigate the relevant chatrooms.

It was not long before Tracker found a delicious prospect named Natasha Petronovich who—except for the pictures, retrieved from some porn site, of "Natasha" lying in the grass with long blonde tousled hair, or wearing a short denim dress and climbing in a tree—was entirely fabricated by Tracker's hairy male co-worker, who devotedly corresponded with Tracker for the latter part of the winter. "Natasha" convinced Tracker to fly to Moscow after his long winter, where he arrived with two hundred condoms and several cartons of Benson and Hedges menthol cigarettes that had expired in 1996. He had bought these items in McMurdo at "Natasha's" recommendation, and hoped to sell them on the Russian black market.

What follows is the correspondence between Tracker and "Natasha Petronovich." Hundreds of misspellings have been corrected for ease of reading, though the intentionally bad English of "Natasha" has been left intact.

Tracker to Natasha:... You asked me why I'm coming to your country in October or November instead of right now, well, where should I start? No, I'm not coming there because of work reason, I'm coming to see you and your country, to have a great vacation. Who knows what might happen between the both of us, only our good lord knows, I'm sure it's good, whatever it might be, I can tell by looking at your face, you're a good person. I look forward to meeting you soon, SINCERELY I DO. The reason I can't come to your country right now is because I'm at the South Pole, Antarctica. I work for the United States government, and the National Science Foundation, researching the ever changing weather conditions in our world. It's very cold here right now, 91 below zero today...

Natasha to Tracker: So nice to read your letter. I am happy that you find my picture pleasing to look. I do not think am so beautiful but it make me feel good in my heart to hear your kind words saying I am. Thank you very much.

So you are scientist at the south of pole? That is very exciting! I do not know people live there. If I can ask, what is it you study there? Do you have the bird penguin there? I see them in movie and think they are very nice bird. Make me laugh when I see.:)

91 degrees below the zero? Brrrrrrrrrrr! (Is correct word?) Is very cold in Moscow winter but that is too cold for me. I think you very brave and strong to live in such place. Am very proud to have a friend who do this! Me? Like I said, I am just secretary. Not important like scientist. Secretary is just ok job. I do not get paid a lot of moneys but am happy for now. I share apartment with two friend with names of Beta and Tamsin. They are long time friend and we have many funs together...

In University I study accounting but also study dance. To be dancer is what I really want. We have very famous ballet here in Moscow called Bolshoi. Ever since young girl I dream one day to dance with Bolshoi Ballet. Is dream of many girls in Russia. Sadly, I was in accident when 20 and hurt my back and now will never dance with Bolshoi. Oh, my back is better and I can do most things but to do ballet dance hurt too much.

That is why I am secretary now. Am lucky I also study accounting in University or have nothing. I still love to dance and tried other job as dancer in club. They want me remove my clothes while dancing. I did one night but was too embarrass so did not do again. It was good monies but not right thing to do. So I am secretary and for this time am happy with that.:)

Oh, I could tell you more but then you know all my secret! That is no funs. I think I will be like book. Each letter like page in book. The more letter you read the more you learn of me.:)

You must tell me more of south of pole where you live. I think is very exciting!

I find other picture to have put on this letter. Hope you also like.

Tracker:... I hope you didn't get the wrong impression from my last letter, but here goes again. I am not a scientist here, I just work for the NSF National Science Foundation. The work that I am here doing is, I am a crane operator, a pipe welder, and an iron worker. I build new labs and buildings for the scientists as you can see in the picture.

In response to your profession I think you to have a very important job. All companies and businesses need secretaries too, to do many jobs for them also. So don't think your job is so bad.

By the way, I'm sorry to hear about your accident, everybody should be able to pursue and for fill there dreams. Maybe it was for a reason, good or bad, who knows. I too like to dance, but not to ballet. I like to dance to disco and southern rock. I think if you like to dance, then you should do so, no need to be embarrassed about it, you're a beautiful lady...

Let me ask some questions, for my book.

When is your birthday? What size pants and shirt do you wear? Do you have a phone I could call you at work or home? Can I mail you a letter or package? If I could send you something what would you want the most? Do you have a car? Can you read English, or if I called you on the phone would we be able to talk to each other?

What do your friends think about us writing to each other?

The end of the Questions for now. I really hope you continue to be like a book, I love to read. I wish to know the name of your book, is it Natasha or Tasha, you tell me, I'll keep reading it, because you have caught my attention. Ha Ha I wish to read all your pages, then maybe we could start a new book, who knows, it could be a perfect book between the both of us...

Natasha: I have just return to Moscow from visit to my family home in Nizhniy. Is south and east of Moscow. I was hope to spend my summer holiday on Black Sea like last year but not enough money so I go to visit my parents and Taki. It was very nice time and my good friend Tamsin accompany me. Oh, we have moneys to go to Black Sea but Tamsin and Beta and I are saving for new apartment. We are on list for two bedroom. We live now in one bedroom and is not so bad because we are such good friend. Tamsin and Beta sleep in bedroom and I have small place to sleep in main room.

Sometime in winter there is no heat and we all get in bed together for warmth. Then is real nice sometime. I like best when I am in middle and my two friends on each side to make me warm. I will act as if asleep and Beta and Tamsin will begin touching me. Is a game we play when together in bed. They touch on my arms and legs and stomach and then my breast. It make my nipples stand like tiny soldiers! I am still pretend to be asleep and they will touch my other places. Tamsin has good English and she says is called "pussy". Like pussy cat. Is that correct? They touch me there and then is very difficult to pretend sleep! It become very wet and I am so hot that I open eyes and say "What are you doing! You evil girls are being bad and not letting me sleep!" Then we all laugh because they know I not really asleep. Sometime Beta or Tamsin will kiss me on pussy and use the tongue to pleasure me. Ohhhhhhhh that is very nice I think! I very much like to be pleasure that way. Sometime I pleasure Tamsin and Beta with my tongue but is better when they do to me.:) Tamsin and Beta have boyfriend and they get very jealous when we play our bed game. I have boyfriend last winter he was sometime also jealous. Now am single so no boyfriend to be jealous and can do bed game all of time.:)

I hope you are not suprise by me telling this to you or think I am bad girl. Is just a silly bed game that we girls like to play. I have understanding that Americans are very open about sex so I am try to be like American girl for you.:)

...You ask about phone? I do have handphone but have turn off now to save moneys for apartment. Maybe in next month when move I can turn on again. Can you make call from south of pole? Is amazing to me! Is very much suprise to learn things of such place...

Oh. You ask name of Tasha book? Hmmmmmmmmmm... How about name "Tasha's Magik" Do you like this name?...

Tracker: I hope this letter finds you in good health and spirits, as for me, I'm doing much better now that I received a new page in your book. I like the name Tasha's magic for your book...

Tell me, what part of Moscow do you live in? Is there a nice hotel to stay in, or a rooming house close to you? If so please send me the phone number to it, so I can make some travel arrangements to come there soon.

I'll be leaving here the 20th of August, I hope to be there sometime in mid-September. How's that make you feel?...

Your letter this time was very surprising to me, it really didn't sound like you, compared to your last three letters. Although it was sweet to hear such things from you, and you and your friends can play in that way, that's very nice.

Let me be the first American to tell you this, American girls do not speak so freely about their sex lives. It is a very personal thing between lovers to keep their sex lives private. It is nice that you and your girlfriends can have such fun with each other, maybe you shouldn't tell their boyfriends, as for me, it's ok, I'm not the jealous type....

I hope to hear from you soon, so take care and stay safe and healthy.

P.S. I like your new photo very much. I would really like you to answer the many other questions I asked you in the other letters.

Natasha: So glad to read your letter. I am so very much sorry for not writing sooner. I have had much things to do and very busy.

I have good news to tell though. I was chosen for the new job AND my friends and I received word that we got the new apartment! All this happen last week and have been so busy with everything... The company I work for is Zenon and is very exciting. It has many things to do with the internet. Internet radio. Internet banking. Email provider. Oh just everything. You can look. www.zenon.net That is company web site.

The moving has been a great stress. So much stuffs we have! I think maybe throw it all away and begin with new. Cost too much moneys though. We borrow a car from the boyfriend of Beta and make so many trip. It is funny sometime because the car does not like to work and sometime just stop. Tamsin says is "Piece of shit!". I am not sure what it means "shit" but Tamsin says is very high curse word.

I did see about hotel for you. If first time to Russia it be best to stay at Intourist Hotel. It has much experience with foreigners and are able to speak English very well. It is very close the city centre with clubs and stores and sights. Also my new company is very close...

Here is hotel information.
Intourist Hotel
3/5 Tverskaya St.
Moscow, 125124
Russia

So do you see dear [Tracker]? I have been good secretary for you even if bad pen-pal!:)... Do you really wish to see my country? Where would you like to see? I like Black Sea best. It has many tourist but also lot of small places and town where tourist not go.

You ask so many question I not remember them all. My dress size? I usualy wear small medium. I am 168cm tall and weight 50kg. If you post me something in mail the address at my work is probably best. Mail at appartments is often stole. I will get address for you soon. Oh! Is right here in front of me!

Natasha Petronovich

Zenon

19,1,1st Yamskogo Polys St.

Moscow, 125124

Russia

I have to go. Will write you again soonest. PROMISE!:) I have another picture with this and also suprise picture. It is my good friend Tamsin. She also wishes to meet you and tells me to say hello to you. Is so exciting that you are come to my country.

Lots of love and kisses!!!!

Tasha.

Tracker: Well I see and hear you're doing fine, as for me, I couldn't be better. I was very proud to hear you got the job, I'm sure you were proud of yourself too. You have been a very busy girl, moving and things like that. Thank you for the information about the hotel, my little secretary, you did a very good job for me. Yes you have been a bad pen pal, I worry about you too much already. When I don't hear back from you for a while I think something is wrong... I wish to be a big part of your world, so don't leave me worrying about you so long. Be a better pen pal and friend, ha ha, just playing with you baby. I really can't wait until I'm there to see you in person. I anticipate an emotional meeting between the both of us, which is all right. I look forward to it. I hope I'm everything you wish for. I really love your pictures, so I know you're everything I'm wishing for. You're a beautiful lady, my heart is warmed of the thoughts of seeing you very soon. Yes, I wish to travel in your country. I hope you are going to travel with me, the Black Sea, it sounds great. I wish to do a lot of shopping for some old art, and I would also like to buy a diamond ring for myself, so if you know anybody that has a nice diamond for sale or any old paintings let them know I'm coming soon, and I wish to see them and maybe we can come to a reasonable price to buy it. Tell your girlfriend that her picture was nice and I look forward to meeting any friend of yours, Tasha, but I'm coming there to see you. Thanks for answering some of the questions I asked you, that will do for now. Let me tell you something, it was 102 degrees below 0 yesterday, I really wished you were here, I think I could have been warmed by you, I don't think so, I know so, BRRRRRRRRRRRR.

Sincerely Love from the South Pole

[Tracker]

Natasha:... To happy to read your letter. It always make me smile to see your letter awaiting me in email box.

We three girls are busy busy busy on the weekend. We have bought paints and are painting our new apartment. It will be so lovely for you to see! It was funny because we go to disco last night for dancing and some boy ask why I have blue parts in my hair. I use blue color to paints my room and have some in my hair but did not know it! It was funny I think.:)

[The 'blue hair' segment is notable in that Tracker's hairy male co-worker who invented "Natasha" had at this point in the winter tried to dye his hair blue. It worked poorly, but well enough to leave a noticeable blue tint, obvious to everyone, even to Tracker, who nonetheless made no connection when he swaggered into work and proudly read aloud the emails of the blue-haired "Natasha" to his blue-haired co-worker.]

...You ask of paintings and diamond to purchase? These things can be done in Moscow. There are many shops and stores. Is better though to buy from some person who is not in store. In Moscow we have what is called Black Market and everything can be purchased this way. Is against our law to do this but everybody does. Even policeman buy things black market. Sometime many things are not in store that you need so just go to black market person and they can find. Black market persons like American dollars and give better price when you have them. As I said, Russia moneys are not good...

Lots of love and kisses from Russia! Stay warm in cold South of Pole. I will send warm thoughts to help you.

Bye for now... Tasha.

[Tracker]
Date: Mon, 13 Aug 2001
Subject: Leaving soon.

It's me again, how are you doing? I'm doing fine. I hope that this letter makes you happier, you know why? Because I'm leaving in just four more days. My plane is coming on Monday, August 20th. Isn't that great news? I have a few more questions for you to answer ...If I could bring anything, what do you need the most of? Toothpaste or shampoo or soap or makeup, stuff like that? On the black market, can I bring some cigarettes or some jeans or pants, please let me know soon. What sells the best?

From: Tracker
Date: 16 Aug

Well I just would like to say I am getting stir crazy, I would really like to be on the plane right now, if you know what I mean. Everyday I read my e-mail, I am warmed to see your letter there, you are warming me up, up, up, up. I will bring the items you said would be the best to have on the black market for trading things, cigarettes and condoms, I have already seen the doctor here and got two hundred condoms just for you and me, how many more should I bring for the rest of your country. I have a very big smile on my face right now, I hope you do too.

From: Natasha Petronovich
Date: Fri, 17 Aug 2001
Subject: Sunshines and Flowers

So wonderful to read your email! Do you know, when you say that I am most beautiful girl in whole of world it make me so happy. It make me all warm inside and big smile outside! Such a kind thing for you to say… 200 of condoms just for us two? WOW! That is very many! I will need new bed after you visit I think for mine will be all broken!:)

Oh. I talk with Tamsin and Beta my two good friends and they wish to buy all 200 from you. They say that now condoms are two and three American dollare for just one and hope that maybe you will sell to them for less moneys. The boyfriend of Beta does much selling and buying of things and he is most interested. He says however many you bring he can sell very quickly. He also tell me that paintings like you wish can be arrange but may take time. He ask when you are to come and will begin asking. You also ask for diamond? He think this is not problem. He say is "piece of cake" but I do not know what he mean by this. English can be very confusing for me.

…Many loves and kisses and I am counting of the days until I see you! Tasha.

[Tracker]
Date: Sun, 19 Aug 2001
Subject: You won't believe this one.

I hope this letter finds you in the best of spirits and health. As for me I'm not doing too good. First of all, I made the mistake of deleting your last letter, the one where you thought your legs were too fat, forgive me for saying this, but you could stand to put on some more weight. But don't get the wrong idea, I like you just the way you are.

Well, there is a snow blizzard blowing here right now, so that means they can't bring the plane in right now, so until the weather gets better, I'm stuck here … …But it's coming one of these days soon. No I can't give you an arrival date yet, but as soon as I know I will let you know. I will try to make it for a Friday afternoon, your time, O.K.

Now for some more bad news, like you haven't already heard enough. I'm sorry I don't mean to bring you down, so here goes. I was at a going away party last night, and I broke my left hand. The doctor here says it will get better in a short time, maybe be all better when I can give you a big fat hug, hug, hug. I'm sorry to give such bad news, but it will be better soon. Please send picture soon, will cheer me up, up, up.

Sincerely yours
[Tracker]

[Tracker]
Date: Sun, 26 Aug 2001
Subject: I'm getting closer to you everyday baby.

Guess what. I have left the New Zealand country, and I'm in Australia: Sydney, to be exact. I'm going to the Russian embassy in the morning... My friend Paul is also coming for three days... Keep on smiling, I'm coming. I believe I will be staying for two lovely weeks with the most lovely woman in Russia: you, baby.

From: Natasha Petronovich
Date: Mon, 27 Aug 2001
Subject: St. Petersburg

You are in Australia now [Tracker]? I was thinking you were in the New Zealand. And you are also have friend to accompany you for coming here? Oh this will be wonderful! We can have large party when you come. His name is Paul? Is he handsome like you [Tracker]??:) This is so much good time for the two of you to come. You see, just before I left Moscow Tamsin become in very big fight with her boyfriend and is not together with him now. She wished for me to ask if you had any handsome friend for her to corresponding with. And now you are bringing friend with you! You must can see into my mind and know what I am thinking [Tracker].

I am happy to hear you are to recieve visa for trip tomorrow. I told you that my country in very friendly to foreigners and welcome all to visit. I did not think you would have problem and now I see I am correct.

... I will be home tonight and make ready the apartment for you and your good friend Paul. Beta and Tamsin will be of so much excited to learn you are bringing friend. Is he also from south of pole?

Must go now. Very many smiles and love. I pray for your safe trip [Tracker].

Very happy now from writing to you. Tasha.

[Tracker]
Date: Tue, 28 Aug 2001
Subject: So very glad to hear your voice.

Yes I did get my visa ...Yes my friend Paul is from the same place, the south pole. Yes, I'm looking forward to seeing you very soon... No, I do not think Paul is good looking, but then again I do not look at men. That will be for you and your friends to decide. I will be leaving here tomorrow, so let me say this Tasha, I really look forward to seeing you soon, and may God reach down and touch you on the head and say, future good luck will always come your way.

From: Natasha Petronovich
Date: Tue, 4 Sep 2001
Subject: So exciting!!!
Dearest [Tracker]! So happy to read your letter! Oh I can not keep sitting sometime I become so exciting from the thinking of you coming. Tamsin and Beta both laugh at me and say I am acting as silly girl. I can not help it. I have never had someones to come visit me from so far away as south of pole!

I have clean our beautiful new apartment many time and then see something is not right and clean again. I wish for all to be perfect when you stay with me... Tamsin and I both will be waiting...

Lots of love and excitings from Russia!!!! Tasha.

[Tracker]
Date: Fri, 07 Sep 2001
Subject: Delayed a day
I'm so sorry I can not be there on the day that I said. We missed plane and will be a day later. I'm sorry to put you through such a hassle, but I promise to make it up to you when I get there...If at all possible, I need for you to notify the hotel that we missed the flight... We had a driver that was to pick us up at the airport, unfortunately, he would be there at the same time you would be there. If at all possible, if you could not pick us up, let the hotel know to pick us at airport on Saturday at 1:35 PM. When me and Paul arrive on Saturday, you can come to the hotel if you can't make it to the airport to pick us up.

I'm so sorry baby, but you must take care of this for me baby, because there is nothing I can do from this end at this point in time. Reply as soon as you get done reading this to let me know if you can take care of these things for me. Looking forward to seeing your beautiful face as well as your beautiful country.

[Tracker]
Date: Sat, 08 Sep 2001
Subject: I'm here in town.
You need to call me as soon as you read this letter, or come see me.
Phone-0952370514 or 9598157 I'm in Moscow, where are you? I'm staying at the Hotel Academicheskaya, room number is 1204. Look forward to seeing you soon. You can call and leave messages at the front desk. If you don't reach me, I'll probably be in the restaurant. O.K. I got to go now baby, hope to see you soon.

From: Natasha Petronovich
Date: Sat, 8 Sep 2001
Subject: Re: I'm here in town.
Dear [Tracker],

...I wish you a good time but have to sadly inform you that Natasha will not be meeting you...

I have to thank you though for the past few months. I have really enjoyed writing to you and everybody here in McMurdo has definitely enjoyed reading your letters. You have become somewhat of a cult hero as everybody asks me each day for the latest news of your travels. There is even a fraternity house in Florida that is demanding pictures of you...

I really have to tell you that everybody here was quite impressed with the way you took all the condoms from the bathroom in 155. We really laughed about that. Also the large purchase of cigarettes that you made in the store prior to your departure...

It has been difficult to keep a straight face over the months while you talk about this girl that we invented in our shop. Oh, I suppose you should be angry with me but when you put an ad on the internet you have to expect to be fucked with a little bit... The sad thing is that once everybody in town knew that the Russian girl you were chasing was just a hoax, everybody laughed about it. Out of 200 people here not one person told me that you did not deserve to be treated in this manner... You came to McMurdo bragging about how bad you are and how good you are at welding and ironworking... Well, I'll admit that this place is a drag but you could not even deal with six months here. That tells me (and everybody else here) that you are pretty weak. Soft. Pussy. (as in "pussy cat") Whatever... Getting Paul to go along with you was a real bonus. Please thank him for being stupid also. Got it?

Not missing you here in McMurdo!!!!!

Tasha.

[Attached photo of 30 people in Southern giving the finger]

Appendix II

ASBESTOS MEMO 1

Date: July 2, 2001
From: Jim Scott; McMurdo Area Mgr.
To: Tom Yelvington; Program Director
Organization: RPSC
Subject: Asbestos
McMurdo Asbestos Issues

In response to recent asbestos issues at McMurdo, summarized below is an overview of the situation.

BUILDING 165: This building has been undergoing room by room renovations. Most of this has involved "non evasive" work such as removal of drop ceilings, etc., with minimal disturbance to the building structure. Prior to initiating this work, FEMC reviewed the comprehensive AECOM Asbestos Survey Report (1992) in an effort to avoid disruption of asbestos containing building materials. This survey included analysis of sample building materials using phase contrast microscopy with polarized light and dispersion staining. This provides positive identification of asbestos through refractive index, morphology and color analyses.

During the performance of this survey thirty-seven (37) building interior samples were taken and analyzed. With the exception of vinyl flooring, asbestos was only found in joint compounds (1-5% asbestos by weight), not sheet rock.

Concern about the presence of asbestos occurred recently during renovation at two locations in the building:

• In room 207 after a piece of door trim/frame was removed and the underlying material looked suspect.

• In room 119/120 where glued corkboard was being removed from sheet rock on the walls near ceiling level.

As soon as the materials were deemed suspect, work was halted and samples were tested using a rudimentary field test kit for hazardous waste characterization. While one sample indicated the presence of asbestos, the test kit is subject to false positives from contamination of other materials mixed with the asbestos. It is possible some joint compound could have been mixed with the tested materials. All other field tests were negative. The more accurate AECOM tests indicated the other building materials to be asbestos free.

When it was determined the materials could contain asbestos, air sampling was conducted to assess the exposure hazard. Initial samples indicated levels inside and outside the rooms to be less than 1/2 the occupational standard. The rooms were isolated with poly. Subsequent samples indicated levels outside the rooms to be less than 1/10 the standard, and in several cases, non-detectable.

BUILDING 203: This building has been 95% demo'ed, to date. Because it is relatively new in comparison to building 165, it was considered to be asbestos free at the start of the work. The AECOM survey was not referenced. This was an oversight. The survey does indicate the building to be asbestos free (12 samples) with the exception of approximately 100 square feet of vinyl flooring in the vestibule area. Although this was unknowingly removed, asbestos in embedded vinyl materials is usually tightly bound, minimizing airborne exposure during handling. In addition the vinyl was removed as a single sheet.

This building was sampled for airborne fibers and found to have levels less than 1/10 the occupational standard for asbestos. It should be noted this sampling method counts total fibers – it cannot differentiate the asbestos fibers from non-hazardous fibers consequently, it overestimates the results. A comparative sample taken on T-site, where no asbestos materials are present (new building) indicated total fiber levels 4 times those found in 203.

Current Situation

While some asbestos containing materials may have been disturbed in the renovation of these buildings, based on the quantities involved, time, and the conservative (over estimating) sampling methods, it appears the exposures were very low. In most cases, levels were well below the permissible limit. The isolation of the subject rooms in building 165 has resulted in levels in adjacent areas considered safe for public use. Building 203 also meets these criteria, though work was initially suspended in the building pending further evaluation due the sensitivity of the issues.

Additionally, 9 out of 10 very recent samples taken in both buildings using the field test, indicated negative results. This included dust residue, drywall, and ceiling tiles. The only positive sample was for vinyl flooring.

While there were oversights in our renovation management planning process, we feel we responded responsibly to minimize exposures after suspect material was identified.

Appendix III

ASBESTOS MEMO 2

From: Blake, Steven
Sent: Tuesday, July 03, 2001 10:58 PM
To: Scott, Jim - Denver
Subject: Asbestos at McMurdo

Dear Jim Scott,

We are writing in response to the memorandum that you sent to Tom Yelvington on July 2, 2001 regarding McMurdo Asbestos Issues that in turn was forwarded to us. In this letter we wish to correct some inaccuracies in the memorandum specific to the remodel project at 203A.

In addition to the vestibule that had 100 square feet of asbestos containing vinyl flooring, we also removed vinyl flooring from 4 bathrooms (16'x12' each = 640 total square feet) and the laundry room (16'x14' = 224 square feet). 964 square feet is approximately 10 times the amount of square footage listed in your memo. In the 1992 AECOM survey the vinyl flooring in the rest of the building was never tested, but was stated to be homogenous with the vestibule flooring.

In your memo you stated that the asbestos containing vinyl flooring was "removed as a single sheet". We know as workers who participated in removing the flooring that this is not correct. We cut, ripped, and scraped the floor off causing the flooring to be torn in numerous pieces as well as greatly increasing (not minimizing) the airborne exposure during handling. This will be proven if the asbestos sheet vinyl is removed from the construction debris flat racks.

We have a discrepancy concerning the statistic you listed for the field tests in which you state 9 out of 10 samples tested negative for asbestos. On June 14th 4 field tests were performed, two of these tests came back positive for asbestos in the bedroom drywall and joint compound. On June 16th 4 field tests were done, 1 field test came back positive for asbestos in the vinyl floor, of the 3 negatives, 1 test was a control done on new uninstalled drywall implying a degree of accuracy to the field tests. The following week a field test was performed in which drywall joint compound from another bedroom tested positive for asbestos. The correct statistic is 6 out of 10 samples tested negative, 4 were positive.

In regards to the recent air samples taken in 203A this is not representative of the poor air quality throughout the remodel process. Multiple penetrations were cut in each bedroom and lounge with circular saws emitting clouds of drywall dust which permeated the entire building. Additionally, the dust from these cuts and other drywall alterations was swept on a daily basis intensifying the amount of airborne particles to the point of low visibility. We are sure that anyone who worked on the building will attest to this. We are confused at how you determined that during renovation the exposure levels were low and well below the permissible level. Could you please explain this?

In closing, we recognize that you took proper action after the asbestos containing materials were identified. However, it is obvious that the facts are being misrepresented regarding the quantities of asbestos containing materials involved, the levels of exposure, and the validity of air sampling after a vast majority of the renovation has been done. This letter highlights many of those misrepresentations. It is important in assessing a situation of this magnitude that the facts and the amount of exposure should be represented accurately by workers involved in the project. Considering the information that we have now provided you with and the serious nature of asbestos exposure, we hope the situation will be handled in a more appropriate and professional manner.

Below is a letter from FEMC station manager Gary Teetsell addressing the asbestos issue, pertinent passages from the Raytheon Supervisors Safety Handbook, and attached you will find the memorandum written by you which we have been discussing.

Sincerely,

S. Wilson Blake
[And co-workers]

GLOSSARY

125—One of McMurdo's two apartments for Distinguished Visitors; self-contained, with its own shower and toilet, kitchen, and spacious quarters

155—The central hub of McMurdo Station, housing the Galley, the store, the barbershop, the radio station, HR, Finance, the Recreation Office, the ATMs, and many dorm rooms

AGO—Automated Geophysical Observatory. Automated data-collection devices placed around the plateau to collect meteorological and seismic data

ANG—New York Air National Guard 109th Airlift Wing, provider of logistical support to NSF for the U.S. Antarctic Program

The Antarctic Sun—Weekly NSF-funded paper published in McMurdo during the summer

The Antarctic Treaty—Multinational agreement governing the use of Antarctica

ASA—Antarctic Support Associates, USAP prime support contractor from 1990 to 2000; a joint venture of Holmes & Narver Inc. and EG&G Inc.

BFC—Berg Field Center; supplies field camps with equipment and provisions, such as tents, sleeping bags, sleds, and dried foods

Boondoggle—any non-routine trip away from station

Bug Juice—Kool-Aid

Carhartts—insulated work overalls

CD—Canterbury Draft, New Zealand beer

CDC—Clothing Distribution Center, in Christchurch, where those going to the ice are outfitted with clothing appropriate to their jobs

Central Supply—McMurdo dispensary for office supplies

The Chalet—NSF headquarters in McMurdo; USAP administration center housing the offices of the senior NSF Representative and senior management of the prime support contractor

CODF—Commander of Operation Deep Freeze

CONUS—Continental United States

Crary Lab—Albert P. Crary Science and Engineering Laboratory; main lab in McMurdo, named after a geophysicist and glaciologist

DA—Dining Attendant, a Galley assistant who washes dishes, scrubs pots, tends the condiments, and mixes Bug Juice

Daybar—Morning bar hours for nightshift workers, held a few times a week in Southern Exposure

Delta—all-terrain transport and cargo vehicle, with large tires for snow traction

Denver—RPSC management headquarters in Denver suburb, Centennial

DNF—Do Not Freeze (refers to cargo itself, or the building in which it is stored)

Discovery Hut—Robert Scott's hut at Hut Point, across the bay from McMurdo Station; probably the most famous historical landmark in Antarctica because of the great number of miserable explorers who sought refuge there over the years

The Dome—Central hub of South Pole Station before completion of the New Station

DVs—Distinguished Visitors, such as politicians, journalists, high-ranking NSF Reps, and celebrities, such as explorer Sir Edmund Hillary, astronaut Jim Lovell, and Princess Anne

ECW—Extreme Cold Weather clothing, including everything from socks and long underwear to UV-blocking sunglasses and a heavyweight parka

EO—Equipment Operator

EPA—Environmental Protection Agency

FEMC—Facilities, Engineering, Maintenance, and Construction; department includes tradesmen such as plumbers, ironworkers, and electricians

Fingee—Fucking New Guy (not pejorative, so contempt may be expressed by "Fuckin' fingee" without redundancy)

Fleet-Ops—Fleet Operations; responsible for making and maintaining roads, runways, and the Ice Pier; also responsible for all explosive handling, snow removal, and crane operations, and in charge of most of the heavy equipment fleet in McMurdo

Fortress Rocks—Staging and processing area for Solid Waste; formerly McMurdo's landfill

F-Stop—Field Support Training Program, in which professional guides and mountaineers train people in outdoor survival techniques; also responsible for measuring ice thickness to determine safe travel routes over sea ice

Fuels—Department responsible for supplying fuel to all buildings, as well as fueling aircraft and orchestrating station resupply from the yearly fuel tanker

GA—General Assistant, Antarctic equivalent of a temp worker for manual labor, assigned to departments as needed for such tasks as shoveling snow, taking inventory, cleaning, and other undesirable jobs

Gallagher's—McMurdo's non-smoking bar

Galley—Kitchen and cafeteria

Grantee—a scientist who has received a grant from NSF; NSF refers to scientists as "grantees" to remind them of their place

Hagglund—Two-compartment tracked personnel carrier that floats

Happy Camper School—Outdoor survival training run by F-Stop

Haz Yard—Hazardous Waste Processing Facility

Heavy Shop—the garage, or the Vehicle Maintenance Facility (VMF)

Herman Nelson—A powerful portable heater used primarily to pre-heat cold equipment that won't start

Highway One—The main hallway in Building 155, where people run into each other at lunch hour and trade quips about work, or run into each other after work and make plans for later

Hotel California—A dorm with very small rooms for people with no Ice Time

Housing—The Housing Department or Office

HR—Human Resources Department, the intermediary between the company and the employee

Hut 10—Large apartment for community social functions

Hut Point—Site of Robert Scott's Discovery Hut, across the bay from McMurdo

Ice Time—The number of months one has worked either in Antarctica or in Denver; a factor in determining one's housing allocation

IAP—International American Products. Subcontractor in 1996–1997 that provided food, janitorial, barber, and laundry service for the USAP

I-Drive—Community drive for sharing photos on the McMurdo network

IGY—International Geophysical Year. From the 2002 USAP Participant Guide: "The 1957–1958 International Geophysical Year (IGY) emphasized antarctic exploration and included research by 12 nations at 67 stations in Antarctica. For the first time, year-round stations were maintained in the continental interior, and the distribution of stations was sufficient to permit synoptic studies. It was the greatest coordinated scientific assault on Antarctica ever mounted."

ITT—ITT Antarctic Services. USAP prime support contractor in the 1980s

Jamesway—Canvas and wood-structured tent used at the South Pole and field camps, made famous in the Korean War

JATO—Jet-Assisted Take-Off for aircraft; also, the pure-grain alcohol stored in barrels that people sometimes drink at parties

JSOC—Joint Space Operations Center

Lower Case Dorms—Less desirable than Upper Case Dorms, with community bathroom and smaller rooms

MacOps—Call sign for the McMurdo Field Operations Communications Center. MacOps is the center for all VHF and HF communications with the deep field and the Dry Valleys (who must call in at scheduled times), as well as vessel traffic in the summer and communication checks with Pole in the winter. Those who leave McMurdo must first radio MacOps to give vehicle information and departure/return times.

Mac Weather—McMurdo Weather; its main task is issuing weather forecasts for aviation. Mac Weather is part of Aviation Technical Services (ATS), which also includes air traffic control and airfield ground electronics, provided by the Navy's Space and Naval Warfare Systems Command (SPAWAR).

Mainbody—Summer season, from October to February

MCC—Movement Control Center, administration center for cargo and worker transport

MEC—Mechanical Equipment Center, the garage for snowmobiles, generators, chainsaws, and other light equipment

medevac—medical evacuation

Medical—The Medical Department; also the hospital

Midrats—Midnight Rations; nightshift for Galley workers

MMI (Mammoth Mountain Inn)—Another dorm with very small rooms for people with no Ice Time

Nansen sled—A wooden type named for Arctic explorer Fridtjof Nansen

Navchaps— Members of the Navy Cargo Handling and Port Group, trained to load and unload merchant breakbulk ships, container ships, and military controlled aircraft, and flown to McMurdo to assist with Ship Offload

Nicoletti-Flater Associates—Company contracted to administer psychological screening for wintering Antarctic personnel

NSF—National Science Foundation, manager of the United States Antarctic Program, under the Department of State

Nunatak—an isolated mountain peak projecting through the surface of surrounding glacial ice

Ob Tube—Observation Tube, a hollow steel cylinder about 30 feet long with internal rungs and a window near the bottom, poked through the sea ice to allow underwater views

Offload—Annual station resupply by cargo ship

Operation Deep Freeze—Formerly, Naval unit established in 1959 by the Department of Defense to support activities managed by the National Science Foundation in Antarctica; now designates flight support by the Air National Guard, or more generally all military activities within the USAP

OPP—Office of Polar Programs, the branch of NSF responsible for the United States Antarctic Program

Orientation—Introductory company meeting where the employee is introduced to the stick (HR), the carrot (Finance), and to the terminology that will govern these forces

OSHA—Occupational Safety and Health Act

PAX—Passengers

Pegasus—Pegasus Airfield, a blue-ice runway for wheeled aircraft on the permanent Ross Ice Shelf

Pickle—M4K Case forklift, dark green

POC—Point of Contact

Polies—South Pole residents

PPE—Personal Protective Equipment

PQ'd—Physically Qualified

Preway—Simple, nonportable space heater typically used to heat Jamesways and fish huts

QA—Quality Assurance

Quonset hut—Half-cylindrical building invented for military use, usually of galvanized steel sheathing over a frame of lightweight steel arch ribs

R&R—Rest and relaxation, unpaid leave for those with winter contracts; known in Denver as "Preparatory Leave"

Remediation—environmental clean-up

RPSC—Raytheon Polar Services Company, USAP prime support contractor that supplanted ASA in 2000

Sastrugi—Hard wind-formed ice ridges

Scott Base—New Zealand base near McMurdo Station

Silver City—emergency shelter near Scott Base on the Castle Rock ski loop, where people sometimes stay on weekends to get away from town

Skidoo—snowmobile

Skua—A large, aggressive gull whose predatory and scavenging nature has inspired the use of its name to refer to voracious hunting and collecting through station "skua piles" (free-piles of abandoned but reusable commodities)

Skylab—lounge and band room at South Pole

Southern—Southern Exposure, McMurdo's smoking bar

SPAWAR—Space and Naval Warfare Systems Command. Provides air traffic control, meteorological forecasts, and airfield ground electronics maintenance for the USAP.

Spryte—One-compartment tracked vehicle; a field camp workhorse

SSC—Science Support Center, administrative hub of science support operations

Summer Camp—Array of Jamesways used for accommodations at Pole in the summer only

Terra Bus—Personnel transport vehicle, almost 50 feet long with room for about 56 passengers

Toasty—Mentally dulled from too much time on the ice

Triwall—Large reinforced-cardboard box used for cargo and for trash disposal

T-Site—Hub of radio transmission in McMurdo

U-barrel—urine barrel (either the barrel itself or the outhouse built over it)

Upper Case Dorms—Most desirable dorms, with one bathroom per two rooms and a sink in each large room

USAP—United States Antarctic Program

UT—Utility Technician; maintains heaters, furnaces, washers and dryers, and other appliances

Vermiculite—a flaky, absorbent mineral used to pack chemicals for shipment

Willy—Williams Airfield, a runway for ski-equipped aircraft

Winfly—winter fly-in, from August to October

Winter—season from February to October

Winter-overs—winter residents of the stations

Winter Quarters Bay—bay that separates McMurdo Station from Hut Point

BIBLIOGRAPHY

AECOM Technology Corporation. *Final Asbestos Survey Report for McMurdo Station and Amundsen-Scott South Pole Station, Antarctica, Vol. 1.* ATC, May 29, 1992.

Aldridge, Don. *The Rescue of Captain Scott.* Tuckwell Press, 1999.

Amundsen, Roald. *Belgica Diary: The first scientific expedtion to the Antarctic.* Bluntisham Books/Erskine Press, 1999.

Anonymous. *The Semi-Basement News, Vol. 2.* June 19, 1991. [A McMurdo newsletter.]

Associated Press. "FBI agents, mediator sent to Antarctic bases: Visitors to probe assault, staff dispute." *The Atlanta Journal/The Atlanta Constitution,* Oct. 14, 1996.

Ayres, Philip J. *Mawson: A Life.* Melbourne University Press, 1999.

Bara, Michael and Richard C. Hoagland. "What is Happening at the South Pole?" *The Enterprise Mission,* retrieved May, 2001 from http://www.enterprisemission.com/antarctica.htm

Behrendt, John C. *Innocents on the Ice: A Memoir of Antarctic Exploration, 1957.* University Press of Colorado, 1998.

Bickel, Lennard. *Shackleton's Forgotten Argonauts.* The Macmillan Company of Australia Pty Ltd., 1982.

Bickel, Lennard. *This Accursed Land.* The MacMillan Company of Australia, 1977.

Blass, Thomas, ed. *Obedience to Authority: Current Perspectives on the Milgram Paradigm.* Lawrence Erlbaum Associates, Inc., 2000.

Burke, David. *Moments of Terror.* New South Wales University Press, 1994.

Campbell, Victor. *The Wicked Mate: The Antarctic Diary of Victor Campbell.* Bluntisham Books and Erskine Press, 1988.

Carter, Paul A. *Little America: Town at the End of the World.* Columbia University Press, 1979.

Charles Wilkes v. Samuel Dinsman. 48 U.S. 89, US Supreme Court, 1849. Online, LexisNexis Academic.

Chipman, Elizabeth. *Women on the Ice: A History of Women in the Far South.* Melbourne University Press, 1986.

CIA, *Polar Regions Atlas.* National Foreign Assessment Center, 1978.

Crawford, Janet. *That First Antarctic Winter: The Story of the Southern Cross Expedition of 1898–1900 as told in the diaries of Louis Charles Bernacchi.* South Latitude Research Limited, 1998.

Darby, Andrew. "Cold Comfort from Skies for Polar Woman." *Sydney Morning Herald,* July 12, 1999.

Davidson, Keay. "Big U.S. outpost is icy trash dump." *San Francisco Examiner,* Jan. 10, 1989.

——. "Journey to the end of the Earth." *San Francisco Examiner,* Jan. 8, 1989.

Didion, Joan. "Insider Baseball" from *Political Fictions.* Alfred A. Knopf, 2001.

Erb, Dr. Karl. *Testimony Before the House Committee on Science, Subcommitte on Basic Research.* June 9, 1999.

Fiennes, Ranulph. *Mind Over Matter.* Delacorte Press, 1993.

Fox, Robert. *Antarctica and the South Atlantic: Discovery, Development and Dispute.* British Broadcasting Corporation, 1985.

Frazier, Commander Paul W. *Antarctic Assault.* Dodd, Mead and Company, 1958.

Gardyasz, Joe. "North Dakota native among Antarctic firefighters sick from fumes." *Bismarck Tribune,* June 4, 2001.

Gore, Al. "Postcard Antarctica: Unbearable Whiteness." *The New Republic,* Dec. 26, 1988.

Gurney, Alan. *Below the Convergence: Voyages Toward Antarctica 1699–1839.* W.W. Norton and Company, 1997.

Guy, Michael. *White Out!: Michael Guy's true account of Air New Zealand's DC-10 crash on Mount Erebus.* Alister Taylor Publishing Limited, 1980.

Hathaway, S.R. and J.C. McKinley. *Minnesota Multiphasic Personality Inventory ~2.* University of Minnesota Press, 1989.

Hoare, Michael E., ed. *The Resolution Journal of Johann Reinhold Forster 1772–1775.* The Hakluyt Society, 1982.

Hornblower, Margot. "At the Bottom of the World, Unremitting Cabin Fever." *Washington Post,* Feb. 4, 1981.

Hotz, Robert Lee. "Last Journey To The Last Place On Earth: At the South Pole, Nothing Can Grow Except the Spirit." *Los Angeles Times,* July 8, 2001.

Huntford, Roland. *The Last Place on Earth.* Atheneum, 1985.

Huntford, Roland. *Shackleton.* Carroll and Graf Publishers, 1985.

Hutchinson, William. "On the Sea Scurvy." *A Treatise on Naval Architecture.* T. Billinge, 1794.

University of California Riverside. "Judges on Trial in NSF-Funded Project at UCR." June 12, 2000, from *http://www.ucr.edu/SubPages/2CurNewsFold/UnivRelat/cranor.html*

Law, Philip. *Antarctic Odyssey.* William Heinemann Australia, 1983.

Lennhoff, Eugen. *The Freemasons: The History, Nature, Development and Secret of the Royal Art.* Lewis Masonic Books, 1994.

"Lifeline to Antarctica." *CBS,* July 8, 1999. [CBS website]

Mawson's Antarctic Diaries. University of Adelaide, 1988.

McMahon, Patrick. "Emergency Flight Heads for Coldest of Winters." *USA Today,* July 9, 1999.

Milgram, Stanley. *Obedience to Authority.* Pinter and Martin Ltd., 1997.

Mohsberg, Margot. "Smooth Landing." *The Capital,* Nov. 26, 1999.

Nansen, Fridtjof. *To the Ends of the Earth.* HarperCollins UK, 2002.

National Science Foundation. *External Panel Report.* NSF, 1997.

National Science Foundation. *Safety in Antarctica: Report of the USAP Safety Review Panel.* Publication no. NSF 88-78, 1988.

National Science Foundation. *http://www.nsf.gov*

NASA/NSF. *Use of Antarctic Analogs to Support the Space Exploration Initiative.* NASA/NSF, 1990.

"A New Bounty and Its New Demands." *Affiliates Meeting: American Association for the Advancement of Science,* Feb. 13, 1998.

Nordwall, Bruce D. "Aviation on Ice Unlocks Antarctica." *Aviation Week and Space Technology,* May 25, 1998.

Palinkas, Lawrence A. *On the Ice: Individual and Group Adaptation in Antarctica.* University of California, 2000.

Philips, Eric. *Icetrek: The Bitter Journey to the South Pole by Peter Hillary, Jon Muir and Eric Philips.* HarperCollins, 2000.

Piatigorsky, Alexander. *Who's Afraid of Freemasons?: The Phenomenon of Freemasonry.* The Harvill Press, 1997.

Poulter, Thomas C. *The Winter Night Trip to Advance Base: Byrd Antarctic Expedition II 1933–35.* 1973. [Typed notes and memos, bound with tape in Canterbury Museum Library, Christchurch, New Zealand.]

Preisler, Jerome. *Cold War.* Penguin Books, 2001.

Raytheon Company. *Ethics: Your Integrity, Raytheon's Reputation.* Raytheon Company, 2000. [brochure]

Raytheon Polar Services Company. *http://www.polar.org*

Reader's Digest Services. *Antarctica: Great Stories from the Frozen Continent.* Reader's Digest, 1985.

Rodgers, Eugene. *Beyond the Barrier: The Story of Byrd's First Expedition to Antarctica.* Naval Institute Press, 1990.

Ronne, Captain Finn. *Antarctica, My Destiny.* Hastings House Publishers, 1979.

––. *Antarctic Command.* The Bobbs-Merrill Company, Inc., 1961.

Rose, Lisle A. *Assault on Eternity: Richard E. Byrd and the Exploration of Antarctica 1946–47.* Naval Institute Press, 1980.

Roylance, Frank D. "Mercy flight heads to end of the Earth." *Baltimore Sun,* July 8, 1999.

"Senators at the South Pole." *The Washington Post,* Jan. 19, 1998.

Siple, Paul. *90° South: The Story of the American South Pole Conquest.* G.P. Putnam's Sons, 1959.

––. *A Boy Scout with Byrd.* GP Putnam's Sons, 1931.

Sullivan, Walter. *Assault on the Unknown.* Hodder and Stoughton Ltd., 1961.

Taylor, A.J.W. and A.G. Frazer. *Psychological Sequelae of Operation Overdue Following the DC10 Aircrash in Antarctica.* No publisher or publishing date listed. Latest reference in text is 1980.

USAP Participant Guide, 1998–2000 Edition. National Science Foundation. Publication no. NSF 98-117.

Verrengia, Joseph B. "Budget Thaw in Antarctica." *Rocky Mountain News,* May 12, 1996.

Wells, H.G. *A Short History of the World.* Penguin Books, 1953.

World Health Organization. *Selection of Personnel to Work in Circumpolar Regions,* WHO Regional Office for Europe, 1984.

ACKNOWLEDGMENTS

Without exception, my crew supervisors in McMurdo have been excellent bosses and a pleasure to work for. So, first thanks go to Lester Bracey, Bob Radke, Bill Poulson, Susie Heyob, and James "Wheel" Mickelson.

There are many people whose keen eyes and thoughtfulness have contributed valuable details to what otherwise would have been vague and uninteresting anecdotes. Though it's impossible to recognize all those whose conversations and expertise I've relied upon, I'm particularly fortunate to have known Robert Zimmerman, David Zimmerman, Doug Wing, Jeff Truelove, Chris Teske, Slim, Liesl Schernthanner, Jeff Ryan, Scott Phillips, Randy Noring, Alex Morris, Rick Monce, Jessica Manuel, Sue Long, Michiel Lofton, Libor, Rob LaBarre, Chris Kugelman, Stephanie Koetzle, Susan Kaspari, Brandon Holton, Peter Hobbes, John Hatcher, Dale-Lynn Gardner, Ted Dettmar, Nelson Corcoran, Jay Cairns, Tony Buchanan, Wilson Blake, and Deb Baldwin.

It would be an insidious oversight not to recognize Keros Johnson, who is the funniest person I've known on this rock, and a goddamn rock in the worst of winters.

Roren Stowell is a phenomenal critic though he's never written a word.

James Penkusky is a sick dog best shot on sight.

Nearby, Brad Johnson should be strung up by his balls.

As Jake Speed dances a merry dance.

And Kathy Blumm shows up just in time to peddle extra rope and ammo.

The librarians at the Canterbury Museum Library in Christchurch many times went out of their way to assist me in finding obscure materials.

For commenting on the first draft of this book, I'm grateful to Sara Lorimer, Dylan Sisson, and Dagwood Heinrich Ludwig Reeves, whose suggestions were either ignored or implemented, and in both cases were invaluable.

More than anyone, it is Jason Anthony who has added to my understanding of this book. We were roommates in Christchurch during the year-long period in which it was written. In some strange marriage we sat writing in our own rooms all day and emerged in the evenings to drink wine and eat fine New Zealand cheeses and discuss Richard Byrd's turds and Antarctica's capacity as a mirror for our culture while outside our window the Kiwi "boy racers" screamed down Worcester Street in their extravagant neon-lit rice burners and gentlemen in white suits flocked to the lawn-bowling club across the street. One day our neighbors beyond our wall, practicing for karaoke, repeatedly played "Hey Jude" for four hours straight, and when I then decided to go over and kill them, it was Jason who diverted my attention with stories of Lincoln Ellsworth, who was so obsessed with the Old American West that when he flew his plane over Antarctica he wore a holster and antique six-shooter. It was Jason who suggested, after reading a draft of my manuscript, that I didn't have enough "Antarctica" in my book about Antarctica, and that I should at least acknowledge the popular image of the place before questioning that image. From this advice I relinquished a portion of my selfishness and remembered the process of my experience of Antarctica, a slow metamorphosis from the grand to the absurd to the normal.

The resulting manuscript appealed to Adam Parfrey, a publisher so sensitive to different shades of American culture that he actually liked the book before wondering whether it would sell to the penguin and iceberg crowd.

Due to their ruthlessness and honesty, there are certain artists whose work long ago so influenced me that I consider them a primary internal audience. They are Nathan Cearley and Sean Tejaratchi.

Rar Jungle is a real showboat. A real piece of work.

When Rar and I once crept into Frank Woll's house hoping to startle him, and found him on the couch watching a Nazi occult documentary, wearing a Darth Vader mask, and toying with a ten-inch hunting knife, I knew I had found an interesting friend.

Before I met David Nelson, I didn't know what dry humor was.

To my parents, Dee Johnson and Jay Johnson, I am grateful for a stable upbringing and for their unconditional support despite my erratic and unpromising path through the world.

The old NSF logo: An elite fellowship lights the way from ancient to modern science under the unity of national might.

The new NSF logo: A federal agency assumes stewardship of the globe under the unity of an interchangeable mob.